INDIAN ENGLISH THROUGH NEWSPAPERS

About the Author

Asima Ranjan Parhi is a faculty in English at Indira Gandhi Government (Degree) College, Tezu, Arunachal Pradesh. An Associate Fellow at Indian Institute of Advanced Study, Shimla, he pursues research in the areas of language in print and electronic media, literary theory and its application in curriculum.

Dr. Parhi frequently writes for reputed journals like Journal of English and Foreign Languages, Studies in Humanities and Social Sciences, and Atlantic Critical Review. Also, he writes poems in Oriya and English.

INDIAN ENGLISH THROUGH NEWSPAPERS

Dr. Asima Ranjan Parhi
Reader
Department of English
Indira Gandhi Government (Degree) College
Tezu, Lohit District, Arunachal Pradesh-792001

CONCEPT PUBLISHING COMPANY, NEW DELHI-110059

Cataloging in Publication Data—DK
Courtesy: D.K. Agencies (P) Ltd. <docinfo@dkagencies.com>

Parhi, Asima Ranjan.
Indian English through newspapers / Asima Ranjan Parhi.
p. cm.
Includes bibliographical references (p.)
Includes index.
ISBN 13: 9788180695070
ISBN 10: 8180695077

1. English newspapers—India—Language. 2. English language—Written English—India. 3. Journalism—India. I. Title.

DDC 070.420 954 22

ISBN-13: 978-81-8069-507-0
ISBN-10: 10-81-8069-507-7

First Published 2008

Published and Printed by
Ashok Kumar Mittal
Concept Publishing Company
A/15-16, Commercial Block, Mohan Garden
New Delhi-110 059 (India)

Phones : 25351460, 25351794
Fax : 091-11-25357103
E-mail : publishing@conceptpub.com

To

My father

Bira Kishore Parhi

the most ideal and unselfish human being

I have ever come across.

Centre for Linguistics
School of Language, Literature & Culture Studies
जवाहरलाल नेहरू विश्वविद्यालय
Jawaharlal Nehru University
New Delhi-110067 India

Prof PKS Pandey
Chairperson

FOREWORD

The written word has played a crucial role in the learning of English in India. English education in India in its beginning in the nineteenth century had to rely mainly on the written mode for a vast majority of its users in educational and administrative institutions. The mass media in the country employing English extended the use of the written variety. As is the nature of language as a natural system, with use comes change by chance as well as by necessity of communication in different cultural contexts. The increase in the use of English in the newspapers led to the rise and spread of many novel features in the structure of English. It is quite in accordance with our understanding about the structure and functions of language that Indian English is looked upon as an independent variety.

Dr. Asima Ranjan Parhi has made a valiant attempt at investigating the structure of Indian English found in English newspapers in India. He examines the factors related to mass communication and journalism that have contributed to the growth of English in India. His own writing, as the reader will discern, is a fitting vehicle of his ideas.

13.02.2008

P. K. S. Pandey
Professor & Chairperson
Centre for Linguistics
School of Language,
Literature and Culture Studies
Jawaharlal Nehru University,
New Delhi-110067

ACKNOWLEDGEMENTS

I am happy to have all my family behind my academic achievement and this book.

I am extremely thankful to Dr. Umesh P. Patnaik who had given his best efforts in supervising my Ph.D. work, a major portion of which has been put into this book.

I am fortunate to have got suggestions and help from my teachers at Utkal University (Orissa), ELTI (Orissa), CIEFL (Hyderabad) and JNU (New Delhi) before planning this work.

My wife Ellora has tried to boost my confidence and potential whenever I felt restrained. She deserves mention.

Prof. A.K. Mohanty (JNU) has been very encouraging in this regard. I am indebted to him.

My friends like Sanjay and others in JNU have constantly guided me for its publication. I thank them honestly.

Mr. Ashok Kumar Mittal and the Concept Publishing Company deserve special thanks for getting this novel and unique work see the light of the day.

PREFACE

This work is a modest and novel attempt in the direction of describing Indian English. Its prime focus is on the extent of influence of newspapers in the growth of Indian English.The lexical, syntactic and semantic areas of the English language as appear on the national English dailies have been highlighted with special emphasis on the factors, affiliations of the writers/editors in creating the new expression in terms of words, structures and meaning.

The new entries have been cited with the processes of change and their source. For example, words and expressions like 'winnability', 'privilegentsia', 'line my pocket','saffronisation', 'unbeautiful' have resulted in making Indian English hold its ground with a trendy and catchy colour.

The task based work also paves the way for curricular renewal by providing tremendous feedback.The strategies used in newspaper English can be utilised effectively in the teaching/learning skills of English in schools and coileges of India.The book broadly asserts two things:

1. Indian English is a distinct variety with specific morphology, syntax and semantic features.
2. Indian English dailies contribute heavily towards the shaping of this varicty of English.

The data collected over a period of six years (1996–2002) from the important English dailies in India and interaction with linguists, media persons, professors in the respective field confirm the above statements. The work is significant in the context of Indian English getting more space internationally. The print media is the most influential medium of changing the face of language which is on a fast move. The formal, curricular fields can be abundantly benefited by this shift in words, structures and meaning. It has enlisted plenty of new entries and explores avenues of many more in the process. In the wake of new Englishes worldwide, it stands as the bedrock of freshness to a language that represents the mass and the marginal. It certainly shares the post-modernist and post-colonial points of view that do not discriminate between anything high or low, superior or inferior in modes of language.

Such a work has been strongly recommended for publication by eminent linguists and intellectuals in the interest of Indian English and our curriculum for higher education. Hopefully my aspiration of making it a tremendous help to the cause of Indian English and scores of people who take interest in the growth and use of English comes true with the publication of this book.

Makar Sankranti
14 January 2007

Asima Ranjan Parhi

CONTENTS

Chapter - 1

INTRODUCTION

Statement

Indian English is a distinct variety of English. Culturally India has a diverse identity. So English is used differently in different parts of India. But these varieties retain a commonness that widely depart from the native English users. Geographically India has different regional divisions in terms of languages and dialects. So in the context of the vast number of languages and dialects used, English appears at centre stage as a link language, as a commonly appreciated mode of communication in both written and spoken medium. A number of factors contribute to the growth and present status of Indian English. Among them the English print media in particular takes the prime lead. The Indians have their own form of English as far as the practical usage is concerned. The editors and writers cater to the specific needs of the reader and in the process scramble, play with words and structures that give rise to a new variety of language. It is worthwhile to verify and establish the factors responsible and the areas in which the English dailies have contributed to the enrichment of Indian English.

The book aims at describing the lexical, syntactic and semantic areas of the English language as used in the English dailies since these areas have been substantially expanded by the inflow of new words, structures and meanings which appeal the readers. The use of the new words or structures is systematic, and certainly adds to opening of a new field of research. We would throw light on certain aspects which widely depart from the curricular, text book variety of English, how the English print media exploits the catchy and flexible areas and offers new possibilities.

Though similar cases may be happening with the western or foreign media, here our task is to highlight on the specific change that the readers are exposed to in the Indian English dailies. The work intends to see how that can pave way for a recognised variety of Indian English at some levels.

We briefly summarise the objectives of this study below :

(a) to analyse the factors influencing the editors/writers to coin new expression;
(b) to assess the influence upon the readers;
(c) to study the fertile morphological and syntactic processes in creating new words and structures;
(d) to explore the semantic potential coming out of such coinage; and
(e) the prospect that this distinct variety of English has at the national and international level as well as towards a change in our school/college curriculum.

Background

Indian English has gained a distinct status of its own in recent times. It has been done through a long process of coining and incorporating new words, structures and expressions. It is our colonial past that has given us the English language as a cultural asset. The formal and extra-curricular use of the language has given it a living and vibrant status. It is a fast growing medium of communication in the field of academics such as research work, higher studies, university education; in the scientific study involving cross country exchange in terms of resources, materials, information; commercial sector that is heavily dependent upon common linguistic interaction; political sectors and so on. Economic liberalisation has led to rapid cultural exchange which has given rise to a growing interest in English language as the mode of link. A language, in order to keep pace with the growth of bringing more and more pockets of a society, has to be strengthened by numerous factors that contribute to its store of vocabulary, structure and meaning variation. It is worthwhile to highlight the perceptible changes English in India has undergone over the years. Various political, socio-economic, cultural factors, intellectual needs have worked in tandem and pressurised the language to undergo such a shift. This change has been always in the interest of the people and their ethnic background. It has been a steady and promising growth since our independence. We have successfully made it an Indian language at all levels unofficially. Indian English literature has already established itself as a concrete mode of expression of a people in the international arena. It has never been absolutely British but wonderfully Indian. So, English in India has fared well not only in the socio-politico-economic and scientific spheres but as the vehicle of the creative and critical writing in this language.

The importance of English language in India could be well understood in the following lines from Kamala Das (1965):

> The language I speak becomes mine,
> Its distortions, its queerness all mine,
> It is half English, half Indian, funny perhaps, but it is honest.
> It is as human as I am human, Don't you see?
> It voices my joys, my longings, my hopes, and it is as useful.[1]

Today an educated Indian may use 'Indian English' as an assertion of his right to his known standards leading towards a linguistic self-determination. For conversation, Indians are already using 'Indish' (English mixed with Indian languages) and 'Hinglish' (English mixed with Hindi). Even in Britain there is a willingness to admit these fresh varieties as Randolph Quirk (1967)[2] observes:

> "Nevertheless, even if a plentiful supply of excellent teachers becomes available (with our help in this country), we must plainly recognise that an independent, Indian standard of English may well crystallise."

The British Council Report says, "fresh dialects of English will arise abroad—as they have always done in English-speaking countries, standards of acceptable speech will vary—as they do in Britain itself". The languages' assets may indeed be increased rather than diminished by wider use; overseas varieties of English may continue to contribute to the richness and resources of the language as a whole, as they have done in the past. In the face of fierce linguistic nationalism in India, English has come to be regarded as a complementary second language and never wholly as a 'foreign' language even by the fanatics.[3] Historically we have realised the importance of the study of this language in our context for a variety of reasons. The socio-cultural reforms, compulsion of understanding the western liberal humanistic thought have been the factors that could be propagated only through our interest in the English education which Raja Rammohun Roy well understood. India has never been robbed of its national character and culture by the imposition of English. It has been only in our benefit. The usefulness of English in the context of multilingual India may be summarised in the words of Jawaharlal Nehru who is reported to have said in 1961:

> "All regional languages must be developed and promoted, but that did not mean that English should be discarded. To do that will amount to closing a window on the world of technology... It was no use getting into an intellectual Prison after achieving political independence."[4] Akbar S. Ahmed, a Pakistani scholar and Civil Servant says:
>
> > "In spite of continuous pressure India retains English as the lingua franca. The retention is through necessity, not love of the language. It is the only language all the ethnic and linguistic groups are agreed upon. The result is a flood of babu English. Academics use English with facility and this has allowed them to be established internationally. It is the intellectual mainstay of the men of ideas. Key values and concepts—liberalism, secularism, pacifism—long ago imparted into India, are now Indian partly because of the medium's world standing, which reinforces them. Through English the Indian remains witnin the mainstream of contemporary ideas."[5]

That clearly states how English has played a part in shaping our political consciousness, the part played for the growth of a cultural heterogeneity. That we have the capability to mould the language to our own peculiar requirements is a proof of the 'Indianness' of English. Today more than fourteen million people in India use English which is larger than Australia where English is the mother tongue. In terms of function and use, today 'Indian English' may well be treated as an Indian language.

We briefly assess the nature of English in India in the past and present below :

Importance of English in Past

1. It was the most elitist language being used by the coloniser, rich and powerful class.

2. Confined to a very limited section of Indians who pursued it due to status, awareness and affluence.
3. Rigid, known as the Queen's variety, a very strict grammatical pattern and vocabulary, researched by a few and highly formal in nature. It was used with a mixture of Indian words by the babus and then looked down upon as the inferior variety.

So in past the kind of English used was just a language of some formal paper work in Indian context, meant to be comprehended by a handful of bureaucrats and clerks.

Importance of English at Present

1. English is the associate official language of this country. All academic, political, intellectual activities are highly dependent upon it.
2. It is the language of science and technology which has flourished in this country significantly after independence.
3. It has served as the urbanised link language for trade and commerce inside and across the globe, professional achievement in India and abroad.
4. With the information revolution and dependence upon the computer and internet services, English has been the only possible and preferable link language.
5. Rather than having an elitist flavour it has successfully captured mass recognition, acceptance. Since everybody is striving towards cosmopolitanism and success in terms of material needs and professional achievement the language of English has been the medium to be relied on irrespective of the specific ethnic and regional identity.
6. It has been the communicative link to bridge the gap between North and South India.
7. It is today the language of youths, students instead of belonging to a few intellectuals as in past, has become a more familiar, comfortable language, in the process has got the identity of our own language shedding its foreign touch.

So English has systematically offered to deliver the goods for mass culture and mass sentiment. It has torn apart its colonial, formal garb. We have made it informal, fashionable, flamboyant. It is also the link between the urbanised and the local in terms of new, colloquial rustic words and structures like : relief, rigging, anganwadi, food for work, e-commerce, internet, cable channel, BPL (Below Poverty Line) rice and so on. These words are used both by the inhabitants of the city and interior village. The aforesaid language has been greatly benefited by a number of sources. Among them, the English print media is considered to be the most influential one in general of which the Indian English dailies constitute the major source contributing to our English. Our newspapers offer a separate, distinct medium through which we have fashioned the language to our needs. India has a multi religious, cultural, ethnic society. Such a diversity has been reflected in the thoughts and language which our mainstream newspapers as well as regional ones have been trying to put on their columns. English language here has also been twisted to meet the expectation of the readers having a strong regional flavour.

Significance

English has been a part of Indian life since last four hundred years. Although Indian English has gained weightage in terms of creative writing, common usage and changes that are taking place in its status as a language, we still do not use it as our model. Instead we follow the British English variety as the base for any form of research, formal and creative writing. We do not have textbooks written in Indian English, or grammar books or a dictionary on it. So this work is in the direction of creating such a model that can contribute to the study of Indian English as purely a curricular, textbook variety and so on. The prospect of Indian English as a language of mass communication is also studied in this work.

In the context of rapid change and growth of the Indian English today, it seems very important. It observes the specific areas of change, factors of change and the application of it for studies in English. The present work is in perspective with the nature of language change and furthers the investigation of ELT in India. The curriculum can be the chief beneficiary of the process that makes Indian English an accomplished language like that of American, Canadian, Australian, Singaporean English. It paves way for making it a mass language in the context of India breaking the earlier rigid framework.

Newspapers offer a very challenging and fertile field of research taking into account the variety and abundance of language exercise in them.The areas under survey give a wide opportunity for strengthening as well as modifying the way English can be learnt and applied.

The book aims at emphasising change, that is on fast move in the field of language use. It is of immense importance to language practitioners, students and Indian English studies in general. It gives great support in establishing English truly as a mass language. It gives an opportunity to the mass in sharing our cultural heritage, tradition and skill. It gives the scope of an integrated approach to the study of English in India. It is required to throw some light on certain works done before and then categorise the areas of departure and further avenues that this book concentrates on.

Earlier Research

Some genuine research has been done in this area with the focus on certain specific branches as discussed below :

(a) On Indian English language

Braj B. Kachru's[6] works have been significant in this field. His dissertation, "Analysis of Some Features of Indian English: A Study in Linguistic Method", articles like, "The Indianness in Indian English", "Indian English : A Study in Contextualisation" have thrown light on different aspects of this language.

R.K. Bansal's[7] "The Intelligibility of Indian English" (1966), S.V. Parasher's[8]. "Certain Aspects of the Functions and Forms of Indian English: A Sociolingustic Study", Ph.D. Dissertation (1979) have been useful works in this regard.

Yet much more needs to be done in the areas of Indian English for its growth and practical usage in all fields—the formal, textual, curricular levels and as a mass language.

(b) On Newspaper English in India

Labru's (1984) view is that English in India is a complementary second language *vis-à-vis* the languages in India whereas Australian and American English have usurped into other existing varieties. In that case he establishes the moderate nature of Indian English. His data is taken from five regional dailies in India and projects the view that they are more closer to the language of average Indian English. He has surveyed the Weinrich model and Kachru model of contextualisation in his description of Indian English. He further states Indian English as :

(i) a second language and not a foreign language,
(ii) a deviant form of English,
(iii) a compound of both formal and socio-linguistic features, and
(iv) Manifesting a tacit acceptance of English as an Indian language.

He is also of the view that Indian Newspaper English is characterised by marginal structural deviance and considerable socio-linguistic deviance. He further goes for an acceptability test by foreign (British) students providing them the Indian newspaper content from the local dailies. In result the test is not that satisfying for acceptability. He observes: Indian English is neither an established fact nor a fiction but a trend and gives it the status of a deviant variety of English.[9] Vinod S. Dubey and Rani Rubdy have also worked on this issue. Rani Rubdy[10] in her dissertation titled "A Study of some Written Varieties of Indian English" is of the opinion that Indian English is not completely different from the native English grammar except in a restricted area. She talks of Indians' use of lexical items and does not give emphasis to our idiomatic usage in English.

She opines that our incompetent mastery of rules is responsible for the deviation. She hints on the standardisation of Indian English. But the processes of change and specific words and usage do not get core emphasis.

Vinod S. Dubey[11] in his book "Newspaper English in India" talks about the complex and information oriented structure of the national dailies. He has focused more on the comparative status of the news columns, editorials, letters to the editors etc. The thematic organisation and compressed informative confusion take the front seat in his study. So it seems much work has not been done in the area of Indian Newspaper English to reflect the different facts it characterises.

This work departs from the data presented by Labru's, rather concentrates more on the national dailies since they represent the body of Indian Newspaper English as well as Indian English in the widest mode. We have not included the phonology of Indian English and instead confined our scope within the lexical, structural and semantic categories. No other work has emphasised the exact nature of contribution of Indian Newspapers towards Indian English (IE).

This work has given a list of the contemporary usage in terms of lexis, structure and meaning that Indian Newspaper English has created; it describes and explains the British as well as certain Indian linguistic processes along with some new striking processes for such a change, the extent of effort by the writers and editors towards such a change, the changing social environment that influences the change both in writing as well as the taste of the readers. Moreover it clearly focuses on Indian Newspaper English and only comprehensively analyses Indian English; finds Indian Newspaper English as a deliberately patterned language, often poetic in certain areas, with a mixture of strange and codified variety of language and its own sense of grammar. It seeks to establish the fact that curriculum in English in India can be heavily contributed by Indian Newspaper English.

REFERENCES

1. Kamala Das, "An Introduction", *Summer in Calcutta* (New Delhi: Everest Press, 1965).
2. Randolf Quirk, *The Use of English*, 1962 (London: Longmans, sixth impression, 1967) 13.
3. V.K. Gokak, *English in India, Its Present and Future*, (Bombay: OUP, 1964).
4. Jawaharlal Nehru, *The Times of India*, 24 July1961.
5. Akbar S. Ahmed is quoted in "A Pakistani Comes to Delhi", *The Times of India* (Sunday Review), 11 September 1983.
6. Braj B. Kachru, diss., University of Edinburgh, 1962; *Word* 21 (1965) and *In Memory of J.R. Fifth*, Eds. Bazell et al. (London: Longmans, 1966).
7. R.K. Bansal, diss., University of London, 1966.
8. S.V. Parasher, diss., CIEFL, Hyderabad, 1979.
9. G.L. Labru, *Indian Newspaper English* (New Delhi: B.R. Publishing Corporation, 1984)151-54.
10. Rani Rubdy, "A Study of Some Written Varieties of Indian English," diss., CIEFL, Hyderabad, 1981.
11. Vinod S. Dubey, *Newspaper English in India* (New Delhi: Bahri Publications,1989).

Chapter - 2

History and the Present Status of Indian English and the Register of Journalism

History of Indian English

The history of Indian English can be traced to the period of colonisation. English came as the source of western education but remained here as our socio-cultural link with the outsiders. The intelligentsia adopted it as a medium of explaining us to the west, getting an access to the western liberal thought. Creative usage in English in India originated as the vehicle of Indian values and philosophy. Indian rusticity and way of life got reflected in the language and style.

The initial attempts

In the year 1813 the educative and civilising initiatives became a part of the agenda that the British India assumed. The missionaries took the task of establishing printing presses that helped in the publication of dictionaries, translations, grammar. In 1780, India's first newspaper 'Hicky's Bengal Gazette' was published. Private schools started imparting English education; established at Madras (1717), Bombay (1718) and Calcutta (1720) later leading to the establishment of the Hindu College at Calcutta, by Raja Rammohun Roy and his friends like David Hare and Sir Edward Hyde East in the year 1817. It became the Presidency College in 1855 making the path ready for establishment of such institutions imparting western education at other places.

The colonial experience of English writing had a number of hazards behind.

(i) It was thought, English language came as an imposition of the foreign culture and religion.

(ii) It was strict initiation rather than experimentation on Indian soil and Indian ethos.

Politics and the English language

Gandhi came as the Messiah of Indian political, spiritual thought at a time when the country was under the veils of darkeness. He was not professional writer. But his speeches, writings in *Young India* gave us the evidence of using the English language in order to link us with others inside and outside the country. The word 'Satyagraha' took momentum out of Gandhi's ideology which has become popular everywhere outside in recent times. It is no doubt an English word now. The concepts and words like 'Swaraj', 'Harijan' got introduced into the English vocabulary from the years of Indian Independence struggle. The main bulk of Gandhian writing in English appeared in his *Young India* and *Harijan*; the papers he edited. With Gandhi, Indian writing in English became functional. Gandhi made English suitable and simple for the Indian. A clarity and pointedness appeared unlike the pompous, Macaulayan richness of phrasing and complexity of structures.

Jawaharlal Nehru represented the elite political class with a very modern outlook and intellectual temper mingled with educationist views. While the Gandhian influence popularised 'Charkha', 'Khaddar', 'Ahimsa' and many such Indian notions outside India, with Nehru came the foreign policy deep rooted in Indian soil and culture; the 'Panchsheel'. The most noteworthy thing about Gandhi is that he really made language a very comfortable means of communication; be it Hindi, English or Gujarati. *Young India* served the purpose of using the English language as the common Indian and made the people aware about the purpose and need of the hour.

> "The introduction of English in India was no ordinary event. When English came to us, the world entered a new stage. India joined the brotherhood of the English-speaking world. It led as I have said, to a cultural upheaval in India, to a wide vision. The barriers of latitude, colour and race were broken down; the east mingled with the West in the sphere of the mind; a great step was taken towards establishing direct human intercourse, and sweeping away national frontiers... today English is ours, and with its aid we can make ourselves felt more than through any other agency. It would therefore be criminal to ignore or neglect English in this country."

Creative Writing

In the field of novel, Indian English writing gained the literary expression bent with typical Indian modes of imagination. The fiction of modern times cashed in on the Indian echoes heard in distant villages, the lifestyle of the common people required the language to be fitted into the colloquialism associated with them. For the first time Indians realised, English in India had to be made more open, more homely than the political intellectual spectrum. And novel gave the scope of writers to persist in their efforts of cutting the language, the medium at their ends, their specific cultural, and social requirements.

The Indian scholars helped the Christian Missionaries in translating *The Bible* which was followed by the translation of western classics. Bankim Chandra's was the first effort that gave us our first English novel *Rajmohan's Wife* (1864). Regarding Bankim Chandra's writing, Annada Shankar Ray says: "The chief question was how to restore the national self-respect. In Rabindranath's time, it was how to bridge the East and the West. In this dynamic age, it is how to identify ourselves with the common people."

Mulk Raj Anand and R.K. Narayan give a promise to Indian writing in English through their mastery in the form of Novel. Anand was a bit bitter, using swear words at times and entering into political controversy. The use of English in Anand gives the impression of him as an angry young artist whereas Narayan has made English in India gain a local tone and colour which he knew would best suit the themes that he chose from the Indian rusticity. There is first time a profound sense of humour, the practice of the comedy form in Indian English Novel, use of Indian cultural and superstitious codes in a language, ironical, satirical and very much Indian from all sides.

Raja Rao's attitude was to incorporate everything Indian, the theme, language and style into the English language as we have mentioned earlier from his *Kanthapura*. On style also he says there. "After language, the next problem is that of style. The tempo of Indian life must be infused into our English expression, even as the tempo of American or Irish life has gone into the making of theirs. We, in India, think quickly, we talk quickly, and when we move we move quickly. We tell one interminable tale" (Foreword, *Kanthapura,* 1938).

Kanthapura is a new variety of fiction, having a fusion of poetry, politics using typical Indian words like 'Vaisakh' and displaying the 'Kartik' festival as here :

> "Kartik has come to Kanthapura... with the glow of lights and the unpressed footsteps of the wandering gods; white lights from clay-trays and red lights from copper-stands, and diamond lights that glow from the bowers of entrance-leaves; lights that glow from banana-trunks and mango twigs, yellow lights behind white leaves, and green leaves; the night curls through the shadowed streets, and hissing over bellied boulders and hurrying through dallying drains, night curls through the Brahmin street and the Pariah street and the Potters' street and the Weavers' street and flapping through the mango grove, hangs clawed for one moment to the giant pipal, and then shooting across the broken fields, dies quietly into the river and gods walk by lighted streets... Kartik is a month of the gods...".(*Kanthapura*, 1938)

There is an attempt, bold and sustained to get the English language set to an articulation of Indian or Sanskritic models of thought and speech. The mixture of East and West, country and city life and culture is well portrayed in Bhabani Bhattacharya's *Music for Mohini* (1952) as Rooplekha says: "We who're so wed serve some real purpose. It's as though we made a bridge between two banks of a river. We connect culture with culture, Mohini, our old Eastern view of life with the new semi-western outlook. Our use of the Western language so can not make us Westerners, it would be again only a bridge of communication, bridge of exposure and understanding each other.

There was a growing feeling that writing in English was a criticism of the Hindu society and its conservative attitude. It was because most of the novels saw through society and revealed the unrest out of the social inequality, hypocrisy and prejudice. Anthony Burgess says on the language while introducing an edition of the novel *All About H. Hatterr* (1970) by G.V. Desani, "a sort of creative chaos that grumbles at the restraining banks... it is, like the English of Shakespeare, Joyce and Kipling, gloriously impure." In the same novel we also find expressions daringly Indian like "In Sarad, Hemant, Sisir, in all seasons alike, sheltered under a canopy fan-shaped, of the lily and the lotus, frozen flowers, frozen in a proud garden of the lily and the lotus-laden snow."

Some of the basic questions have been whether Indian poetry can be written in English, whether the Indian imagery and tradition could be expressed in the medium of English, whether such poetry written now-a-days in English is really Indian and so on. And from time to time writers have also felt that there could be Indian motifs, responses, attitudes and trends displayed in the other language. The images of rain, lotus, peacock as we have seen them, the concept of renunciation, detachment as our sages and intellectuals have perceived have been well put into the language we deal with. Deb Kumar Das says, of the three languages available for tackling themes and traditions on "an all India basis", with impartiality, his vote was for English"; Sanskrit is dead, Hindi is a lexicographer's fantasy; and although English is 'alien', it is at least a living language and can be shared by creative minds, not by grammarians or linguistic experts."[1] Anita Desai talks of a "marvellous elasticity and expressiveness" in the English language and Pradip Sen remarks "If the English language is suitable to express the sentiments and feelings of the Jews 2,000 years ago, I do not see why it cannot express Indian imagery and tradition".[2]

P. Lal affirms, "Without trying to be facetious, I should like to suggest that only in English can real Indian poetry be written; any other poetry is likely to be Bengali-slanted or Gujarati-biased, and so on. Only Indian writing in English can hope to attain the 'Indian' flavour. I cannot imagine a Punjabi writing Bengali poetry, or a Maharashtrian writing Hindi poetry, but there are Tamilians, Bengalis, Punjabis, Gujaratis, Jews, Goans, Sikkimese—all Indians writing in English on Indian themes for Indian readers."[3] It is well realised that Indians across the country have found a creative self-expression through English. Deb Kumar Das again perceives the situation as "The Indo-Anglian writer, in the sense of what he has to be rather than what he necessarily is at the moment, is a new faith in transition. He is the choice and the instrument of a phase of history which, in turn, is only a piece in the jigsaw of human events. What he can do; what he can say; what he can be; what he can achieve. These define him as no other facts or failings can. And on this is built hope, and commitment, and adventure. The whole point about the Indo-Anglian phenomenon, surely, is that it is a dialect of the mind rather than of the tongue. It is the focus of the mirror, destinies in the Indian tradition, the classic Indian and the grafted western; and, in the ultimate analysis, may prove to be more real than either."[4]

A brief summary

In retrospection, ever since the Indian soil saw the publication of Rammohun Roy's tract on 'Sati', our atmosphere got ready for the new generation of 'Indian English writing'. Just like the Aryan inflow of Sanskrit and Muslim inflow of Urdu, English came as the vehicle of the West to us which in turn became our national identity and reflection. A culture is dynamic and healthy when it accommodates as well as makes room within it for another culture. Language is the most significant part of a culture. So was the adoption of English in our main stream. For all practical purposes, from national conferences to business contracts, English has been an 'all India' language and it is the language of the 'dominant minority' since the trendy business community, political class and corporates promote its importance in their fields apart from the specialised use by the academics and professionals.

In the other commonwealth countries English has fared well though they have been free from the clutches of colonisation and so has been the status of English in their national literature, medium and prosperity. The introduction of English in India is in fact the entry of 'Renaissance' in India.

The Status of Indian English at Present

Indian English today has a distinct space independent of the specific creative and critical writing in this area. The media and wide interaction among people of different places which is fast growing due to rapid industrialisation, commercialisation and scientific progress everywhere have enabled the atmosphere rely on the language in its different forms, the easily digestible, comprehensible and trendy manner of expression.

Goffin says "Anglo-Indian is, after all, merely a jargon, a few scattered limbs of speech, whereas Indian English though it began as, and still largely consists of 'ignorant English', does yet show signs of assuming an individual body, or at least a sort of ghostly life—an English far exiled from home." What the forerunners of Indian English dreamt of its status for the future has been a reality today when we get quite a large number of newspapers, periodicals, books, published, circulated across the country starting from the libraries to the small book corners.

A.N. Jha had reported once, "May I, in that respect, venture to plead for the use, retention and encouragement of Indian English ? Is there any reason why we need be ashamed of Indian English ? Who is there in the United Provinces who will not understand a young man who says he is going to join the 'teachery' profession and who after a few years says he is engaged in headmastery' ? Similarly, why should we accept the English phrase, 'mare's nest', and object to 'horse's egg', as familiar in the columns of *Amrita Bazar Patrika* ? Why should we adhere to 'all this' when 'this all' is the natural order suggested by the usage of our own language ? Why insist on 'yet' following 'though' when in Hindustani we use the equivalent of 'but' ? Must we condemn the following sentence because it does not conform to English idiom, even though it is a literal translation of our own idiom ? I shall not pay a paisa, what to say of a rupee...". A little courage, some determination, a wholesome respect for our own idioms, and we shall before long have a virile, vigorous 'Indian English."[5]

Before being content in the established status of Indian English it is essential to see it under the framework of linguistic sciences as Kachru studies it in 'The Indianness in Indian English': "...we have attempted to illustrate that the distance between the natively used varieties of English and Indian English cannot be explained only by comparative studies of phonology and grammar. The deviation is an outcome of the Indianisation of English which has, gradually, made Indian English culture-bound in the socio-cultural setting of India. The phonological and grammatical deviations are only a part of the process of Indianisation."[6]

Due to necessity the editors of the journals disclaim any intention to offer readable writing. The new compounds and derivatives in the field of science and technology are labelled ISV (International Science Vocabulary) now-a-days. The use of ISV has created an interest in the employment of abbreviations in present day writing. Since they save a lot of time and all languages use them and comprehend them their use is more appreciated. A large number of people print R.S.V.P. on their invitation card without knowing the source and significance, whether actually the originators, the French, have stopped using such expressions or not. The process of change of such abbreviations is very interesting to note. 'S.A.A.R.C.' became SAARC and then 'Saarc' in a chain and the 'Society for checking the Abuses of Public Advertising' has become scapa: S.C.A.P.A.; SCAPA; Scapa. How many of the people know that 'FIAT' is the Fabbrica & Italiana Automobili Torino and 'PEN' as the club for poets, playwrights, essayists, editors and novelists. The language is adapting itself to any kind of changing circumstance. There is a tendency to shorten long vowels and a drifting between voiceless and voiced consonants to suit the user and his needs. English is taking the place of French as a second language in Latin America and some European countries. As a trade language its use is immense every where in the world and the influence it has had over the other national languages is a recent (after the eighteenth century) but lasting phenomenon. Over the centuries English has been just a competitor among the European languages but at the world level it has strived to remain indispensable. The text books designed for us at our preliminary learning level of the language has been giving importance to produce grammatically correct sentences and the notions of greeting politely, attend parties with proper language codes at such places.

But recently things have taken a completely different twist. At the secondary level text books have been designed to teach the students the skills of listening, speaking, reading and writing and creative answers, compositions without any strict, imitative, fixed grammatical rules or patterns. Even in the class room the cultural nuances that motivate the teacher and the students have a greater say than how the textbooks are planned to be considered. So there is overlapping of languages, cultures, practices and also the manner of interpretations. When English is taught in an Indian context it acquires an Indianness at the lexical, structural and thematic levels for practical purposes. So even though a specific 'Indian English' has not been prescribed or officialised in reality what we notice is just the opposite, the teaching of a variety, not strictly British or Indian but in between the two.

Indian Writing in English (IWE) is now recognised as one of the dozen or more authentic voices that India has to express itself with. What was created once as the medium to rouse a nation for awakening, self-respect and step ahead in history has now grown into a creative trend, generating literature and a whole way of life establishing a distinct culture of its own. Kachru remarks:

> "In India the English language has blended itself with the cultural and social complex of the country and has become, as Raja Rao says the language of the 'intellectual make up' of Indians. It is the only language, except perhaps Sanskrit, which has been retained and used by Indian intellectuals in spite of political pressures and regional language loyalty. In certain ways the use of English as a link language (and the growth of Indian English) has for the first time created a pan-India literature (except of course, the earlier use of Sanskrit) which symbolises the cultural and socio-political aspirations of Indians."[7]

Such a new culture of Indian English with its regional blends and variations in our country only adds to the other distinct forms; the American English, African English, Canadian English, Newzealandian English, Australian English, Caribbean English and so on. The result is a world literature in English out of the 'Global village' and Indian English becomes a distinct phenomenon to it. Bruce King's *Literature of the World in English* (London, 1974) and *(Kunapipi)*, a bi-annual magazine edited by Anna Rutherford, University of Aarhus (Denmark) which devotes its pages to new writing in English anywhere in the world, stand testimony to the globalisation of English and acknowledgement of Indian English.

At present we have successfully made use of the English language which we came in contact in past. As a language we know English has borrowed a lot. So we agree to its status as a global language. When a nation expresses itself through a medium, it is its own as all its distortions, whims and socio-cultural codes are reflected in that medium. We have got a large body of creative and critical writing in this language, a number of newspapers and journals apart from its status as the intellectual, administrative vehicle.When different people put on the same dress differently it is the specific style that gives each its distinct worth and the dress belongs to the person concerned rather than its owner. The question is suitability and not imitation. Indian English is our suitable self-expression, our medium of self-employment and modernisation in the face of the world. So it is ours being ingrained in our lifestyle, an established and promising genre.

The trend of Indianisation of the English language in the works of art has been well experimented and no one really bothers whether it is officially permissible to write in such a form of the language. It has been the practice today and may be the most acknowledged one and official one tomorrow. It is a kind of literary nationalism that we foresee.The category that seems to be more Indian than English in its use of the English language consists of a group who have created a form that expresses the Indianness of feeling and thinking, conversation in the Indian way, argument and curse, translating the Indian tempo into the English language as we find in Lal Behari Dey, Mulk Raj Anand and Raja Rao.

Meenakshi Mukherjee considers Anand as "the first conscious experimenter" in putting the Indian style into the English language. She also feels in her article "Style in Indo-Anglian Fiction": "The few writers who wrote novels in English in the early part of this century used language carefully, with stiff correctness, but always conscious that it was a foreign tongue and in the nineteen thirties the sudden and vigorous attempt to weild the language in a different way was marked by the experiment of Mulk Raj Anand followed by Raja Rao." Sochee Chunder Dutt gives the touch of Indian words directly translated to give a strange impression to the foreigner in his publication (1845, P. 51), words like 'straw-pallets' and 'low-house' although the exact equivalent of these words in English are available.

In his novel *The Young Zemindar,* it is remarkably seen :

> It was a grand 'mela', and an immense multitude variously reckoned at from ten to fifteen thousand persons, were congregated within the mango-grove to celebrate it. There were all kinds of men and among them from the 'chasa' and the cowherd, who had taken short leave of their fields, to the Hindu 'Mohunt', and the Mahomedan 'Fakir' to take part in the festivity; and even the village girls and matrons had ceased working from the time at their 'dhenki' and with the 'Koola', though such immunity from their labour falls rarely to their lot (P.15). He has also used words like 'asirvad', 'goolmal' in the same novel.

But the significant development can be seen in the attempt of translating Indian idioms of speech into English—the first attempt in Indo-Anglian fiction since the exact equivalents are not available, in the novels of Lal Behari Dey. In his *Govinda Samanta* (1874) the priest and peasant are in conversation :

> "Ho Badan! are you at home ?" said a husky voice at the door of Badan's house one evening, a few days after the celebration of the feast of First Rice. "Who are you?" shouted Badan from the Verandah of the big room where he was sitting and enjoying a pull or two of the peaceful hookah." Come in, Acharya Mahasaya; this is an auspicious day when the door of my house has been blessed with the dust of your honour's feet."

The Indian idioms like "On the head which is already saturated with oil, more oil is spread, whereas we poor folk go entirely oilless" (P. 268) in the same novel really starts a spectacular journey on its way to assert the way we understand the usage to the outside world. The peasant in the same novel as discussed above shouts:

"Rupa's mother ! Rupa's mother !" (P. 6). There is another instance where the peasant Badan asks "Don't you think, mother, it would be a good thing to give Govin his 'hate khadi'? Don't you think, it would be a capital thing to teach Govin 'Lekhapada'?" (Writing and reading, P. 58.). Also Badan Says: "Whatever is written on the forehead by Vidhata purusha must come to pass. × × × The quantity of rice with which he had to come into the world was finished, and therefore he died. It was fate, mother, it was fate." In Indian context "Kapaal Likhan" is a key concept which the author has tried to translate directly. The author himself justified his stand by saying that it is rather better to retain the Bengali identity of the peasants in their use of the language rather than making them appear the Yorkshire or Somerset peasants using the dialects of English. He also uses 'crow-cowing, straw-loft, paddy-straw' which are direct translations of Indian idioms. Here is again the interesting use of the Indian onomatopoeia :

> "...Kalamanik sitting on his toes in a kneeling posture, and resting the milk-can before his knee-joints, went on milking at a great rate to the delightful tune of chan-cho, chan-cho, chan-cho" (P. 143). "Neither of them spoke for some time, we presume, the exquisite music which was produced between them. The 'bhroor-bhroor-bhroor' of the hubble-bubble kept time with 'ghnan-ghnan-ghnan' of the charkha, and the two together evoked a melody." (P. 58)

Mulk Raj Anand's English goes steps ahead in showing signs of Indianness in rhythm of speech, the feeling, blessings and curses, and so on. The trend has been so that, while initially Anand used to give glossary and notes on the Indian terms used in his earlier novels, he later gave up the practice as Indian English had gained a status of its own by that time. But the use of distorted words, wrong pronunciations by the common man in India has been expressed by Anand's novels; words like 'Motu Car' (motor car). In *Two Leaves and a Bud* (P. 111), 'fashun' (fashion) and 'natus' (native) in *Untouchable* (P. 9), 'injan' (engine), 'railgar' (Railway train),'haspatal' (for hospital), (P. 197) in *Coolie*, at times evoke disgust in some critics as a device unnecessary to attract attention as the Indian Coolie never goes for conversation in English. But the point is different.The assertion of Indianness in language is something that matters. Anand's translation of Indian idioms and phrases is more significant qualitatively that has enriched the later trend in Indian English as can be seen here in *Coolie*:

> "Eaters of their masters! They have raised their heads to the skies! They think that just because they have prestige in this world they can do anything!" (P.54). "Muno ohe Munooa O Mundoo! where have you died, you the evil star?" (P.5). "Are you talking true talk?" asked Munoo (P.139). "In your thought do you think it will be possible for me to get a job at the factory where you work?" (P.153)". "Let us mention the name of God, and go on," said Hari (P.154).

It is definitely an innovative Indian style in writing. The language amuses the learned and acts exactly as the Indian way of cursing, suggesting, coaxing happen in common people. Imitating such nuances into the English form retaining all the Indianness except the script is no doubt the trend today. Throughout his novels one finds abusive structures like 'rape mother', 'rape sister', 'rape daughter', 'lover of your mother', 'illegally begotten', 'may your lives burn', 'may the vessels of your life never float in the sea of existence', 'may the vessels of your life be drowned', 'spoiler of my salt', 'eaters of their masters', 'son of a pig' and direct Indian words like 'Suar ka bacha' and 'Haram zada'. Other Indian curses and abuses also have been reported [8] such as : 'You of evil stars', 'You cock-eyed son of a bow-legged scorpion' etc.

The Indian syntactic uniqueness is expressed in sentences like "The meaning of my life is my child" and "Your shoe on my head" in *Untouchable*. Anand says in his paper "Pigeon Indian" (P.1):

> "I believe that Indian English writing has come to stay as a literature of Indian, because it is based on Indian English language of the most vital character like Irish English, American English, Welsh English, Australian English or Canadian English."[9]

Raja Rao uses translations of Indian 'identificational nominals' into English at the risk of violating both English syntax and English collocation, as pointed Kachru. Here we find such cases in his *Kanthapura*; "Kannaya-House people", "Water fall Venkamma", "Temple Lakshamma", "Bhatta's wife chinnamma", "Coffee planter", "Santpur Patwari Venkatramayya", "Norse-Scratching Nanjamma" etc.

Then, there are abusive terms like 'Son of Concubine', 'I will sleep with your wife', 'you donkey's husband', 'you bearded monkey', 'you parian day' etc. In the same novel the use of Indian interjections, vocatives and exclamations can be seen:

> "He is the age our Seenu is, and he and Seenu were as, one would say, our Rama and brother Lakshmana" (P.13). "He chenna, cried Range Gowda, turning towards the inner courtyard." "You had better go to the Big Field and see whether these sons of countries are planting well"(P.24). "You can offer me a king's daughter, out never will I sell my soul to a pariah" (P.66). "O Maharaja, we are lickers of your feet" (P.138). "But our Rangamma was as sane as a cow" and she only said, "One cannot stitch up the mouths of others" (P.138).

About the above we can say it is a mechanical way of producing the Indian tone and words and structures. Similarly the rhythms of Indian ways of life and sensibilities can be seen in the same novel *Kanthapura* :

> "They said Moorthy would come by the blue bus that runs from Lallapuri to Karwar" and well said, "That will be when the *Sun has passed* over the courtyard," and we were at the village gate when the cattle had drunk the afternoon rice-water and gone, and pariahs were already there with blankets and coconuts and horns, and the weaver folk were there with silk upper cloth, and the potters with pots and the betel-sellers with betel-leaves, and even lazy Range Gowda was there, rubbing his eyes and waving his turban to keep away flies and perspiration—so sultry was the day"(P.166). Also "And yet he was as honest as an elephant" (P.18). "More and more men followed him as they did Krishna the flute-player" (P.22). Moorthy said, 'like Hanuman to Rama' (P.53). 'But our Rengamma was as tame as a cow' (P.138) and she only said, "One cannot stitch up the mouth of others." (P.138)

Thus the trend is already on its progressive, promising mode. English has acquired a distinctively Indian shape with the characteristics of an Indian language. The status today of such a language could be well traced from what Anthony Burgess says in his introduction to the 1972 Penguin edition of the novel *All About H. Hatterr* by G.V. Desani:

> "It is what may be termed whole language, in which philosophical terms, the colloquialisms of Calcutta and London, Shakespearean archaism, bazar whinings, quack spiels, references to the Hindu Pantheon, the jargon of Indian litigation, and shrill babu irritability seen together. It is not pure English; it is like the English of Shakespeare, Joyce and Kipling, gloriously impure."[10]

Even though officially there is a stress on regional languages everywhere, the number of entry into the English medium schools, increase in books, newspapers at railway stations, book shops and libraries, the university system clearly shows the steady and established position that English in India has sought to occupy. To the question of its survival, what K.R. Srinivasa Iyengar says in his *Indian Writing in English* (1962) is relevant:

> "Most of our writers are bi-lingual, some equally proficient in English and the mother tongue, and some more in one than in the other. The background and the situations are usually Indian, but the characters may often be drawn from bilingual milieus. The need for exposing the values, varieties, and heartbeats of one culture in the language of another poses its own problems and there is doubtless the inner urge to render in English, the rhythms, idiosyncracies, images, idioms and proverbs of the local speech. At a deeper level language transcends mere translation; the medium is the message, and the soul-charged piece of writing then acquires its own autonomy."[11]

The History of Journalism in India

Journalism is both an artistic and professional enterprise that lifts, records the events that are significant and opinions that are worth discussing, and offers the public a scope of scrutiny and understanding. It has risen to practice as the vehicle of communication among people too and as a reading material with both light and serious sketch of the writing for a wider public unlike the interest intended by serious texts and classics. Even though people differ in their opinion of defining journalism as art or profession, a balanced view must admit that it is factual, databased, brief and so a professional work and at moments of editorial fancy, whims and analysis, opinion based articles it is serious art. C. Rajagopalchari points out : "Journalists are like painters and poets rather than factory workers. They are really creating a work of art."

Newspaper and other journalistic content so provide what can be called the popular literature. It is popular in terms of sales, more acknowledged by all sections of the society, mostly used by people of all trades. Its chief purpose is to entertain and it has an immediate, spontaneous response. On the other hand, the elite literature, the classics are meant to challenge the values, raise new values, become an art form of contemplation and there is a stress on form, style as well as the serious thought content. Popular literature so at times poses a threat to the healthy traditions of other writing and values. So in the present time it presents a more difficult problem than any form of high art which is selective. Today's newspaper content, scope, schemes, sections are overloaded with variety which establishes a new method in journalism outside.

So though the journalistic writing could time and again use the language and content like serious literature, the ego of the reporter or the journalist had to make rooms for the more objective approach and intention to meet the requirements of the reader.

The Indian pluralistic culture and race has raised numerous and versatile issues that have reflected our national heritage and variations offering a big contrast to what is perceived outside.

(a) The Indian journalistic tradition has stood firm beside the colonial rule and issues related to it;
(b) Social reform, especially in the 19th Century at the hands of free thinkers and social activists;
(c) National security, relations with the neighbouring countries;
(d) Political instability, corruption and social change pertaining to education, exploitation and growth both economic and cultural.

The Indian experience of the freedom of Press and a democratic stand is more strong than the developing countries elsewhere since our secular notions have stood the test of time always. If we divide such a long tradition of our journalism, in the first hand we get its role as an:

(i) inspiring force of the liberation struggle and the other as a commentator of
(ii) the flawed democratic institutional experience of an

independent nation which was well perceived in the 'Defamation Bill', 1988.

We get roughly 200 years as the ground for the study of Indian journalistic experience.

The initial attempts by outsiders

James Augustus Hicky launched the first newspaper in India known as the *Bengal Gazette* in 1780, almost hundred fifty years after the first British newspaper came up. The paper became a bit controversial since it earned contempt of the colonial ruler and also being competed by its contemporary rival *Indian Gazette*. Bengal earns the reputation of the birth of journalism in India. In Madras, *Madras Courier* came out as a weekly in 1785. In 1789 *Bombay Herald* and then *Bombay Gazette* (1791) started publishing next. These papers were controlled by the government. The proceedings of the British Parliament could not be published in these papers. *Bengal Journal, Indian World, Bengal Harkarer* suffered from the exploitation of the rulers.The first real journalist in India is James Silk Buckingham who stood for the freedom of Press. He became the editor of the paper *Calcutta Chronicle*, that appeared first on October 2, 1818 which indicated to be a chronicle of political, commercial and literary news and views. Buckingham gave emphasis to the local conditions and news, emphasized the voice and opinion of the Indian people, criticised both the government's policies as well as Indian evil practices like 'Sati' and 'Child marriage'.

Initial attempts by Indians

In the field of journalism in India, the first name is that of Rammohun Roy when we think about the Indian journalists. He founded the *Sambad Kaumudi* (Bengali) in 1821. He was the victim of restriction of Press freedom in his days and strongly stood for it by talking about the unrestrained liberty of publication.This was the time when Indian Press took the social and administrative evils as the chief subject for its body of writing. Newspaper fixed the motto of social reform. He glorified the idea of a liberal socio-cultural tradition first gaining from the liberal West which could be utilised for the political freedom next. He used the Press and his writing in this field as the vehicle of such an ideal.The first Indian owned English daily, the *Bengal Gazette* was published in 1816 by Gangadhar Bhattacharjee. It seems that Rammohun Roy was behind all these attempts, the launching of newspapers at such a time though he did not associate himself directly to them.

The Indian Press continued its struggle against official hostility. During 1831-33, there were 33 English newspapers. Dwarkanath Tagore started the *Bengal Herald* (English weekly), Girish Chandra Ghosh started the *Hindu Patriot* (1953) which later came into the hands of the social reformer Ishwar Chandra Vidyasagar. In 1861, the *Indian Mirror* (an English fortnightly) was started by Manmohan Ghosh. Keshub Chandra Sen converted it into a daily. In 1861 an Anglo-Marathi daily *Indu Prakash* was started by Gopal Rao Hari Deshmukh on which M.G. Ranade ran an English column. Ranade felt a national press and national education were potent means for national uplift. Dadabhai Naroji started his own monthly journal, *Voice of India* on February 1, 1882. The year 1881 had already seen the rise of *Mahratta* (English) and *Kesri* (Marathi) by Bal Gangadhar Tilak. He thought English education was like tiger's milk and had strong favour for it.

The professional momentum

The Anglo-Indian Press which prospered in India spoke through the newspapers like the *Englishman, Statesman, Times of India, Madras Mail, Madras Times, Civil and Military Gazette, Pioneer* of which *The Statesman* and *The Times of India* have changed into Indian hands in later years. Robert Knight founded the *Statesman* in 1875. He had also worked in *The Bombay Times* (1838) which he merged with *Standard* and the *Telegraph* (both from Bombay) renaming it *The Times of India* in 1861. Knight was a versatile journalist and tried to awaken public opinion campaigning to protect the health of Bombay citizens. He actually tried to bring close the Indian and Anglo-Indian journalists. He was more interested in the public than the British Government in India as a journalist ought to be. Both *The Madras Times* (1860) and *Pioneer* (1861) had the intention to defend the British administration and its working against the protest of the Indian Press. *The Civil and Military Gazette* came out in Lahore (1872) merging papers like *Mofussilman* of *Agra* (1845), *Lahore Chronicle* (1846), *Punjab Times* and the *Indian Public Opinion* (1867). Rudyard Kipling was a staff of the *Civil and Military Gazette* who later worked in *The Pioneer*. Kipling describes his attitude in the *Pioneer* as: "I made my own experiments in the weight, colours, perfumes and attributes of words either as read aloud so that they may hold the ear or, scattered over the page, draw the eye." Kipling also said:

> "Western education is an exotic plant... we brought it out from England exactly as we brought out the ink bottles and the patterns for the chairs. We planted it and it grew monstrous as a banian."

A Brief Account of Journalism Today

As it has already been observed in a nutshell before, today's world of newspapers conform to a multi-dimensional objective. The progress of a civilisation always throws wider issues. In modern times inter disciplinary approach is adopted in all spheres. The newspaper is no exception to this experiment. The number of newspapers also have started being growing which necessitate the need of multifarious and more analytic issues for the public. Much of it would be discussed in the next chapter. Here we are just trying to concentrate on some of the features of present day journalism.

Magazine explosion

A revolution in production technique and commercialisation had effected the magazine explosion that began after 1976. The 'news magazine' became a trend. The 'news magazine' took investigative efforts to issues, political and otherwise, it motivated the style, substance, variety, management, circulation, technology, professionalism, marketing and design.

There has been an increase of daily newspapers over the years as follows:

Table 2.1 : Number of Newspapers (1997-2000)

Year	*English Dailies*	*Tri-Bi weekly*	*Weekly*	*Fortni-ghtly*	*Monthly*	*Quarterly*	*Annuals*	*Others*	*Total*
1997	256	18	637	496	2161	1025	133	590	5316
1999-00	371	30	881	671	2734	1210	162	771	6830

Source: *Manorama Year Book* (1997) and *India 2001* (2001).

In the West, sensationalism, violence, sex have been the prime theme whereas in a developing country like India which has cultural, social differences and a political experience that motivated the media for a value based war first which only in later times became a bit melodramatic due to the more liberalised society and open outlook which at times creates gaps with the tradition.

The local dailies

Two factors influence the rapid production of local dailies in modern times:

(i) The newspaper toady is a profitable business unlike that of colonial times, it is being commercialised very fast and at times the news items are suppressed under advertisements.

(ii) The leading newspapers at the national level are more or less confined to metropolitan cities and highlight more about the foreign as well as national news in a broad scale. The local dailies have come up very fast to meet the requirements of the respective states as well as regions. They confine to the news of the state and districts and inquisitively try to see the local socio-cultural problems, from the state of agriculture to the natural calamities and hunger and focus on local talents as far as the columns and articles are concerned. Their role in developing the language and content cannot be neglected. Some of the local newspapers, the *Sun Times, Assam Tribune, Arunachal Times* in the respective states have come very late but clearly assert their regional accent both in linguistic and thematic terms which is a modern development. For example, the *Sun Times* has started writing terms like 'Cuttack' as 'Katak', 'Orissa' as 'Odissa' as they are spoken locally.

Language then and today

Broadly, journalism earlier had a role in the freedom struggle in India along with social reform which required language to be impressionistic and sentimental, emotionally charged to attract mass attention. In modern times journalism became the upholder of democratic principle and a powerful agent of social transformation. English was a new experience for educated Indians of the 18th Century. The language was no doubt imitative and artificial. Direct influence of the mother-tongue and nativity was more than that of later times. English in the West has also changed a lot since then. Rammohun Roy was conscious of the pleasure and variety that the English language offered. His hold on English language in his journalistic practice is observed by Jeremy Bentham, the English writer: "which (his English) but for the name of a Hindu, I shall certainly have ascribed to the pen of a superiorly educated and instructed Englishman."

Speaking things in a roundabout manner was the practice as is seen from a statement by Rammohun Roy: "Every good ruler must be conscious of the great liability to err in managing the affairs of a vast empire and therefore, he will be anxious to afford to every individual the readiest means of bringing to his notice whatever may require his interference". Tilak thought, English education as the tiger's milk. His writing read like speeches. This is an important aspect of most of the leaders of those times when the immediate need of arousing the emotional response of the people for agitation was the goal. So the speech form was reflected in writing. Tilak's sentences were crisp, simple and pointed in approach. He also used quotations from Purans, Sanskrit writing, and he sounded as an editor-philosopher. It created a fire like sensation in imagination. The writing and practice of English was definitely ours as gradually, the emotional appeal of our leaders, our cultural ethos got transferred to the foreign tongue. A person who feels intensely, burning with new ideas in a new context makes a foreign language fitting to this context going for an innovative use of the language which was done effectively.There was also a difference in using the language among the moderates and the extremists in the Congress. Gandhi's practice of English was very simple and lucid. He appealed to the nerves again. His language also was charged with a spiritual idealism. When Tilak says : "Swaraj is my birth right"; Gandhi's voice is more soothing : "We want to overthrow the government, we want to compel its submission to the people's will". Gandhi had a very effective style that of touching the whole of India, from the peasant to the enlightened. He also used no confusing sentence, cliche and stressed on clarity.

A foreign writer once had the view that Gandhi's writing was like painting. He returned again and again to the canvas, adding, shifting, focusing what has already been expressed and was never satisfied with what he wrote first. The stronghold of grammar had a pressure in older times and the editors were formidable grammarians and stylists. Nehru had a much better practice of the language. He was poetic without being hysterical and much sentimental on public issues.

The language of English has gone through serious changes over the years throughout the world due to factors like:

(i) a more global approach.
(ii) corporatisation, consumerisation of societies and free access to one another.
(iii) growing distaste for rigidity of the language.

Indian journalistic language taken on the whole has not yet been so precise. The round about usage of language and mere rhetoricism have been the practice of some columnists in modern times too which misses the point straightaway. The leading newspapers put the business sections in a more catchy and trendy manner. *The Economic Times* (1961) and *Business Standard* (1975) have boldly asserted a kind of language that have been a major influence in the usage of language by the business executives, agents and corporate sector. Whether the medium has been a kind of alienation from the textual English and being so rather has been a more popular medium in such developing countries like India is a challenging question which has to be met and researched subsequently. Journalism throughout these years in India has come to a point of realizing that the themes have been changed and it is a world of creating one's own medium under the global cover of English rather than strict imitation of the past. So any trace of our ethnicity, cultural nuances and social set up through the language is a growing trend and considered as an innovation in our use of English. The journalistic register so has been a complete different field other than the strict imitative modes followed in the textbooks and educational institutions. So it has become a field of improvement and practice and fast change. The intellectual, philosophical as well as marketing needs have affected and facilitated the field of journalistic register. Though officially English is in the retreat in most of the states in India, the expansion of English medium schools, and an indirect rush to express and interact in that medium in all walks of life has created such informal use of English by the English dailies.

Srinivasa Ayengar says :

> "The need for expressing the values, varieties and heart-beats of one culture in the language of another poses its own problems,

and there is doubtless the inner urge to render in English, the rhythms, idiosyncracies, images, idioms and proverbs of the local speech".

The above spheres of change along with the dominance of the advertisement world as a separate discipline and profession on the pages of our newspa pers have shaped the growth of Indian English as a distinct variety.

A brief account of some leading newspapers over a long period of time

The five leading English dailies that have crossed the century mark are the *Amrita Bazar Patrika*, *The Hindu*, *The Tribune* (Indian owned) and *The Times of India*, *The Statesman* which had been British owned and edited (later gone into the Indian hands after India became free). All these have a tremendous role in the national struggle for independence, social reform and towards the growth of Indian journalism and status of the English language.

(1) The *Amrita Bazar Patrika* was born as a Bengali weekly in February 1868 in Bengal (now in Bangladesh). Sisir Kumar edited it writing against the alien rulers which became the mouthpiece of the downtrodden and poor. It moved to Calcutta in 1871 and functioned as a bi-lingual weekly, published news and ideas in English. It became an English weekly later, became a daily in February 1891. It shared its identity with the anti-British wing and dared express it. Its language could be perceived here on its page on August 15, 1947 : "It is dawn, cloudy though it is. Presently, Sunshine will break".

(2) *The Hindu* was founded in Madras on September 20, 1878. It started as a weekly and became a daily in 1889. It was an elitist paper with the motive to express views on the political and social topics attracting the intellectuals of these areas. It brought out a sports weekly, *Sports Star* in 1978 and a fortnightly, *Frontline* in 1984. It made a strong point on its ideology by standing defiantly for Press freedom.

(3) The *Statesman* was started in 1875 by Robert Knight. It has been always the practice of Indians to follow the *Statesman* for its language, style which according to Nirad C. Chaudhury can replace Macaulay's fine English. It shared the rightist

point of view in the 1920s. It was both conservative trying to conserve the best traditions of the country and liberal in trying to be free of dangers and superstitions.

The Statesman wrote on August 15, 1947 : "Now is the appointed day. Now is the day of salvation. If we start right, we can continue right..."

(4) *The Tribune* came up in 1881 in Lahore as a weekly by Sardar Dayal Singh Majithia. In its first issue on February 2, 1881, it said "the aim of the *Tribune* will be, as its name imparts, fairly and temperately to advance the cause of the mute masses... We shall strive as much as lies in the compass of our humble abilities to create and educate such opinion."

(5) *The Times of India* has been the most controversial among the centenarians since its pro-administrative views before independence on most occasions. But its role in making journalistic discourse in English a growing, developed and distinct phenomenon has been immense in course of time. After Independence it has occupied the highest position as a leading mainstream daily in English. It is the oldest English daily in India. It came up as the *Times of India* after the merging of *Bombay Times* and two other papers in 1861. The first issue of *Bombay Times* appeared in Bombay on November 3, 1838. Its first editior, J.E. Brennan wrote in the first issue on the need of education for the people of India "whose capacity for improvement is inferior to that of no one elsewhere but were victims of ignorance and delusion". *The Times of India* sought for abolition of Sati, Child marriage, Widow remarriage, against polygamy and has had a very profound role in social reform.

In 1890 it printed 3000 copies daily. Its name has been associated with both Bennett and Coleman (F.M. Coleman) who facilitated daily newspaper production. K. Ramarao, sub-editor in 1920s wrote that it was a complete paper "carrying the highest prestige in particular for its sports and commercial coverage. It carried more Indian news than many Indian papers." It came to Indian hands in 1946. The *Economic Times* (1961), *The Illustrated Weekly of India* (journal) are associated to it. By 1984 it had the second largest circulation among the English dailies in India.Today it has the highest circulation in this country. Its issue on September 23, 1998 says it has 178 per cent growth in the

Delhi edition's circulation over the last four years making it the fastest growing daily in Delhi. It is based on the Audit Bureau of Circulation figures published for July-December 1997. One of its September issues also quotes from the "world communication report" brought out by UNESCO for 1996 that the *Times of India* figures among the 30 top dailies in the world in terms of circulation. It also says it has a sale of 9,78,000 daily which is the highest in the country, of all its editions combined. The report also says, in 1991, 21 newspapers were sold for a population of 1,000 whereas 67 newspapers were sold for 1000 inhabitants in 1996. By 1997 (the year from which we mainly started collecting our data) it was established as the top circulated newspaper in English with 9,54,619 circulation copies (*Manorama Year Book,* 1997). For the reasons above, we have taken *The Times of India* of the contemporary times as our model and primary field of research for our proposed task.

Also the paper which once was a staunch supporter of the British cause, today offers the widest variety in terms of news and items, and the most important aspect is the twists and Indianisation of English. The numerous changes in lexical, syntactic, structural usage have been influenced by it and it has projected a transformed, distinct way of using English by Indians. Since its widest access to people, it has developed an interest in making our use of English help our English having a distinction of its own. Its role and data can be taken into account to have represented our newspaper English.

Broad spheres of change today

The fields on which newspaper English has cashed in on today for fast change are broadly:

(i) The language of the market; pushed on by globalisation and consumerism.
(ii) Advertisements.
(iii) The ethnic values and transition pertaining to both the identity of one's own as well as accessibility to the macroscopic area.

A Universalised, Yet Individualistic Variety

The tendentious, subjective, biased affiliations both on the part of the columnists and readers project such a strong and strange situation to study the need of such expressions which the third chapter elaborates. It has been marked, though broadly the English newspapers reflect the global English language, the usage remains embedded in Indian soil in terms of the diversity of race, culture which take it towards a separate evolution of the language of our own.

REFERENCES

1. *Miscellany of Creative Writing* ed. P. Lal (Calcutta: Writers Workshop, No. 2, 1960).
2. *Ibid.*
3. *Ibid.*
4. *Ibid.*
5. Reported in the *Ceylon Daily News,* September 28, 1940.
6. Braj B. Kachru, "Indian English, a study in Contextualisation" (London: Longmans, 1966) and "The Indianness in Indian English" (Urbana : Illinois UP, 1966) and later *The Indianisation of Indian English* (New Delhi: OUP, 1983).
7. Braj B. Kachru, "The Indianness of Indian English", *Word* Dec. 1965: 408-9.
8. Braj B. Kachru, "Some style features of South Asian English", *National Identity,* ed. K.L. Godwin (London and Melbourne : Heinemann Educational Books Ltd., 1970) 130.
9. Mulk Raj Anand, "Pigeon Indian: Some Notes on 'Indian English' writing", paper presented at the Seminar on Australian and Indian Literature, New Delhi, January 12—16, 1970: 70.
10. Anthony Burgess, Introduction to *All About H. Hatterr* by G.V. Desani (London: Penguin Publications, 1972).
11. K.R. Srinivasa Ayengar, *Indian Writing in English* (New Delhi: Sterling Publishers Pvt. Ltd., 1962).

Chapter- 3

FACTORS BEHIND THE NEW EXPRESSION IN NEWSPAPER ENGLISH

Focus

Our task at hand is to assess the broad factors governing the journalistic writer who creates the new expressions, and classify the conditions influencing the reader who receives it. The writer and the reader in course of their journalistic interaction lead towards fast change and growth in the field of English language in India. So our focus is to analyse the factors that work behind them and the affiliations they subscribe to, resulting such a change. We seek to highlight certain brief observations before discussing the specific factors.

Basic Observations

1. The English Press in India is a great source of influence towards enriching Indian English. Because it contains various fields— editorial, feature articles, sports, business, entertainment, regional news, advertisements and so on. It is targeted towards all kinds of readers and so works productively in their minds as can be seen:

   (a) "Two to Tango, three to twist" (*TOI*, 4, Nov. 2001) (This is a poetic expression, alliterative with a patterned /t/ phoneme and ironic in appeal as it talks about the present alliance between George W. Bush (American President) and Parvej Musharraf (Pakistani President) along with Indian Prime Minister A.B. Vajpayee).

   (b) "Shahrukh conquers, the Dalai Lama concurs" (on entertainment, the movie *Asoka* and its appeal to Dalai Lama, the celebrated Buddhist monk).

(c) "Chopsucky chutney somewhat Stale" (on film review which gives a pejorative remark).
(d) "Too few good schools, too many good parents" (ironic and rhetorical in nature).
(e) "India out of the woods" (sports, on India scoring good runs to come out of crisis).
(f) "KHUL JA SIM SIM OFFER" (Advertisement of Kelvinator refrigerator).

2. We find that our standard English is not adequate to cater to all our needs. Any language with its rigidity cannot appeal to all kinds of readers. So, there is a need of breaking the language and create new expression to meet the changing requirements. "Khul Ja Sim Sim" (the advertisement above) is an age old proverb ingrained in the minds of common people and so that is catchy enough to attract consumers even though it compromises the conventional rule of English by using another language. So this sort of code mixing has been essential.
3. The above example also confirms that the English Press is bilingual and at times multilingual. In other words the writers practise their respective mother tongue and other Indian languages according to the need. An alliterative usage like "Aap Ki Bari Atal Behari" is a similar mixture of the Hindi language and the Roman script. This reflects our national reality.
4. Language has become trendy and catchy. The terms 'Aussies', 'Kiwis', 'Windies', 'Howzaat' and specific terms like 'Ton-dul Kar', also have taken a deep place in the reader's mind which conform to coming in terms with the global approach as people across the world are well acquainted with the sport events and personalities, countries that provide these terms. The related fields, commercialisation, technological processes etc. are discussed in detail ahead. The writer interacts with the national trend and tone. By that, we mean the special identity that a country subscribes to, the medium that can be comprehensible to the people it constitutes of. Here the writer takes the people into confidence and brings a change that is suitable for the national interest. The terms like 'Hinglish', 'Kargilonomics' (the impact on the national

economy due to the Kargil war) are derived out of the national issues or contemporary fashion.

5. Interaction has been multifaceted. The writer has to interact with the local, family sectors along with the global one. The terms like 'gormint' (from typical Bihari usage), 'Basu *versus* Bahu' (referring to Jyoti Basu and Sonia Gandhi, two political leaders, and Bahu being the Indian term for the daughter-in-law). 'Babudom' (the Bengali notion), 'Punjlish' (Punjabi English) get affiliation due to the local identity of the writer. He also uses terms like 'Fatherji', 'Abbajan' that refer to respectability in family bonds and relationships.When the writer confronts and talks to himself, he also comes with strange, new, often very creative usage of the language. A regular columnist in *The Times of India*, Jug Suraiya uses English according to his own whims and needs that arise out of the content he chooses. He accurately joins the name Rabri Devi with the Bihari usage of the word 'Government' as 'gormint' as 'Rabri gormint' which is pejorative. Terms like 'winnable', 'fightable' have been seen in certain important articles (source cited later) which is in conformity to the prerogative and twist of language by certain eminent writers. The English language itself has been the greatest source of influence in choosing the twisted variety of English. It is because English is a global language, it has come out of different sources other than the English soil and it contains a fertile field of change since its practitioners are from all corners of the country. Since the writers feed their medium to professionals, businessmen, academics etc. it is bound to be in a constant need of scrutiny and flux depending upon the varying area of interest and change. The complexity in this case is due to the different kind of understanding that our readers have that of English due to their mother tongue, regional influence, professional influence and other socio cultural factors they are governed by. So the requirement becomes immense. And on the other side, the writer is forced to create his lexical, structural innovations to suit to these needs.
6. The standard variety of English has limitations. It caters to our needs only upto an extent which is not sufficient. An alternative and twisted Indian English becomes the ideal medium for the writer on which he can build up a language

for all kinds of readers here. There comes the need to break the language. For example, even though for the English language the word 'customisation' is wrong, we must be indebted to it because of the source word 'custom' it gives us which is utilised to create another term for economy. It follows the rule that is observed in words like 'globalisation', 'communalisation' etc. An article is titled "Spectre of Siachenisation" (S.K. Pillai, *The New Indian Express*, June 25, 1999, BBSR). The reader is automatically attracted towards such a coinage and draws his own conclusion of the word as the content reveals. This definitely brings a change in his use of English as he is accustomed to use the word like other words such as 'globalisation', 'commercialisation' and is driven to coin new terms in that light such as 'marketisation' and customisation (Rohit Nair, *The Asian Agė*, June 30, 1999). Similarly the reader whose requirement is that of the material, fashion world is frequently met with words like 'Steam X Press' (Usha iron), 'Sex Press' (sexually express oneself) 'flexigerator'(flexible refrigerator) etc.

The Writer

The writer is a product of the society. His family, local and regional environment, education build up the social personality in him.They condition the mode of his thinking and writing. In the field of journalism, the writer is exposed to diversified areas like the cultural, political, intellectual, professional nature of writing. So his world of writing becomes vast, directed towards the commonplace, professional, intellectual reader depending upon the topic, context and language used. He is also an individual in the sense that he has certain specific interests, capability, knowledge of the topic and language, whims, methods. From the personal tone he moves to the local, regional, national and global spheres in terms of content and language. So in the process we find he controls and is controlled by the above factors influencing him.

The Reader

The Reader is the receiver of message from the body of writing. We come to find that the English Press in India is a great source of influence for the readers who constitute people from different walks of life. The reader who is interested in the political field is naturally influenced by the news items on politics by the writers/editors. The readers in India also have different mother tongues like Hindi, Oriya, Bengali, Assamese, Tamil and so on that diversify their needs.The editors and writers constitute a small section in comparison to the large bulk of readers subscribing to various newspapers. So popularising and acknowledging a word or structure is largely dependent upon the readers who are at the receiving end. Out of the interplay of words and structures between the writer and reader (since the reader's expectation also plays a role), Indian English gets its separate status. But such a strategy has been adopted unconsciously throughout the years, and more so in the modern times due to global, political, social and economic changes. If the writer cannot cater to the needs of the reader, he rejects it. The readers offer tremendous feedback through 'letters to editor' and increase in circulation of the newspaper. The number of influences on the readers have been various and changing day by day. Here too we find that the reader controls and is controlled by the writer. So both the writer and the reader immensely contribute to Indian English as a fertile field of change.

Condition Governing the Writer and the Reader

Socio-cultural factors

Indian social set up covers a wide range of subjects; the people come from rural, semi-urbanite background. It has a developing economy, multi-racial society (the Aryans, the Dravidians, Mongoloid stock etc.). The Hindi speaking north India and the southern states with their respective languages give the writer a multilingual status. In such a context the writer acts as an agent of communicative link whose words represent the plural identity. The writer uses the term 'Amma' as Ms. Jayalalitha (Ex-Chief Minister, Tamil Nadu) is addressed in her state. The newspapers also write the terms 'chudiyan', 'kada' (as used by the Prime Minister of India and President of Pakistan); *TOI* November 6, 2001) which represent the Hindi identity. Similarly any issue covering matters related to West Bengal and Orissa uses the term 'babu', 'bhadralok' etc.

The writer uses such local, familiar words, accents being influenced by the Social undercurrent. Jayanth Kodkani uses the words

'Paan', 'Paanwala', 'gaddi' etc.. (*The Times of India*, Octobar 23, 1998) rather than 'betel' since for the mjority such words are quite familiar. So the writer has no inhibition to use these words as they are known in India reflecting the social force. The social hierarchy in the agrarian, rural India which gives terms like 'sahab', 'huzoor', 'babu' (initially meant the gentlemen clad in white dhoti and kurta; especially the Bengali) denote their own notion of respectability which the writer is eager to use. The use of words like 'Upiyat', Punjabiyat' directly represent Indian social identities, particular provincial coinage. So is the case with 'Bombaiya', 'Mumbaikar', 'Bangaloreans' and so on (source cited ahead). The words 'Kudi', 'Munda' (taken from rural Punjabi expression; girl and boy) are used frequently now-a-days on the body of newspapers relating to films, teen age gathering etc. Jug Suraiya (*Times of India*, October 25, 1998) uses in his column words like 'Kolkata' (of course, recently it has been officially accepted), 'Bongdom' (to mean Bengal dom or West Bengal with its typical Bengali identity), 'Bongness'(their regional bias) and 'biskoot' (symbol of Bengali superiority) to represent the way the words are pronounced there and satirises the superiority complex of its subjects through such strange coinage. It seems there is a compulsion from the social sectors of making English language based on immense Indian nuances. It results in over simplification at times. The socio-linguistic aspects would be discussed in the subsequent sections of this chapter. Since the average reader is bilingual whom the writer keeps as his target, he accommodates all peculiarities associated with our society into the language. The cultural diversity in India (in terms of different customs, festivals, costumes, food habits) is a big factor in motivating the writer to create certain new expression and mixture of languages. In the north 'Gajar ka halwa', 'Sorson da shaag' are very common expressions as far as the food habits are concerned. 'Sambar', 'Chutney' and 'Dahi' constitute some South Indian dishes. Similarly 'Mandap' is a very common word associated with worship, marriage, and .any holy occasion. 'Dhoti-Kurta', 'Pyjama', 'Sherwani', 'Churidaar', 'Salwar' are the common dress codes here. Festivals like Dusshera is very popular throughout India although it is significant in the context of West Bengal and Orissa. So at that time some leading newspapers on their advertisement captions write "Ya devi sarva bhuteshu" (source given later), that contributes to the festive spirit and cultural identity of the people. And the terms 'Dussera', 'Dusshera', 'Dasahara' get used frequently to give weightage to people of different regions as used by them. Similarly 'Holi' is used in all newspapers though while explaining it they coin the expression 'festival of colours'. 'Deewali' is another important festival which is a combination of 'diyas' and cannot be well communicated by "the festival of lamps or light". These factors authenticate our diverse social-cultural identity which facilitates the outcome of Indian English substantially. We here also study the physical, institutional, psychological, political reality of India and so on, that manifest an influence on the writer.

(i) Physical reality

The Indian way of looking at the physical objects around us gives Indian English a distinct stamp. For example, 'Mountain' is used for a height around 10,000 feet and above, 'hill' for a lower height, 'hillock', 'mound' for still lower heights in Indian way of using English. However, in native English any raised surface on a road within fifty feet area can be called a hill. This is a difference in the differing semantic scale arising out of the physical features. In Indian English we use 'rock' for an area or opening with extended rocky surface which is 'cliff' in British English and not for a piece of stone (Labru, 1984). In Indian English 'mess' does not mean an 'Army Canteen', as in native English but a place where pecple stay and have food (like a hostel). This is due to the mixture of different groups of people together that the term is generated to mean different in different contexts.

(ii) Family bonds

In keeping with the demands of the society, there is extra honour given to the relatives, parents, elders in Indian English as Name + Sahib or 'Ji' (in case of superior in status) Father + ji or jan; for official seniority 'Your goodself' and so on (Labru, 1984). This influence at times works on the writer and he writes 'Atalji', 'Mantriji', 'Jyoti babu', etc. Though occasional, it gives an impression on the mind of the reader.

(iii) Local coinage

The term VIP is so common among ordinary people that the use of 'VIP visit', 'VIP meeting' rather than 'high level meeting' or use of 'bureaucrat' become more convenient for the writer. Some words which would be archaic in British English are amply used here which influence the writer to give them validity. This can be called the attested Indian English usage. For example, the British English, 'buy' is replaced at times in Indian English by 'to make some purchases' (Labru, 1984). In formal applications still the practice of 'most humbly' 'respectfully', 'your goodself' are practised by teachers in schools and even in some offices the boss expects such terms as a mark of sincerity, modesty and respect. The terms like *Moksha, Adwaita,* (cultural aspect), *chai, baba log* etc. from local social sphere authenticate the diversity and validity of Indian English.

(iv) Ideological/conceptual influence

There is a difference in attitude between the people of India and the West. 'Thanks' in British English, is replaced by 'thanks very much' which according to the Indian standard is more polite and appropriate. The attitude towards the 'moon' is another such example. In British English, the 'moon' is a sign of chastity (Diana's visage). Moony implies 'sleepy and dreamy'. But in the use of Indian English, we are governed by our traditional concept of the 'moon' as a token of 'loveliness' and so the use of 'chand ka tukda', also the moon is seen here as the maternal uncle (Chanda Mama). It also happens with the use of the word 'blue'. In idiomatic use, 'blue' also means 'a depressing state' and strange, sudden (out of the blue) whereas here we associate romanticity and love with 'blue' (Nilambar, Neelanchal etc.). 'Meeting' in British English, is a pre-planned one for which an appointment is already taken. In Indian English it is used in a broad term. So the writer in this case has to also communicate the essential,vital Indian experience as well as the regional influence.

(v) The political influence

Our political system and experience grow out of the social reality. So though it is a vast area under analysis we consider it a medium generating tremendous influence on the writer within the social base. The detailed entries and sources are cited in the subsequent chapter. The terms 'Moniclinton', 'Monicagate', became very popular during the time of a controversial relationship in the U.S.A. Similarly Indian writers preferred to use the metaphoric expression "the smiling Buddha" for Prime Minister Vajpayee. 'Saffronisation' is another very important coinage in contemporary times after the BJP came into power. So has become the use of 'Talibanisation', 'Islamisation', 'Sia-chenisation', 'Rabri-gormint', 'Sphinx' (for Sonia Gandhi), 'Saffron vs. Red', 'Hindutva', 'Swadeshi' and so on. Politics is such a vital part of our daily experience that we are bound to be governed by it. And the writers are mostly concerned about the field of politics on their columns which acts as a big influence to coin the new expression.

(vi) The economic influence

In recent times economy has a great role in a country's policies. In the columns of newspapers dealing with our economy, business, we get terms like 'Manmohanomics', 'Swaminomics', the new schemes of 'Saral', 'Samadhan', 'Samman', 'Swadeshi policy' etc. On the budget of P. Chidambaram (ex-Finance Minister). *The Economic Times* once wrote "Chidambaram adds UF Sauce to Manmohanomics". V.K. Gokak rightly said "English has been caught in that ceaseless flux which is Indian life and thought at the present".[1] So the need for deviation is determined not by linguistic twist but socio-culturally as well.

Linguistic factor

In the context of India the writer is aware of a number of indigenous languages—Hindi, Bengali, Oriya, Assamese, Punjabi and so on along with English. So the linguistic principles of all these languages come into play at times while he writes on the specific context. The writer is bilingual (Since he is writing in English and has a mother tongue) and attains a multilingual identity when the need comes. He transforms the codes, nuances from one language to the other; for example, he uses the Hindi language and Roman script and forms a mixture of both the languages: "Life Banana Hai!" (An advertisement, *The Times of India,* November 7, 2001).

A writer is exposed to a linguistic field which acts as a fertile area of experimentation. He takes the numerous linguistic processes into active play as a result of which a productive lexical and syntactic system gets validity. The case of article, subject dropping and pattern of interrogative usage form apt examples in this regard:

" Sourav's boys Second best?" (*The Times of India*, 4 Nov. 2001).
"Ours have safety locks".

Earlier, linguists have tried to see the need for such deviations arising out of 'formal' factor as we find in Weinrich's socio-cultural setting (which excludes the political-economic factors) and Kachru's contextual approach. But we find the Indigenous languages are orthographically phonemic unlike English as Labru says *(Newspaper English in India,* 1984). The socio-cultural context has been broadened towards and accommodated the politico-economic areas that motivate the deviant language usage, the bilingual context being replaced by the multilingual awareness that the writers and editors are conscious of.

The writer has to respond to three communicative situations which Haugen[2] specifies as :

(i) Primary speech community (where there is complete understanding);
(ii) Secondary speech community (where there is partial understanding; and
(iii) Tertiary speech community (where there is no understanding at all).

The writer is conscious of what J. Spencer says:

> "Clearly, if development is to be assumed in this increasingly complex process, the linguistic means must be adequate. This poses a most difficult question of linguistic logistics: how to ensure an adequate supply of sufficiently competent bilingual (or in certain cases trilingual) speakers of the relevant languages at the appropriate places in the developing social and governmental structure."[3]

The pressures on the writer do not just confine into the bilingual, multilingual or contextual areas but extend towards the socio-cultural boundaries.The sociolinguistic awareness may be observed here:

> "To understand the mechanisms of social changes, political pressures, economic development or cultural patterning is a task we leave to other specialists. Yet language is a factor in, and is itself acted upon by, the forces and pressures which operate at all these levels in the complex life of a society."[4] So the socio-linguistic attitude does not more concentrate on the language

structure as it does with the language function. The writer is also conscious of the social, functional task he has taken up through the mass media. An important factor that facilitates the innovation of the writers is that we treat English in India as a second language, or one of the languages we have at our possession and not as a foreign language. It is on this approach that John Holloway says:

> "English in India is genuinely what I was being told it was all the time, not a foreign but a second language; one which the Indians build into their culture and through which that culture itself, in its modern form, in part built... In a hundred different ways, it is something for home use in the subcontinent."[5]

Holloway asserts that English is not an outside language for Indians but a second, alternative language. Next he says the Indians use this language suitably, so by breaking it at necessary junctures for their cultural voice and by such process their own culture is also impregnated. Because when they build a word or structure; for example, 'Ya Devi Sarva Bhuteshu' (an advertisement caption on a leading paper; source cited ahead) where the cultural notion (acquaintance of Sanskrit; natural to our ear) gets reflected. Similarly "Saturday Review" (*The Times of India*, 19 August '98) writes, The 'blame game' instead of 'game of blame'.

(i) ***Style/Politeness***

There is excessive politeness which makes the writer imitate it.

(a) Thank you very much indeed.
(b) I am extremely grateful.
(c) At the feet of our parents.
(d) I beg to submit.
(e) Our most beloved gentlemen and ladies etc.
(f) Brutal unabashed aggression.
(g) Charmingly beautiful.
(h) Saddest event.
(i) The happiest lad on earth.

There is an earnest attitude and moral tone here.

We are fumbling in our pockets for this key today. If we do not recover it in good time, we may lose it for ever. We need this key to throw open to our youngsters the window that will give them a world perspective of the problems of humanity and their possible solution.[6] It seems we are fond of hyperboles, and exaggerations. There are also instances of flowerbed (nuptial bed), dead womb (barren womb) and 'Himalayan blunder' (Mahatma Gandhi's phrase) which are used purely from the Indian regional, cultural experiences and expectations.

(ii) *Slang*

Slangs grow out of the specific culture. The use of slang in British English and Indian English are poles apart as it is an area rooted in the colloquial local understanding of affairs. Indian abusive terms are curses unlike that in British English.

(a) 'You of evil stars';
(b) 'Pig's daughter' or 'son of a pig';
(c) 'May the vessel of your life never float in the sea of existence';
(d) 'You cock-eyed son of a bow-legged scorpion' (Kachru).

Since slangs are culture specific, we get ample such usage in our linguistic system. Example: Nannies, Amma etc., terms like 'Maths' 'Exams', 'Civil Mains' would be slang in British English. In India slangs refer to abusive terms, unparliamentary languages and curses. In British understanding the words that do not have formal acceptability and not necessarily vulgar or rough could be slangs which is not so in Indian use of English. So the writer is also under its influence when he handles the Indian understanding. We can cite Indian English slangs such as 'Munda', 'Kudi', 'Punjab da cockney' etc. used by Nikhat Kazmi (*TOI*, details in the next chapter); Raw Dadaism' (1 May 1998, editorial, *The Times of India*).

(iii) Indo-Anglian writing

The rapidity and recognition of Indian writers writing in English has given impetus to large scale infiltration of Indians words, idioms, structure, style, nuances that inspire the media writer and editor to give those usage a more popular breakthrough as newspapers only can enrich such usage appealing to larger sections of the society. The novels of Raja Rao (*Kanthapura*), and Salman Rushdie (*The Moor's Last Sigh*) etc. are full of Indian English usage that have been discussed in the previous chapter. Vikram Seth in *A Suitable Boy* writes :

> "Ah, Huzoor has brought his presence to the Secretariat at last ! Adaab. Making a Kabab out of our honourable Home Minister..." The structural twist is prominent in Salman Rushdie's *The Moor's Last Sigh:*
>
> "Baap-re ! Krishnaesqe behaviour, chhi, Bewaqoof" and so on.

So the linguistic influence leads towards a pull of the linguistic structures of the mother tongues of India which in turn govern the linguistic competence of our readers.The habits of the mother tongue get reflected in the second language. So it is a kind of translation of the syntactic structures of the first language into that of the second language. When we do not perceive any clear distinction between the two syntactic structures we say it a 'positive transfer'. In other cases that of the 'negative transfer' puts the idea of deviation in the mind of the linguists. Majority of the readers form the deviating section because of the stress on the regional languages, pluralistic cultures and the whole process on move is that of legitimizing the deviation and accept the change as progressive and real. So we find the readers of the newspapers are now prepared for the deviating structures implicitly. The only thing to do is to provide indigenous structures which may seem deviant but can be of productive usage.The strong linguistic deviations are perceived in case of advertisements. Advertising has only one purpose to help the manufacturers sell their products, to gain popularity. Some of those captions are innovative enough and attract the readers and easily motivate, influence them. A good advertisement does two things :

(a) It attracts attention to itself.
(b) the caption is short, striking and strange to be remembered and gets learned easily; for example :

(i) "Neighbour's envy; owner's pride (ONIDA);
(ii) Limca, the Zing Thing (Limca);
(iii) "Taste the thunder" (Thums up);

(iv) "Eat Cricket Sleep Cricket, Drink Pepsi" (PEPSI) and many such ads are easily influential because of the strange words (Zing Thing), structure (Eat Cricket, Sleep Cricket), antithesis (Neighbour's envy owner's Pride) etc. and remain in the minds of the readers for good. Sometimes when an advertisement with its deliberate deviation of linguistic patterning of the target language catches our mind due to the attraction of such deviation we are not concerned whether it violates the strict grammatical core of that language; but are more interested the new role, code that such violation builds and establishes for the future usage. The L_1 Structure (bachcha diya, bachcha paida kiya) controls the English equivalent for economy by converting the noun into a verb:

"Moore babies" (*The Times of India*, 30 Octobar '01) (Julianne Moore is a Hollywood actress). Such violations can be positively exploited which marks another morphological sequence that is acceptable to the readers.

Institutionalisation

Journalism has been well rooted as an institution by now. It is definitely a point of advantage to journalistic identity. The new breed of journalists are trained with uninhibited style and curiosity. Professionalism has replaced sentimental journalism of pre-independent era. Being a powerful separate organ of public opinion, watchdog of the country's interests, promoting impartial and fearless voice to the state, journalism has been experiencing freedom from all fronts which makes it easy to dare new usage that can attract readers to the issues with fresh colours. The earlier journalists worked with newspapers on trial and error basis. Today the university offers a degree or diploma in mass communication and specialised mass media institutions have flourished with greater intention than mere reporting.

The All India Institute of Mass Communication that came up in 1965 and the Press Institute of India (established in 1963) with its workshops and interactive seminars provide avenues for its practitioners the scope to establish their own standards in the use of language and content deviating from that of the text book variety. The coveted profession of journalism is an aspiration as well as a challenging study for fresh students. The variety that the political, commercial, sports, women magazines present cannot simply be rewarding by being documents or imitative of British English. Rangaswamy Parthasarathy in his book *Journalism in India* speaks of the need of journalism as an organ of social monitoring which was felt in the post-independence era. It was also thought deeply that it has to be a constructive critic, the stimulator of debates on public issues, a medium of feedback, a watchdog of democracy, a balancing wheel in the governmental structure, a great social vitaliser, a big enemy of tyrants, the right arm of liberty, an exposer of public corruption, an interpreter of public events and a professional forum for investigative and interpretative journalism. It was also thought that the reporters had to bring dynamism by keeping their feet on the rural soil. Also the need of freedom for the organisation, the 'authority' gave it a separate body of scrutinizing everything in public and private life. K. Rama Rao, who had been a staff member of *The Times of India* believed journalism to be our out and out professional body with the trained, tutored group of journalists for the specific purposes they are supposed to perform. He said that a school of journalism teaches the essentials which being an associate to a newspaper for years cannot be learnt. All these demand greater vigilance and stability of journalism as a body, licensed to check and alter, see through and amend the nature of things which creates space for new models of expression in particular.

Technology today

We have entered into the world of computers, internet and cyber space. There is greater space for economy of expression in the advent of the latest technology. The way world communication is influenced by the high technology giants like computers and e-mail, newspaper can not afford to avoid it. In the world of limited time and fast movement, people in the urban, metropolitan areas are in need of messages in codes than sparing time for detailed reading of articles and honey coated phrases of earlier days. The newspapers also respond to such innovations immediately. Some articles that speak about such developments seem obscure at first sight. For entrepreneurs, traders of higher status, executives, NRIs and academics the computer has been the store house of almost a separate medium, language which the newspapers also try to have access and put into their features. Here are some examples:

(i) Vajpayee and Co. (Refers to Vajpayee and his BJP colleagues; Vajpayee and the allies of a coalition government), *The Times of India,* 16 Nov. '98.

(ii) Bangalore's Got IT : *The Times of India* news, 7 November 1998 (editorial).

(iii) 'Swadeshi enterprise', titles Farrokh K.R. Mehta in his article (*TOI,* 7 November 1998). He also writes 'desi entrepreneur' in it.
It refers to the fact that certain general notions have to be expressed by economic global connotations as they rule the world now.

(iv) In 1960s, due to computers, the term 'hardware' created the necessity for a new word 'software' to mean the programming thereon. From it came 'vaporware' that means the non-product (which the company promised but couldn't meet the deadline).

(v) Television—Marathon has become
'Telethon' and an unending stream of faxes becomes a 'faxathon';
'talkathon' (an advertisement of a cell phone, refers to unlimited talk on phone), *The Times of India*, 26 November 2001.

(vi) 'e-lancers' are 'free agents who are electronically linked to other soloists for specific projects and move on when the work is done.

(vii) The 'electronic mail' that came up in 1977 was shortened to 'e-mail' and so came 'e-bucks', 'e-ticket', and so on.

Inter-disciplinary approach

In modern times no particular subject is independent by itself. Registers from all disciplines jumble together and get validity through the register of journalism. Newspapers in general have been the meeting point of professionals from all departments. The journalist keeps in mind the above fact and creates a medium that can interest the variety of readers. Journalism is both an art and a profession. It is the art of structuring reality and not a mere record of facts as we find in the analyses of the editorials and columnists. So the technique of journalism has been to an extent analogous to that of fiction. The readers become the market for the product that is the newspaper from the professional point of view. It has to provide space for every type of brain.

(i) "Tendulkar Inc." has been used in the wake of success of a personality as well as personalities being promoters of global access to companies and products. Cricket and corporate sector merge through a new expression simultaneously attracting the reader for its strangeness.
The newspaper has come up to secure the role of a historian, reporter, analyst, communicator, advocate, salesman and so on. The purpose behind it has been both to inform as well as influence them. So it cannot live with its advocacies alone but on its total presentation of its image. And the total image is that of a highly diversified, heterogeneous mixture of disciplines and languages meeting the demands of all sections that find a place in them. Certain kinds of deviations are facilitated by both switching over to different disciplines as well as individual idiosyncracy and innovative quality.

(ii) Shastri Ramachandran writes in *The Times of India* on 13 November 1998: "Basu and Bahu, Congress coat and Communist Tail" where he has used a variety of metaphors like Sonia Gandhi; the Indian daughter-in-law, the present alliance of political parties. The discipline of politics, poetry (being alliterative) and political satire (the nexus between the two leaders) are taken together. 'Bahu' is a typical Indian way of referring to the daughter-in-law. So the use is undoubtedly giving importance to Indian way of expressing the exact notion.

(iii) Similarly one writer writes:
"The language of bhakti", *(TOI* 12 Nov.'98) using words like 'puja', 'archana' in the process. When the medium of English displays the discipline of the spiritual or the Indian ritualistic tradition, then comes the automatic need of deviating from the main language and making room for the Indian words that fuse to such practices. So the writer does not feel like writing "the language of devotion" and 'worship' rather incorporates his own medium.

(iv) On 19 November 1998, Edward Zurick writes on *The Times of India,* "Celluloid Stereotypes of Islam" where he uses an expression like 'Islamically incorrect' that clearly projects the autonomy of the writer as well as putting different subjects (say for example, the world as moral or aesthetic) as if they bear the similar word function and so instead of quoting it as "Islam thinks it to be morally incorrect" he uses the term as an adverb.

(v) "Biharisation of Politics". Here, 'Biharisation' clearly refers to 'criminalisation'. So the word is first used as a trait and speaks of a distinct stereotype.

(vi) e-mail which comes from the discipline of electronics, opens up the application of the usages, like e-text, e-speak, e-money, e-ticket etc.

(vii) The Sanskrit word for 'price' (vasna) gave the word 'ware', says William Safire in his article "Coin your own, for fun and Profit" *(The Times of India,* 12 November '98) which later got used as 'Hardware' than 'Software' and 'Vaporware' (the non-product Software). The process clearly shows how in different disciplines the same word gets new expression for its applicability so that a word moves and remains alive as a kinetic one.

Globalisation

In the economic sphere 'globalisation' stands for 'free market' situation worldwide making the consumer choose a product that comes from any country. It is availability and freedom. In other words language does not remain aloof from such a phenomenon that has hit society at present. So journalistic discourse also adopts the process of making its raw material (words) freshened and reshaped to attract the consumer in the shape of readers. We mean to say, the impact of the global reach requires the journalist to create a new expressive mode both at the lexical and structural level. An advertisement of an iron by Usha Company writes 'Steamxpress', which is coined for economy and due to the pressure on the writer to imagine a deviating way to attract all kinds of readers and consumers from all parts of the world. In colonial times the newspaper did not have the role of spreading business and advertising ideas. In the changing times it has become itself a profitable business containing separate sections of advertisement, fashion schemes, and in the process a commercialised medium has taken precedence. The world today is integrated through new market products. The editors of newspapers cannot create attraction for the readers by using old words for certain products. Certain catchy words and phrases enable the customers to get attracted into the details. New products so have better access if they are being launched with new words on the newspaper columns. Globalisation has also affected the living style of Indians. British lexicon has lost popularity among the students, executives, computer personnel etc. which get due coverage on newspapers. When American English is used by writers that also gets Indian colour. Most of the times when the editorial covers a news on French or German politics, a write up on french cosmetics, we find ample use of French and German mixed with English too. So here the need comes out of purely from the intention of making all events of the world integrated into a common mode, medium.

Examples: *The Times of India* on 30 October 2001 features an article on famous actress Rekha and writes: "Director's 'Diva', many believe that the quest for the 'femme fatale' ends with Rekha. Another article on actress Manisha Koirala on 4th November in the same newspaper writes the form of speech by the actress:

> "Dunno what it's about me, I generate controversy". ('Dunno' replaces 'don't know') and again by the columnist: "Her performances in *Bombay*, *1942—A Love Story*, *Khamoshi* were performances that 'wannashines' only dream of."

An article is titled : " The weather: Knicker warm in South, stormy bra in north" (27 June 1999, *The Asian Age*). The columnist is Dave Barry who is not an Indian himself and the use here for the public is a bit off. beat. Naturally the reader is drawn into the content and finds that the issue is on American news correspondents on TV forecasting the news (in this case weather reports) being completely naked or topless. And that issue is fashionably presented under such a structure which makes use of an uncommon and metaphoric language. It is definitely a commercialisation of the language. As language is saleable, the writer is concerned about drawing attention of the very busy reader today by coining a new or changed expression. It is the rule of the market now. There are dependent markets and interdependent economies. When world recession takes place if affects all individual economies. When money is devalued in India, it also significantly targets the Asian and World economic scenario. So the limitation of a language, strictly based on one stereotype rules is bound to be overcome. The *New Indian Express*, on its feature (25 June 1999) writes : " 'chickenin' out in the kitchen? Well, if you got to eat your mistakes, you'd better garnish them with lots of spices". The whole sentence is a mixture of cooking features, words like 'chicken' being used as a verb replacing that of cooking that too in a twisted and whimsical manner. It does not write 'chickening' but 'chickenin'. Like the mixed words, 'Hinglish', 'Punjlish' etc., in the sphere of latest music, 'Indipop' is a word which is popular because of its Indian roots and western touch (*Indian Express,* 25 June 1999). Flexibility in governing the structures of the parent language (the basic English language) has become a necessary step in the present global interaction among people and corporates. So language is amply influenced by the values of globalisation.

Assertiveness

Writing in English has been global and local simultaneously in order to cope with the cosmopolitan identity of the writer as stated before. It has taken up writing English with Indian nuances, words and structures in order to assert the status of 'Indian English' as a respectable genre of English at the international sphere. The *Oxford Advanced Learners' Dictionary* has already accommodated quite a good number of words of Indian origin. The journalists are in a rush to make Indian English more and more popular and they have the intention of making it a choice for anyone opting different kinds of English. We come to know about this by the prepared questionnaires that have drawn opinions from journalists, linguists and readers. The Indian creative writing has though taken a firm stand in this regard, it has a limited scope and elitist reach. Newspaper is a part and parcel of many Indians who are even partially educated. So the words incorporated by Indian English novels and poetry may not popularise the trend satisfactorily. The journalistic discourse has shouldered the unique responsibility of handing over the world a peculiar English of our capacity, reach and taste. It is the projection of our linguistic notions that govern some of the writers who are fast using many Indian words and structures. And when the mainstream newspapers use number of such words and structures freely it certainly is a sign of assertion of Indian usage since they are read across the world too. *The Times of India*, the largest circulated English newspaper in India, has been immensely rich with Indian words. Frequently, we notice a number of Indian words (that are systematically put and analysed in the next chapter) being deliberately fitted into the format that could be avoided by the English equivalents. Indians have come of age through such massive mention of the words which are very common to all. And when they are repeatedly used, it seems (as the field study reveals) the newspapers have asserted the Indian self to express itself by the kind of English they are comfortable with. To make one's presence felt outside, such a task serves a great purpose. The newspapers also assert their stand on Indian English by reproducing some of the public speeches, interviews of leaders, artists, public figures with mixture of Indian, regional or our own idioms well rooted in our peculiar social systems, ceremonies.

A special report on the Prime Minister of India, A.B. Vajpayee appeared on "The Sunday Review" (*The Times of India*) as "Aab Ki Bari Atal Bihari". Though it is the mixing of two codes of Hindi and English (Hindi language and assertiveness in expressing it in an alliterative framework, the outsider has to accept it even before he is briefed about its implication in the context. It suggests the bilingual nature of our editor/writer. Cricket star Tendulkar's exceptional performance made him appear on the sports column as 'Ton Dulkar'. It further contributes to the morphological process of blend. 'Ton' suggests heavy and 'Dulkar': a befitting strong response. His top scores get reflected by it. A special review also came on the KonKan Railway (*TOI*) titled as "No Chai Cuphee on the KonKan Railway". Similarly Indian cricket captain Sourav Ganguly is referred frequently as 'Maharaj' as he is known at his native place. The need for assertion creates the need for new expression, new lexicon, be it peculiar, sounding strange or good. As it has already been mentioned, certain local, dialectical expressions take precedence with the motive of both attracting the category of people who are accustomed with that expression (their local expression) and asserting the local usage in particular and the Indian peculiar variety of English in general as seen here:

> "The Rabri gormint": 'Government' in Bihar is popularly pronounced as 'gormint'.

Most of the times anything on Punjabi music comes as "Balle balle" as it is a typical catch word of the Punjabi folk. 'Saffron' earlier stood for commitment and sacrifice. Journalism has today turned it to pejorative usage since it has been identified with a particular fundamentalist creed in recent times. So 'saffronising education' has been a catch phrase in journalistic register standing for 'narrowing education' to certain dogmas, communalisation and such a usage comes from an assertion of such creative vigour of the writer.

Competition and Attractiveness

Rise of journalism as an influencial area and various social, scientific changes have created a vast scope for a number of newspapers, periodicals, weekly magazines. All these can only survive through tough competition among themselves. So language as a medium remains at an advantageous position by being healthily contributed out of the individual newspaper's attempts at new structures. As a result a mixture of strange structures and words come into use and gain popularity among common folk even.

(i) Spelling

It occupies an important position in attracting attention of even the non-serious reader. *The Sun Times* started writing 'Cuttack' as 'Katak and 'Orissa' as 'Odissa' which can be termed as both a regional assertion as well as a trick to survive by establishing its own genre of journalistic innovation. Words like 'Distinkt', 'Kwality', 'Caliber' (new brand of Kawasaki bike), 'Ushafone', 'Splendor' (another bike) etc. fulfil this purpose.

(ii) Metaphors & neologism

The Telegraph has written; 'Nuclear Twins' to mean India and Pakistan (25 November 1998).

Jug Suraiya regularly writes for *The Times of India* and habitually coins words in jocular vein which show journalistic flexibility and attract readers. One such example from his column is "Plology lesson" (22 November 98) where PIO stands for Persons of Indian Origin.

The Assam Tribune writes 'Swadhin Ahom' (means Independent Assam) since the 'Ahom Kingdom' had been a significant ruling class in this area and there has been continuous fight for independence of the state of Assam. This is how one strange word gets validity in normal usage. We can say competitiveness creates a deviation which looks attractive initially and becomes a part of normal usage. Deviation in the language structure effectively attracts readers either due to its uncommonness or because of opening new avenues for language users. An interview with Mira Nair, filmmaker, on 24 November. 1998 in *The Times of India* is titled as "Salaam Masala Mira" which comes from her film *Salaam Bombay, Mississippi Masala* and her name Mira. On 25 November 1998, Pranay Sharma writes in *The Telegraph*: "Vajpayee reloads bofors gun". A magazine article writes in bold letters: "Sexpress Yourself". The coinage 'Sexpress' certainly means 'Sexually express'. Whether the term 'Sexpress' gains legitimacy or not is a question for future. At least it attracts, is read and so is acceptable. It is acceptability that guarantees the validity of a language. Similarly the advertisement that goes like, 'Kwality Icecream' does not raise the eyebrow of the reader or scepticism of the proprietor of newspapers for display. The media that gives popularity to such deviation in fact popularises such attractiveness of the language. The spirit of competitiveness and tough fight for survival through a separate lexical and idiomatic medium has hit the media which is on a process of fast change and growth. In turn the world of language validates such needs and legitimizes the deviations in a sphere beyond the textual, strict academic one thereby displaying our assertiveness. Earlier the word 'Hinglish' had been popularised by such attitude of the print media. Gurmukh Singh on 2nd December 1998 writes in *The Times of India*: "After Punjabi-Hindi, get ready for Punjlish" (Title of the news). This step ahead is taken out of borrowing the word 'Hinglish' which can be termed as keeping the foot on the right genre and the chief aim concentrates on attracting the onlooker.There is no clear yardstick to decide the beginning and end of the structures and lexis of English in today's pluralistic society. Pluralism believes in individuality, the discrete and the setting of a personal standard. So anything that a news writer writes with the slightest deviation creates the particular newspaper's own step in regard to such reform in English.

The Telegraph on 21 November 1998 writes : "Cesspool for Atal's highways". The news actually talks of a levy on Diesel which the task force on it has suggested. The individual papers cite their metaphoric mettle uninterruptedly. William Safire from *The Newyork Times* service writes on 4 December 1998 in *The Times of India*, in his article: "Touching base with Cuckolds" about the strange roots of English words and concludes by saying: "Once again, English shows itself to be an equal opportunity language". There is a lot to be guessed out of this observation for future expressions. The way the world is liberalising itself of all its past rigidities in all spheres, language would be a safe victim of such reforms in making it more and more accessible to the common man. Nikhat Kazmi writes on Bollywood films giving language a twist according to the film she is reviewing. On 5th December (*TOI*) she uses words like 'Biradari', 'mofussilman', 'aam Indian' etc. and she says that the films of Govinda have proletarianised Indian cinema since they have a subaltern approach as was with some of Amitabh Bachchan's films in the 70s where the hero represented the labour class and not the typical English gentlemen. This can be a part of the attractiveness formula of the paper in general and columnist in particular. *The Week* (22 November 1998) has written: "Madam versus Behan" on Mrs. Sheila Dixit versus Mrs. Sushma Swaraj on the eve of Delhi going to polls and shapes the popular public figures as they are addressed by people there to attract and Indianise.

Simplification and Economy

Journalism cannot afford to contain lengthy and old, pedantic expressions and stock phrases in the world of rapid industrialisation and corporatisation. Every individual in such a world is running short of time. So the writers keep their eyes on economy that could attract popular attention. Many readers are from a section who can only provide time for the headlines only. They need to be fascinated by the freshness, newness, deviation, innovation. Some readers are whimsical and read the articles here and there. The pressure of business, lack of concentration might produce readers who follow newspapers for facts alone. There are also people who need to be responded in such a way that the newspaper could form a pastime enjoyment for them. Such extensive reading pressurises the writer for economy of expression. The drafting of headlines constitutes an important journalistic technique which can meet the hasty reader's requirement. So other than giving a label or indirect title, some writers hint at the information directly through the title. A writer had given a theoretic standing on it in one column of *The Times of India i.e.* words which are otherwise used get expression through one word which acts as representative of all others. Here economy, rather than exact, appropriate word becomes the motto.

(i) In the language of headlines, compact, contract, agreement, engagement, convention, covenant, stipulation, armistice, pledge, truce, treaty become a pact;

(ii) a proficient, experienced person of any capacity: an 'ace';
(iii) any purpose, design, object, or intention become an 'aim';
(iv) any prohibition, restraint, refusal become 'ban';
(v) any offer, endeavour, or attempt become a 'bid';
(vi) Superintendent, Supervisor, Overseer, Governor, Manager, Director, Commander: a chief;
(vii) any abridgement, abbreviation, shortening, curtailment, reduction: a cut;
(viii) any negotiation, transaction, bargain : a deal;
(ix) any concerted or coordinated effort : a drive;
(x) decree, public pronouncement, proclamation, declaration, regulation, ordinance, enactment : an edict;
(xi) messenger, emissary, ambassador, representative, delegate, intermediary, intercessor, mediator, go-between, minister, herald : an envoy;
(xii) any undertaking, enterprise, achievement, occupation, performance, concern, task : a job;
(xiii) assembly, convention, congregation, conference, conclave : a meet;
(xiv) petition, application, appeal, request : a plea;
(xv) investigation, inquisition, interrogation, examination, scrutiny, exploration: a probe;
(xvi) conflict, collision, disagreement, controversy, contention, altercation, dissension, dispute, squabble, discord : a row;
(xvii) unexpected obstacle, sudden difficulty, impediment, adventitious hindrance, or accidental hitch : a snag;
(xviii) address, allocation, oration, lecture, monologue, harangue, palaver, discourse, conversation : a talk;
(xix) a trial, striving, experiment : a try.

Apart from the above compression of meaning into one, we have the processes like 'back formation' and 'blends' which get utilised heavily. In the process of blend, parts of two different words get mixed to coin a new expression. An expression like 'Panaphone' comes from the company brand 'Panasonic' and 'phone'. Another example is that of 'Sex Press' (Sexually express), Oxbridge (Oxford and Cambridge) and so on. In the process of back formation a clause or part of a sentence is compressed into a phrase or compound word.

Example: Bridge course—'a course that bridges the gap'. The later brings the former in this process. 'Play of power'— power play. Other examples : snap decisions, key industries, crash programmes, end products etc. The chief purpose of such usage then is to give variety and power to simple yet touching words rather than searching for the exact, equivalent synonyms. By doing so, English in general is amply strengthened. At the specific level the kind of English the newspapers provide by standing on the feet of difference and versatility both at lexical and syntactic levels enrich a standard Indian variety of English. It also fulfils the needs of a hasty reader, a die hard professional, a person who never would bother for authenticity of the appropriate traditional use of words but prefers something that makes him comprehend the whole thing by referring, suggesting rather than strictly defining. It so takes English not to the disciplined practitioners of the English language but to the people from all walks of life making it comprehensible and accessible widely.

Thematic and Situational Influence

The print media takes up various issues from the cultural, social, political, domestic spheres. It discusses national and international issues. It accommodates different sections dealing with different items such as entertainment, sports, politics in detail, art, literature, fashion and special reviews. It is not that the writer takes all these separate themes into concern to innovate the requisite structures, but as if the readers are in search of a change in words, style and structures from one theme to another.

The newspapers have used terms like 'saffronisation', 'saffron brigade' as a school of thought identifying with 'Hindu fundamentalism'. Naturally all readers take up this context of 'Hindu revivalism' as pejorative and so 'saffron' becomes pejorative in appeal. Later in their use, they do not share the idea to which 'saffron' originally stood for.

Example: The editorial (*The Times of India*, 5 December 1998) writes: "... those on the saffron side of the rationality have employed this emotive isue...". So it gets ingrained in the mind of the readers and fossilizes itself. Now we can say the 'real situation' is where we acknowledge the old positive notion of the symbol saffron (commitment, sacrifice). There is a 'visual situation' which creates a new theme and context to suit the occasion; the birth of Hindu extremists. And the print media uses the term 'saffronite' for one political wing. And the readers are influenced by the visual situation. On 8 December 1998, *The Times of India* comes with an article on opening up India's insurance sector into foreign companies. The writer uses the word 'foreignisation' along with privatisation and admits of coining the former word as the theme presses him. The exact context most of the times presses for an appropriate new word or structure as perceived here and the readers naturally accept it and legitimise the influence at that particular moment making room for future usage. It shows that the reader is both controlled by the writer's influence and controls the writer according to his taste and interest.

Influence due to applicability

The readers who are impressed by the new usage take the positive advantage of it and impregnate the language by using it through their interaction, socially and even on formal occasions thereby empowering the genre of Indian English. The catch words and phrases gain currency out of the popularity the readers render it by taking such usage into more broader fields like the professional fields, domestic chats, club and recreational moments.

"The Sunday Review" of *The Times of India* on 13 December 1998 gives two titles like "The goodbye girls" and some "Good home cooking" which have nothing to do with 'goodbye' as such or 'home cooking'. It is a kind of fashionable coinage attracting the reader into the depth of the news which reveals that 'good bye' and 'home cooking' are two music albums. The title also does not use the capital letter. The readers are quite enthusiastic about such whimses of the columnist who does not harm the language but gives the scope for flexibility and change to freshen and enliven the language. An important fact is that certain words and structures are sharpened and popularised by the newspapers though they might have existed before. That acts as the prime influence on the common reader, and the majority. During the mustard oil adulteration the word 'dropsy' was popularised. During the Clinton-Monica Scandals the words like 'intern', 'subponae' came to limelight and words like 'Monicagate', 'Moni-Clinton' were coined both for economy with metaphoric reference and were accepted by the readers without any missing link for communication. The controversy on the film *'Fire'* made even common people accessible to the term (lesbianism); a woman-woman relationship. In fact it is newspapers that popularise and give validity to a language making the readers accessible to it and use it by its influence which otherwise would have been stored in a dictionary.

Influence from the writer's whims

The writer is both an experimenter in positive language skills as well as a motivator of certain strange usage. It influences the reader both theoretically and linguistically. Language is changed according to themes.

Some examples :

(i) The Femina advertisement caption; "a ma - in - law and a good maid." (27 December, 1998, *The Times of India*). This mixture of the Indian 'ma' and British 'in-law' looks strange and may be alright for an advertisement but if the reader is influenced to use it elsewhere in formal writing it seems to be a whimsical use as it hasn't yet got wide practice.

(ii) Nikhat Kazmi writes on 5 December 1998, *The Times of India,* on the violence shown by some TV serials about ministers, bureaucrats and their corrupt practices. She titles her essay as "Kill-Kill, bang-bang and the babalog". This is done deliberately to attract and communicate indirectly with visual pleasure for the deviation. But the coinage is definitely on whims which can influence the reader to use such phrases with economy later on.

(iii) Similarly *The Telegraph* on 29 November 2001 writes 'The Good Ol' days' (for 'good old days' which is whimsical.

(iv) Jug Suraiya's columns on *The Times of India* also gives exposure to such whims of the writer which can easily influence the reader to use all those words for his communicating process. He uses a title: "Comma Sutra" (*TOI*, 23 Feb. '98) and uses phrases, words like 'cheating baazi', 'hangama', 'Aare yaar', 'maramari', 'Dilli', 'Missis' (Mrs), 'baqwash', 'dhanda' etc. He says: "The polls are the do-it-yourself Kama Sutra".

(v) There is another instance when a reader writes a letter to the editor on the same day as above on the same newspaper addressing "Sari Sonia" (for Sorry Sonia).

(vi) *The Telegraph* advertises the Cielo car on 20 Febaruary 1998 as "Valyou for Money". These things have influenced the readers to write on cards '2tu' (Tutu), B'bay (for Bombay), U'rs (yours) and may influence them to use it in more formal fields too.

(vii) Febaruary 28, 1998, *The Times of India* uses the term 'Up-iyat' (means the interests and identification with the quality of this state) and says the words like 'Punjabiyat', 'Kashmiriyat' are on the move. This does not harm but adds and gives scope for further personal usage contributing the language in general. It may further coin the terms 'Oriyayat', 'Gujaratiyat'etc.

(viii) *The Hindustan Times* advertises the cola, 'Thums up' on 19 March 1998 as
"Don't be a Bunder!
Stop Monkeying around
Grow up to the taste of thunder!"
Use of the Hindi language as well as the poetic form is used here.

(ix) On 23 March 1998, *The Times of India,* we get a word 'Suradhyak-sha' (liquor shop in charge).

(x) The Cricket appeal as 'How is that' is written 'Howzzat' (as one word) which the common reader can easily digest to use it so.

(xi) Whirlpool advertises on its flexible door model of its refrigerator on 6 April 1998 (*The Times of India)* 'Flexigerator'. This is a nice mixture creating a single word for two.

We can easily estimate the extent and nature of such usage that has influenced and will always influence the reader to feel at ease with the language of English even if it sounds illogical or absurd.

Influence of noted columnists and journals

Even the most cynical, pedantic reader is pressurized to accept the new expression when he sees its usage by a noted writer/columnist or editor. Throughout our history, writers of eminence have taken steps in pursuing change, development in the language system. Chaucer freed English from foreign influence, Shakespeare made it more flexible, Donne made language logical, a medium of day to day conversation, Bacon purified it more and added a flavour of modernism; economy of expression to words and structures. Every age and every genuine writer shares this great tradition of shaping the language. So the noted columnists and writers who have established their influence on the pages of journalistic writing give a command to the varieties of changes and influence the linguistic capacity of the readers. Modern times have modern idioms as can be seen :

(i) Jayanth Kodkani on a special report in *TOI* writes, "We have, indeed, been living in a pressure cooker for the last decade".

(ii) Dipankar Gupta writes in *The Telegraph* (29 September 1998) : "Black is unbeautiful". He gives stress to the word 'unbeautiful' to highlight the American affiliation of the blacks in America rather than with their African origin. No one asks about the grammatical accuracy here but the strangeness attracts as well as establishes the change in language. So the writers and their intellectual, social status act in influencing the readers.

(iii) *The Telegraph* writes on 27 September 1998, "Satanic years, Rushdie, The midnight's child". It also titles its editorial : "The Midnight's end" to hint the lifting of death sentence on Salman Rushdie (Salman Rushdie is the author of the novels *The Satanic Verses* and *Midnight's Children*).

(iv) *The Outlook* writes: "No Biz like Chow Biz". The usual 'Show Biz' refers to the cinema world and cine stars. Since they own some restaurants and fast food counters the editor replaces 'Show Biz' with 'Chow Biz' (Chawmin stands for the fast food here).

(v) *Femina* on 15 December 1996 writes : "Sexpress yourself". These words and structures are adopted and highlighted due to the popularity of the journals.

(vi) Sunil Sethi (28 Feb.'98 *TOI*) coins the words 'Up-iyat', 'Kashmiriyat' etc. which are discussed later on.

(vii) Jug Suraiya (*TOI*) writes : "Lotus and Robot in 'Hindustrial' India" by mixing 'Hindu' and 'Industrial together'.

(viii) Praful Bidwai (9 April 1998 *TOI*) in his article "Not by Numbers Alone" uses the term 'out Bhandaried' in the Ramesh Bhandari (ex-Governor, UP) ouster case.

(ix) Jerry Pinto on "Sunday Review" (*TOI*, 26 April '98) writes: "No chai cuphee on the Konkan Railway".

The use of 'chai', 'cuphee' in unusual new spelling order does impress the reader and can be legitimised.

(x) Editorial, *TOI* on 1 May 1998 writes : "Raw Dadaism" (on Shivsena activists disrupting the singer Ghulam Ali's concert).

(xi) Nikhat Kazmi writes : "Sunnyish style" (means the Sunny Deol style of social realism), *(The Times of India,* 27 April '98).

(xii) M.D. Nalapat writes : "Too many Kooks Spoil the Broth" in place of "Too many cooks." He refers to the pressure of Indian opposition parties on the issue of India's nuclear test. He changes the word deliberately with his authority (23 May 1998, *TOI*).

(xiii) "Artha, not Dharma Propels the BJP" writes Taufiq Subhan on 24 May 1998. Also frequently he uses the word 'mantra' in his article.

(xiv) K. Subramanyam writes "Politics of Shakti" in *The Times of India,* 27 May '98, since the term "Shakti" gained special importance after the Indian nuclear tests which were named the 'Shakti tests'.

(xv) The editorial on 28 May '98, *TOI* writes : "Stree Shakti" as its title. So here the word 'Shakti' and its significance facilitates the use of another word (stree).

(xvi) On 23 June '98 (*TOI*), a news item by Jayanth Kodkani is titled: "A byte of the 'paan' on the net". There is also frequent use of the word 'paan', 'paanwala', 'meethapaan', 'gaddi' etc. throughout the whole news.

(xvii) Nikhat Kazmi in her article (*TOI,* 8 Oct. '98) uses the word 'bankable' just like cashable, reliable etc.

(xviii) Jug Suraiya uses words and expressions like "Momma T" (Mother Teressa) 'not a Bong!' (as people of Bengal said that she is not a Bengali and can not be counted as a Bengali getting a Nobel prize); "Amartya da biskoots with them" and titles his column as "Amartya takes the biskoot". He deliberately satirises certain aspects through such coinage but it influences the reader (25 Oct. '98, *TOI*).

(xix) Manisha Koirala (noted Hindi film actress) in course of her interview in the columns of *The Times of India* ("Sunday Review", 4 November 2001) emphasizes on gender neutrality of the term 'actor' which is otherwise known to be a masculine one. "I'm primarily an actor", she says, yet again says "I love being a woman". So her intention is very clear regarding the term 'actor' which is not just a slip of tongue.

The Affiliation of the Writers and Readers

The writers as well as the readers of newspapers are subject to varieties of influences, pressures from all around. It results in change in language items, their usage, modification and application when the need arises. Both constitute the system of effective communication and reception. The writers well understand the readers' interest and feed them with the distinct interests that the people behind them might have in order to fulfil the political, cultural, social and linguistic requirements in the process. Such identities persist throughout the journalistic discourse and largely depend upon the bulk of appreciation and saleable factors. We here briefly highlight certain distinct affiliations they are subject to.

The writer's world of affiliation

The columnist is conscious of the responsibility he has to undertake while writing an article or a news item from all the angles. The social, cultural and political background serve the primary factors upon which a writer has to cash in on. Objectivity is a relative term taking into account the nationalist, regional, local issues. So the objective writer is he who has to balance all these factors operating behind his writing and sound a note of freshness, authentic personal gesture through the issues he has taken up. So he cannot be free from the distinct influences from all sides. Here is a list of some of such affiliations that the writers subscribe to.

(a) Socio-cultural affiliation

Every writer is aware of the socio-cultural milieu and ethos he consciously and unconsciously associates himself with. When Nikhat Kazmi writes 'down market biradari', 'Punjabiat' (related to people like Daler Mehendi who have made the language popular outside), 'aam Indian', 'mofussilman' (*The Times of India*: "Real Life Heroes in Unreal Showbiz"), she certainly has a strong affiliation of the Indian common man's sense of the language, the rustic and naive notions which have entered into a special linguistic culture.

The Assam Tribune writes (6 Dec.'98): "Mamta's new avatar". The article is on Mamta Kulkarni (film actress) and her new, traditional role which contradicts her earlier off the guard roles. The word 'avatar' is well known to all Indians, especially from our myths which talk of incarnation of gods. Presenting it justifies the cultural identity of the editor/writer.

The word 'Kavi' (Poet) has special artistic significance which is attached with some famous poets like Pradeep known as 'Kavi Pradeep' (*TOI*, 13 July '98) who wrote "Ye mere watan ke logo" (sung by Lata Mangeshkar). "The Business Times" of *The Times of India* on 14 July '98 writes, "How will the economy escape from the Chakravahyu?" The word 'Chakravahyu' is very much an old Indian practice of war strategy that engulfs the enemy. This kind of a metaphor used in the corporate and business sector is clearly a clean chit to the journalist's cultural ethos getting fairly represented.*The Times of India* on its entertainment column (30 March '98) uses names from *Mahabharata* like Judhisthir, Draupadi, Panchali not just as names but it seems the writer deliberately wants to force upon the reader his obsession with the cultural ethos he wants to represent and his sense of the past and myth that he wants to share with the reader. Example: "Draupadi's passion in Kathak and Verse". Newspapers like *The Times of India* also have created space for our ethos separately on special columns like 'The Speaking Tree'. Devdutt Patnaik on 2 April '98 on this column writes "A Hanuman for all seasons" and fills his article with plenty of Indian words like 'brahmacharya', 'Siddhi', 'Stri-rajya', 'bhakti-marg', 'maryada-purushottam', 'jivatma' etc. On 29 May '98 *The Times of India* in one of its articles writes "A Nuclear Lesson from Bhasmasura" (Siddhartha Varadarajan). The 'Bhasmasura' episode is known to the Indians (especially the Hindus) from their childhood which is interesting to share with.

The editorial of *The Times of India* on 6 June '98 writes "Sops and Tantrums" which is strange to make out. 'Tantrum', 'Tantrik' are words well associated with tricks related to necromancy and black magic. That metaphor is appropriately chosen to trace the kind of relationship the BJP allies (Mamta Banerjee in the present context) have with the ruling one. Similarly Namita Devidayal writes "Looking for the true guru" (*The Times of India* 9 June '98). A special report in *The Times of India* on the same day writes "Mera PIO ghar ayaa?" on the Persons of Indian Origins investing here being modelled on a popular modern Hindi film song "mera piya ghar ayaa". This is an affiliation with the world of entertainment that the writer has in his mind.

An editorial in the same paper on 27 June '98 writes "Madonna's Mantra" which seems to point out so many things simultaneously :

(i) there is alliterative use of the language,
(ii) juxtaposition of the western pop star with Indian hymns,
(iii) the real message; that of Madonna learning Sanskrit.

A journal, *Politics India* (Vol. 11, No.12, June '98) on its cover page boldly writes "Awakening the Kundalini" on the Pokhran tests where the use of the word 'kundalini' is synonymous with the magician, saint of earlier days and the rituals related to them highlight a cultural affiliation. Under the distinct social identities the customs, fashion, entertainment, sex, sports related issues come up to contribute new models of word and structural changes. On 25 October '98, Anita Katyal (*The Times of India*) writes, "RSS propagating Hindutva through Textbooks". "Murli Manohar Joshi fails to lend a Saffron halo to the education system" and again, "One of their deepest desires is to go to Mecca for a darshan of a Shivling". All the above deviations both come out of the social, cultural context in which these news items, articles are designed. A veteran journalist, James Cameroon had said, "Indian Press had not the purposeful stubbornness of the communist press, nor the meretricious stupidity of the pop press of the West, it was semi-literate, ill-argued, imitative". A headline in *The Telegraph* writes: "Salmans run amok in MP" after Salman Khan's 'black buck' killing episode. Such usage gains legitimacy and the social condition then accepts such usage. 28 Oct. '98 sports news, *TOI* (V. Srivatsa): "Cricket promotion within the country hit for a six". "The authorities did not 'bat an eyelid' in dumping the BBC and give TV rights to a Private channel"; "thumbed its nose at the state owned Doordarshan...". All these subjective use of the language in a supposedly objective medium of the media is in relation to the factors prevalent in contemporary times. In a film review by Nikhat Kazmi (*TOI*), the title is "Seeking a Tikamgarhi by the Thames". Actually Tikamgarhi is a place in Rajasthan. The review of the film *Hero Hindustani* shows that it relates Indian culture with Western locales and so on (28 October '98).Pritish Nandy writes in the *Assam Tribune* (21 October '98): "The enemy at the gate: Let us understand what all this natak is about." He also writes 'Masiha' (Laloo is the Masiha of the downtrodden), 'dehati' ('this remarkable dehati women') etc. 23 Oct. '98, *The Assam Tribune*, editorial : 'Gill's eye view' like "bird's eye view". It is structurally Indian. Another news in the same newspaper reads as 'Meiree-making waves'. Later one comes to know that *Meiree* is a Manipuri film. But the foregrounded structure of 'meiry-making' is chosen in order to visually attract the readers which owes to the writer's social identification with the entertainment world.

The Telegraph (30 Oct. '98), "Affordable Moronism".

This is on Indian pop music. As the pop music today in India is a mix of old and new tunes, instruments and a lot of noise, that idea of remix also is displayed in the making of a word 'Moronism' (not modernism). It relates to the affiliation to such a world of entertainment. On 28 Oct. '98 (*TOI*), another item comes like 'Utterly Butterly Kurien'. It is an interview with Dr. Verghese Kurien, the man behind the National Dairy Development Board (NDBB). And because of the department of Dairy the word 'butter' and so 'butterly' is used (Rachana Burman is the interviewer). *The Telegraph magazine*, 30 Oct. '98 also writes 'Preity Zintabad!' (from the name of the heroine, Preity Zinta). Again on 29 Oct. '98 (*TOI*), an interview with Power Minister P.R. Kumarmangalam is titled as "Electrify and be Dammed". From 'Dams' the verb is coined as the interview talks of electrification, irrigation etc. and the consequence could be also negative to the common people somewhere. So all sides are taken into notice and the phrase is structured so. On 12 June '98 *Indian Express* (BBSR edition) editorial writes: "Walkoutathons". It refers to the AIADMK which walked out of the Lok Sabha. On April 27 '98, Nikhat Kazmi writes (film review, *TOI*) : "Social Realism, Sunnyishstyle" that refers to actor Sunny Deol's style of social drama. "The Sunday Review" of *The Times of India* (3 May,1998), gives a news item : "Aaj Ka Abhimanyu" on a Keralite District Collector fighting the liquor lobby, where the outsider is forced to understand the significance of the name of Abhimanyu to our society and the source behind.The social affiliation with certain catch words and phrases of our past traditions and systems takes the writer to directly reflect those phrases instead of relating them by their English equivalents, as can be seen in an article (9 June '98), *The Times of India* by Namita Devidayal:

"Looking for the true Guru": Ideally, the relationship would result in a seamless system of imparting knowledge, spiritual, intellectual and physical. This is what came to be glorified as the "guru-shishya

Parampara". In an age of satellite classrooms and cyber universities, however, the Guru-Shishya bandhan is perceived as an outdated and oppressive institution. The use of the word 'dakshina' has been frequent also. *The Competition Success Review* (March 1994, Editor S.K. Sachdeva) gives the title to its cover: "Kapil Da Jawab Nahin". It also speaks about the affiliation of a regional notion. In our social field most of the people are illiterate and use words in a twisted, broken way which the writer affiliates with and gives voice to as in an article by Sonal Nerurkar in the "Sunday Review" (3 January 1999, *The Times of India*): "Cool comes to the Movies"; the concept of 'cool' has been central to the article here as a notion that captures the films today unlike the hot headed debates of some earlier films. And the subtitle also uses the word 'phillums' since the writer identifies with the innumerable viewers who perceive 'films' as 'phillums". *The Sunday Statesman* gives a report on the bureaucrats who also are good writers and titles the section as "The write bureaucrats" which attracts the reader due to its recognisable deviation.

Similarly, *The Telegraph* writes (13 July '98), headline: "Zedane headers move France to the crown". Zedane is the French player whose heading the ball actually gained France the match in the final football match (World Cup). The *Film Fare* (July '97) writes : "The Sweet smell of Sexcess" which indirectly means 'excess of sex' in films and the coinage of a single word easily communicates the backgrounded meaning. "Silence, Action, Cut" is the title of an interview with Mujaffar Ali, film maker by Neetalal (*TOI*, 5 Sept. '98) which naturally owes to the idea of identifying with the directorial instruction while taking shots. "The Sunday Review" (*TOI*) writes on teachers' strike for hike in salary (23 August '98) : "To Sir, with love and more money". This is based on the title of an English novel which adds interest to the title and speaks about the present unrest among the teachers. 'No asha ki Kiran' is the title of a news (30 Aug. '98, *TOI*) for the people living in custodial homes. Also 'bachchon ka jail' is one such usage.

Jug Suraiya (*TOI,* 6 Sept. 1998) gives voice to the present crisis and adulteration of mustard oil as 'Tels of terror':

(i) he tells the tale behind the 'tel' (mustard oil).
(ii) And 'terror' because of the deaths in the news he talks of. Also 'garib hatao' is changed to 'hataoed garib' in his article.

He also gives voice to the harassment of common man by the security officers everywhere; "niklo yahan se sale." A drive against polluting vehicles in Delhi (the bullet driven auto-rickshaws) was termed in these terms:

> "It is end of the road for the 'phatphati'. The Indians only understand what 'phatphati' means."

Jerry Pinto writes in "Sunday Review" (*TOI*), 20 Sept.'98: "Sleep well Mantriji" on Indian politicians being more involved in sex and social corruption than Clinton (ex-President, USA) as the issue was raised then. The socio-cultural sector is a very broad field which covers the fashion and entertainment norms of changing times too which get reflected in the use of the English tongue as a natural progressive phenomenon in the register of journalism.

(b) Political affiliation

Indian journalism is a product of the political scenario of 19th century, the colonial situation and the conditions related to it. So journalism in India has been more drawn into the politics everyday rather than that of the western counterparts. The writers, proprietors and editors in course of time have directly identified themselves with certain parties and wings and represented their points of view. So every writer has had to respond to any political turmoil from his angle modelling the language accordingly.

(i) On Clinton's extramarital relationship one clip comes "Yatha Praja, Tatha Raja". Feb. 28, '98 (*The Times of India*, editorial).

(ii) "UP's Bhul-bhulaiya"; relating to Kalyan Singh's sudden ouster and coming back to chief ministership (*TOI*, 28 Feb.'98).

(iii) March 2, '98 *TOI*; Ratan Manilal (columnist) hints at 'Mandalisation' and 'Yadavisation' to denote the conflicts in UP and other places. The words come out of the politics of caste.

(iv) When Chandrababu Naidu flies to Delhi to support the BJP government, *The Times of India* writes (8 March, '98) "Flying Alliance Air to Delhi".

(v) Kofi Annan's talks with Iraq is reflected in the newspaper as "Toasted Kofi" (2 March, '98 *TOI*).

(vi) Terms like "Janata Darbar" (PM's Janta Darbar) and "Sangh Parivar" are popularised by today's journalism only which comes from the political wings.

(vii) 'The Onion-way' became a catch phrase after the unprecedented price rise of onion (29 Oct.'98, *TOI*). "ONION-POLL-ITICS" becomes the title of a columnist on the same day. It referred to the opposition's agenda to win the people.

(viii) The concept of foregrounding is not new to language practitioners. Newspapers also practise it in their convenience and even with abnormalities. But it is nonetheless attractive and contributory in nature. One newspaper wrote the name A.B. Vajpayee in the wake of the nuclear tests: "A (tom) B (omb) Vajpayee". Similarly Raja Menon writes (Aug. 1, '98, *TOI*) "Exploding myths : Power and the gory of Nucleonics".

(ix) Structurally certain sentences have adopted the current political turmoil and upheavals which are exposed through the linguistic foregrounding of Indian words.
Example : Madhu Kishwar in *The Times of India*, 2 August, '98 (Title of the column— "Making a home of hell") writes: "Being Indian also demands living at the mercy of a whole army of 'Sarkari Parasites'. Our 'Maibaap Sarkar' understands only two codes : a 'ghoos' from below or a 'Sifarish' from above".

(x) July 7, '98 (*TOI*): "To skirt China is to skirt the issue". *The Oxford Advanced Learner's Dictionary* talks of 'Skirt around' (a phrasal verb). The use of skirt without the appropriate collocation here is a liberal use definitely.

(xi) Editorial, *TOI*; 21 July '98: "Promises for keeps"; since the editor has to highlight the silly promises made by politicians or the futility of genuine promises being made by them without implementation, he has to speak in a language fit to the context.

(xii) *TOI*, editorial (col. 3), 29 Oct. '98 writes "Buck fever" which can be understood if one goes through the whole column. It is related to the black buck poaching by film actor Salman Khan which gives the scope to the writer for using such a cliche.

(xiii) *The Sunday Times* (1 Nov. '98) titles "When will the computer conquer babudom?" The concept of 'babudom' is well known to the people here, the bureaucratic and clerical harassment, files being dumped in offices become the constant source to use the word legitimately. So 'babudom' immediately evokes the idea of harassment, corruption, negligence and bossism.

(xiv) The writer is also aware of the politicians making the people fools by projecting their fake innocence as in case of a politician milking a cow. So the incident which is occasional gives a new idea to the writer which he uses through his language. *TOI,* 27 Oct.'98 — editorial (col. 3):

> "Milking Democracy". This pejorative use of milking and the kind of democracy we have can be made out after one reads it. On similar vein one finds titles like "Vegetable Soup", on price rise of vegetables. *TOI,* 28 Oct. '98; editorial (last column) talks of the 'Tantra Sutra' (an Indian classic presented to Bill Clinton in which Shiva explains Parvati about meditation which here refers to Clinton being advised at a crisis). And the implicit word behind is 'Kama Sutra'. The title is "Shiva in Oval Office". Any reader gets perplexed initially unless he believes in the confusion above and goes through to discover who this Shiva is and what he does in the oval office of the United States of America.

(xv) Oct. 28 '98, *The Economic Times :* "Securitisation in vogue : some fundamental facts" (the lexical deviation due to the constant and overwhelming practice of security officials everywhere now).

Oct. 27, '98. *The Telegraph*: "Dalai Lama melts Sunshine" (title). And the news item is also round about, extremely metaphoric, subjective (news items are actually meant to be objective) and oblique. "Offering Calcutta warmth in exchange of protection from Sunshine, the Dalai Lama has blown away the cloud on his brethren's annual winter woollen roadshow in the city." The real message is that it is a request by the leader to lift the ban of sale of woollen garments by the Tibetan Lamas on the streets of Calcutta.

(xvi) "Polls Do Pyaza" is the title of the editorial (col. 2) of *The*

Times of India on 26 Oct.'98. The metaphor of food here suggests (on reading the news) that the politicians make food of small issues at times. The onion issue is being made a political weapon and so a food for the public to enrage them.The editorial on the same day has also used a word like 'autarchic' which the writer means 'autocratic' and 'anarchic' both. The sentence goes like " ... despite an autarchic policy ... ".

(xvii) Bengali identity is reflected on a news item in the use as follows : "Bongness" (the Bengali land), "I'm told Amartyada biskoots with the best of them (This is on the attitude of some Bengalis towards Dr. Sen receiving the Nobel Prize).
The Economic Times writes:

(i) "Illiquidity hurts" (26 Oct.'98), on Profit, loss of the stock exchange etc.
(ii) Also "Re (de) fining the rules of the game" on refining the structure of certain companies.
(iii) "Taking good care of thy child's future", where the structure teaches archaism, a tool of poetry.
(iv) "Aphrodisiac for the bulls" (Yashwant Sinha and Vajpayee are the bulls) — on corporate sector.
(v) "Playing Santa Claus to the markets".
(vi) "Mine your business." The title first evokes the impression of a conative, command based on the structure "mind your business". But on reading it one finds it is an interview with a Managing Director of Orissa Mining Corporation.
(vii) To confuse the readers the title in one of the news items in *The Economic Times* is "Tata sons buys bagful of Tisco, Telco Shares". Later one comes to know that it is "Tata Sons Ltd." one group constituted together and not ungrammatical as the title projects it to be. It is deliberately coined.

On 25 October 1998 *TOI,* "Sunday Review" writes: "On Your Marx, Get, set go", modelled on 'On your march, get, set, go' and the message is related to the world's leftist, Marxian ideology.

15 October 1998 (editorial), *The Times of India* writes: "Sen and Sensibility" on Amartya Sen and his sensibility in welfare economics.

And the pattern is taken from *Sense and Sensibility* by Jane Austen, an eminent English novelist.

The Statesman (15 Oct. '98) gives a headline: "Jungle Jammin". On 9 Oct. '98 *TOI* raises the status of the word 'Bangaloreans' as a word to mean the people of Bangalore.

Bachi J. Karkaria says about 'Monickergate' modelled on 'Watergate Scandal'. She talks of Monica and the scandal she was related with and the Clinton episode.

While Robin Cook, foreign secretary of UK was touring Brunei, the news item came on 21 Sept. '98 (*TOI*); "What's cooking in Brunei?" (means what he is doing there).

"Thalaivar Vajpayee in Dravidanadu", says Shastri Ramachandran in *TOI*, 27 Sept. '98. Thalaivar refers to the leader and Tamil Nadu is written as Dravidanadu.

Expressions like "Clinton cloud" (*TOI*, 13 Sept.'98), "a gift horse in the mouth" (oral sex, editorial, *TOI*, 5 Sept.'98) refer to the Clinton-Monica scandal in US politics.

The Times of India also on its editorial titles 'Sahib Biwi and Ghulam' (means Sahiv Singh Verma, Sushma Swaraj and the common men) in the wake of Sahiv Singh's ouster as Delhi Chief Minister and Sushma Swaraj's new Chief Ministership. Political affiliation is the most significant factor as all newspapers and journals cover political events more, that ensures, guarantees and provokes the writers to pattern new words and structures making English popular among all sections.

(c) *Global commercial affiliation*

Advertisements boost the products of their respective companies through a deviant language and the newspapers display them.

Coca Cola advertises, "Eat Cricket, Sleep Cricket, Drink only Coca Cola". If one minutely observes, one can find a deep sense of the 'poetic' (may not be serious poetry) within this caption. The alliterative use of alphabets, the crispness and strangeness, absurdity of the message are due to such innovative strategy by the advertising agency in order to cope with the higher competitiveness and numerous entry of all global products in a limited market condition.

Another advertisement frequently draws attention : "Utterly Butterly Delicious" which gives a positive meaning to the word 'utterly' instead of a pejorative one and creates a new word like 'butterly' to suit the rhythmic pattern of the clause. 'Too Cool' is a title given to the two actresses Manisha Koirala and Tabu but in fact the word 'too' has been used as if it were two (the numbers, the two actresses are cool); advertisement of *Film Fare* in *TOI* , 5 Nov. '98.

On 6 Nov. '98, Jagmohan (columnist) writes in *TOI* : "Steel of the Iron man" on Sardar Patel where he means strength and depth in the word 'steel' which has reference to the idea of survival.Tanushree Podder (Nov. '98, *TOI)* writes: "Ode to the Onion" on the present crisis on onion sale and price. Also on 7 Nov. '98, L.K. Sharma (*TOI*) writes a news item: "Sinha dishes Indian Onion soup to UK audience" on Yashwant Sinha's (present Finance Minister) use of the metaphor of onion as it is so precious, at a conference in London. After so much of attention to the 'Swadeshi' cult in Indian politics, economy and culture, titles come frequently as "Swadeshi Enterprise" (Farookh K.R. Mehta, *TOI,* 7 Nov. '98).

The editorial, 7 Nov. '98 (*TOI*) writes : "Bangalore has got IT." The structure is resembling 'Bangalore has got it'. But after reading the news one knows the capital letters 'IT' stands for Information Technology.

On 8 Nov. '98 (*TOI*) Ranjit Madgavḳar writes 'Cyberruse' which means both 'Cyber use and cyber ruse'; it relates to the gamble between Videsh Sanchar Nigam and Private Net Services.

Similarly the editorial, 23 Nov. '98 of the same paper gives a name to Indian bureaucracy: 'Steal frame' instead of 'Steel frame' as it talks of corruption and dishonesty.

The Times of India, 8 Dec. '98 records an article on the entry of foreign insurance companies into India; "Insuring the Future" by K.R. Malkani (a BJP M.P. at present) who uses the word 'foreignisation' and privatisation. The concept of the new suffix comes only out of the other words that use such suffixes and because liberalisation has forced such a word to get validity.

On 6 Sept.'98 (*TOI*), an advertisement reads as: "AKAI MEGATAINMENT". This caption adds the words mega entertainment without violating the whole pattern and rhythm which is so worth noticing. The commercial affiliation presses the writer to think for economy and attractiveness.

Film Fare, July '97 advertises on some costume items as: "Spring xxtravagance".

August 12, '98, *TOI* advertises for APTECH Computers and coins the word 'Aptechites' like the 'Delhites', 'Ravenshavians,' 'Nittians' 'Bangaloreans', Guwahatians, Bhubaneswarites and so on.

The Statesman on 18 July '98 writes: "SINGING THE GENERATIONEXT TUNE" on the music gharana of Amjad Ali Khan. This practice is also used in a number of newspapers even for some soft drink advertisement (Pepsi drinks).

An advertisement of a water bottle company (Cello) writes on the same paper "Waterrelief!". On 26 July '98, *TOI* uses the word 'River Sutra' (the idea taken from 'Kama Sutra') on the dispute of Cauvery Waters and the solution out of it. The global touch lies in connecting the traditional with the modern issues and products.

One marketing financial organisation writes DISTINKT (not Distinct) ENERPRISES (30 July '98, *TOI*).

The Statesman writes 'Saarc' (31 July '98) which could be termed as a naturalisation of gradual changes in abbreviations due to global reach and flexibility.

S.A.A.R.C. → SAARC → Saarc

"No BIZ like Chow BIZ"; writes *Outlook* (26 Jan. '98) on film stars (from them comes the idea showbiz) who own fast food centres and restaurants (Chowmin-Chowbiz). *The Telegraph* advertises for the CIELO car as "Valyou for money" (20 Feb. '98). Thums up advertisement (*TOI*, 19 March '98): "Taste the thunder!"

On 30 March '98 (*TOI*), Swaminathan Aiyar writes "MITI or Mitti ?" The first term is "Ministry of International Trade and Industry" which he says has turned muddy and worthless; so can be used as 'mitti'.

The Asian Age on its "Travel Page" talks of 'Silvery Tea' highlighting the imperial hotels of Delhi, and similar is the use of 'Silvery welcome' (31 March '98 and 1 April '98. Hero street (motor bike) advertises (31 March '98, *TOI*); "Gear lagao, Gadi badhao".

On 5 April '98 *TOI*, Jug Suraiya writes: "Lotus and Robot in 'Hindustrial' India". By it he means the Hindu world turning industrial and combines the lotus (Swadeshi) and Robot (Videshi) norms.

Whirlpool company advertises : "Flexigerator"(on a model of its refrigerator) to highlight its 'flexible doors'.

Siddharth Varadarajan talks of "Swadeshi Talk, Videshi Thought" on the BJP Budget (6 June '98, *TOI*) which is deliberately poetic and under the influence of the present day concept of global or local economic reforms and policies of the world. From the concept of PIO (Persons of Indian Origin) who invest in India; the word Piology is also formed by certain other news items. On 26 Oct. '98 (*TOI*) another advertisement writes: "DAM IT, MIX IT, FIXIT" instead of "Damn it, Mix it, Fix it". 'Manmohonomics', 'Swaminomics' are words that came only after the frequent affiliation the persons have with the economy and areas of economics in the country. *TOI*, 23 Oct. '98 titles : "Nu-Power" instead of 'Nuclear Power' by Susan Davis who probably attracts the whole world of readers to such deviation as all can easily guess the word in the wake of the nuclear tests. Day by day the world is turning global. Regional, local influences though exist, years ahead, one cannot afford to keep aloof from his identification with the global way of life, dress codes, manners, products and so on. So language has to be modelled on this new attitude and model. Newspapers and journals are more open receptors that expose to these affiliations instantly. The common man is so easily influenced and heavily contributed by the usage due to such affiliations of the writers.

(d) Affiliation with the owner/proprietor

A reporter generally subscribes to the kind of views the owner of the newspaper identifies with. Generally the writers would not like to go against the owners' points of view and rather reflect their interests by consistent display of such views. *The Competition Success Review* has published one essay on its March 1994 issue which gives the result of a study conducted in this field. The U.G.C. sponsored study on journalism revealed that nearly 89 per cent of journalism graduates with the media feel they do not have the freedom to write according to their views. Only 5.6 per cent people differed from this view. Of them who talked of pressures, 90.3 per cent said there are different kinds of pressures and it also revealed that most of the pressures were from the proprietors. The Government and the editors came in the second and third next pressurising categories. We are here concerned with the owners who influence and motivate the reporters and editors and not the political influence.

According to *Press in India* (1984), published by the Registrar of Newspapers there were 83 common ownership units in 1983:

(1) Benett and Coleman Company (15 news interest publications)

(2) Express Group (31 news interest publications). The big units dominated not only English journalism but also vernacular journalism.

The percentages (1982) are :

(i) English — 85
(ii) Bengali — 70.9
(iii) Gujarati — 81.4
(iv) Hindi — 41.2

In 1982, Hindi led all newspapers with 5655 papers (28.4 per cent). English had 3689 papers and Bengali 1537 papers (7.7 per cent).The Press Commission said, "when newspapers are controlled by other big businesses they become vehicles of expression of the ideology of their owners and the selection, presentation and display of news in such newspapers would be dictated by that ideology. The newspapers industry in their hands becomes involuntarily the cultural arm of other businesses and industries and takes a vested interest in maintaining the existing socio-economic system." It also questions whether there should be a code of ethics for the journalists and newspapers who frame the news. So the problem (big affiliation) is the big business ownership of multiple newspapers.The Commission had said "It appears to us that a very significant part of the press in the country in general and a major portion of the important daily press in particular is controlled by persons having strong links with other businesses or industries". But it cannot be altered in our context. Since high circulation needs to be built up, newspaper had to become an industry of earning money other than its pre-independence motto of revolt. Unless readers felt interested and attracted high circulation would not be possible. Newspapers also have to spend a lot towards the well-being of high professional journalists. So the proprietors' control becomes an inevitability because of their financial investment to run the newspaper industry and their commercialised interests get reflected. Language becomes crispy and commercialised than literary or figurative. New idioms, figures of speech replace the old ones.

The Sunday (magazine) writes on BJP leader Ashok Singhal in these words (10 —16 January 1999): "Singhal- minded agenda" (It is modelled on the phrase 'single-minded' and here it highlights the assertiveness of Mr. Singhal in the BJP). Similarly journalists use the terms, 'saffronisation', 'Hinduisation' etc. Affiliation to the owners of the newspapers generally distorts the news and the language of distortion is always oblique, round about and confusing.

(e) Regional affiliation

Real India has never been seen in its cities and posh areas. Regional, local issues, ordinary events constitute the basis of the newspaper corpus here. So the regional bias is well observed in the local newspapers. There was a time when Indian Press had an urban and middle class base thereby limiting the process of development of language of the mass. Now the gap has been fought over with the entry of a number of local newspapers. So newspapers have alienated from the colonial attitude of English to that of Indian languages heavily invading the mainstream English as exposed on news columns.The Press Commission had said: "It is the language Press which is becoming increasingly relevant to the bulk of our people with growing use of Indian languages as the media of education." So there is a fast move on the process of Indian English getting Indianised and establishing itself as a new promising genre. *The Sun Times* in Orissa has adopted the process of getting new colours for Oriya words: 'Odisa', Katak (instead of Orissa, Cuttack) and so on. *The Assam Tribune* has used the word 'Asam' instead of Assam in the article, "Swadhin Asom" as the word is pronounced so there. *India Today* (7 Dec. '98) gives a feature on the popular Hindi film "Kuch Kuch Hota Hai" as 'Kuch Kuch Kyon Hota Hai' by Namrata Joshi and Nandita Chowdhury which owes its deviation to both the regional, popular affiliation of the Hindi tongue as well as the contemporary entertainment news items. An interview with Pakistan's High Commission Asraf Jahangir Qazi by Janak Singh (*TOI*, 7 Dec. '98) is titled as "Kya Karega Qazi" (this is part of a popular proverb in India).

A number of times newspapers use the reference of "capturing the gaddi (meaning power, chair, position) which owes to our popularity of the Hindi medium. An advertisement from the property tax department of Municipal Corporation of Delhi writes (*TOI*, 11 Oct. '98) "Sampattikar Samasya? Let's find a Samadhan together". We have already cited about the process of using the words 'Upiyat', 'Punjabiyat' and the possibility of 'Oriyayat' and so on. On 23 March '98 *TOI* comes a news item, "Atalji will make the mandir possible". Editorial (March 25) of the same paper gives the title 'People's

Pratinidhis' and uses 'nidhi-pratis', 'mantripad' with confidence and natural flow. Soli J. Sarabjee writes on 10 April '98 *TOI*: "Privacy, Chupa Rustam and Holidays" on Narasimha Rao's book *The Insider*.

April 10, '98 *TOI*: "Pakistan's Ghauri is India's Agnipariksha." We include all the above examples as a natural local affiliation which adds to our comfortability. "Raw Dadaism" is the title of an editorial column on 1 May '98 *(TOI)*. *The Times of India* on 4 Nov. '98 discovers the term 'wife house' from the concept prevalent so in north Kerala where it is the most commonly used word not found in the English dictionaries. The local practice of husband staying at the wife's house for a long time gives it validity. Similarly the words like 'Amartyada', 'Kapilda' gain popularity out of the popular Bengali affiliation.The Punjabi 'Bhangra' and other words like 'balle balle', 'kudi' are freely used by all newspapers. "Sunday Review", 19 July, *TOI* writes on Bhangra music by Sonal Nerurkar: "Ho gayi balle-balle".

27 July, '98, Nikhat Kazmi *(TOI)* titles her column on films as "Balle-balle", "a kudi, a munda and bhangra". The same paper on the same day also has another article by Bachi J. Karkaria: "From Yoni to Yeti". And the article is appropriately termed so as it discusses the transformation of Pratima Bedi who had come to the hills (Himalayan valleys and the Yeti Tribes living there); from the world of sex (Yoni) and Kama Sutra [Puja Bedi's (her daughter) advertisement etc.]. 29 July '98, Chaturvedi Badrinath (*TOI*) writes, "Meaning of Moksha: Path to freedom from Tamas".

On 50 years of Independence a special report (*TOI*) Aug. 9, '98 writes, "India : Kal, aaj, our kal". F.K.R. Mehta (*TOI*, 7 Nov. '98) uses a number of Indian words to assert the regional notions. He also questions the paradox between the global and swadeshi cults. "Does the desi entrepreneur have the dum (he means guts) to combat the heavies from Harvard?" He uses the words like; lungi, havaldar, chowkey, Loks in minits (about news locks in minutes), phoren companies, magazins, dekho, aarey etc. It is found that the prevalent vernacular items gets reflected in the process of writing.

(f) Subjectivity

A writer feels most free on one front; his whims and subjective licence. He is absolutely autonomous to coin new words, structures and validate certain syntactic deviations to either attract the readers, or contribute to the language and new mediums of communication and for saleability of his papers. *The Telegraph* writes (editorial) 7 January '99: 'No sense of gilt' which is due to the writer's subjective choice, and gives a shape to the Indian pronunciation system and the deviation throws light for further linguistic survey in this direction. The editor and writer's point of view easily gets access of the mass and when the mass gets acquainted with a new mode of expression, it starts identifying with it easily than the textual, formal, strict grammatical, pedagogical English. And again objectivity which is supposed to be the essence of newspaper language is a relative concept. Any news item which different reporters interpret for different newspapers bound to differ from one another and become personal yet objective in differing contexts. *India Today* (January 25, '99) has the cover news "Courting controversy" on the controversy between the President and the Chief Justice of the Supreme Court on the appointments of judges. The idea of 'courting' may seem absurd but does communicate a lot. It serves the purpose of rhetorical communication.

The Times of India (1 Feb.'99) writes :

(i) "Sachin's *ton* goes in vain" (his century).
(ii) "Progressive *Middle Kingdom*" (on Madhya Pradesh)
(iii) No Cinema please, we're *Cyberabad* (from Cyber — cybera and from Hyderabad — cyberabad as Hyderabad film festival used high electronic gadgets).

The Telegraph again writes on Sachin's century and effort going in vain as "Pak snatch win from Sachin's Jaws", 1 Feb. '99. Similarly the title "Polls Do Pyaza" is one such change in choice of words (26 Oct.'98, *TOI*). On 27 Oct. '98 *TOI* writes :

(i) Rabindra Sangeet,
(ii) Oxbridge (Oxford/Cambridge educated)
(iii) Have a 'Cuppa/Cha' (Punjabi accent) and so on.

The Economic Times (26 Oct.'98) writes 'Illiquidity' which is an editorial invention.

On October 11, '98, C.P. Surendran (*TOI*) writes: "Currying favour with the Brits" which means 'begging favour' and uses the word 'curryholics' on the model of alcoholics. *The Telegraph* (17 Oct.'98) on its front page writes, "Salim one up on deer son Salman";

the word 'deer' is used instead of using 'dear'. And again it is known that his father Salim also harbours the endangered species of deer himself. "The Sunday Review" (*TOI,* 30 Aug. '98) writes an article on the best selling novels of Shobha De, the novelist : "De after De" (means day after day) which suggests the rapidity of production of commercialised novels by her. The word 'privilegentsia' has been used in a newspaper following the model of the word 'intelligentsia' which is a step ahead in creating new words (Rajiv Desai, *TOI,* 9 Aug. '98). The structure is : "The only one who have benefited are the privilegentsia". An article on the same day comes as 'Whodunnit' (who has done it).

The whole paragraph of an editorial (*TOI*), 12 Aug.'98 is subjective in nature; title — "Mounting Pressures":

"with the build up of steam generated by pressure cooker politics, the BJP led Government must convincingly show that it can take the increasing heat in the kitchen". This metaphoric expression completely owes to the innovative notion of the editor. On 3 January, 1999 Sunday Review, *The Times of India* advertises for 'Head and Shoulders' shampoo; *"Film Fare* helped me rise head and shoulders above the rest", says Urmila "Matha-dho-Kar" (means comforting above others). It refers to the actress Urmilla Matondkar. "Trial by Terror" (12 Aug. 98, *TOI*) is a title modelled on 'Trial and Error'. The *Oxford Advanced Learners Dictionary* talks of robot(n) and robotic (adjective). *The Times of India,* 26 July, 98 has an article "The Computer Doctor" where Sudha Umashankar says : "It has been proved that robotically conducted operations can produce superior results than those by human surgeons". Here robot is used as an adverb.

The crucial point is that there is so much of English all around us, in these less noticed spheres that motivate the common men who count more than the learners in a class room.

Similar is the case with the caption, "It's end of the road for the 'phatphati" since people generally use the word 'phatphati' which is more popular and needs to be given significance than its exact English substitute. On 23 Feb. '98 *The Times of India* writes (Bachi J. Karkaria) words like 'Abba Jaan', 'nani-ma' as this comes from the readers' direct touch and interest to use these words in their actual social life. Similar is the case with the use of words like 'Amartyada' which appeals the people as Bengalis are addressed as 'dada' out of affection. Mahendra Ved writes in *The Times of India*, "Khichidi or Bhelpuri?" On speculating about a Government yet to be formed, the use of a word like khichdi gives colour to general people's gossip. Example—It is a khichdi government (with number of partners) and so on. Again there is another example in *The Times of India* on 5 April '98 'Charity Khichidi'. Similarly the writers keep in mind the mass interest in festivals, rituals, popular traditional ceremonies, cinema, stars, sports etc. which they intelligently fuse in their headlines and content.

Use of structures such as 'The Big B' (Amitabh Bachchan, actor); Dream Girl (Hema Malini, actress); Maharaj (Sourav Ganguly, cricketer); Little Master (Sunil Gavaskar, cricketer) and many other form nice examples in this regard.

The Times of India on 9 Nov. '98 writes 'The Dhamaka Season' (Seema Bassi) on festivities, specifically the Deewali eve. *The Telegraph* writes (8 Nov. '98) "Will the Censors *Zakhm* Puja Bhatt?" (Zakhm is the controversial film made by Puja Bhatt under inspection then).

"Waiting for Naseer" is the title of Nikhat Kazmi's column in *The Times of India* on 8 Nov. '98 on the play *Waiting for Godot* by Naseeruddin Shah.

Also it is very interesting to note how Vir Sangvi writes in *The Telegraph* on Ramesh Sharma (15 Nov. '98); 'Don bad man' modelled on 'Don Bradman' (cricketer), well known to the readers. Similar is the case with the caption, "21st Century Sachin gives India the Cup". *The Statesman* (News item), 14 Nov. '98. Here it suggests two ideas. That Sachin Tendulkar is the 21st century star cricketer and it also talks of his 21st century at Sharjah (the highest number of centuries in Oneday cricket then).

Editorial (*TOI*) writes on 12 Nov. '98: "Language of Bhakti" which appeals to all sections of the people across the country. No doubt the words 'Moni Clinton', 'Monica gate' came out of the writer's subjective indication at certain things. But when it prevailed throughout the pages of all news papers for months together, we can say that the readers must have unconsciously subscribed to the political upheaval that these words have behind their origin.The significant thing is that most of these writings indirectly take the affiliation of the readers into confidence and then Start creating the new modes of expression. It is a two-way process where the writer corresponds to the readers' identities directly. The cultural diversity, linguistic variation and number of political wings in our country provide great scope to be translated into a strange idiom that the people at both the ends are ready to absorb. Indians are more used to metaphoric, euphemistic expressions than a formal, pointed one. So the newspapers adopt the mode to suit them and expressions like "Centre cooks up price battle plan" (*Telegraph* 1 Nov. '98) get generated.

Other such expressions are 'Diet to trim price line'; 'Atalji, Swadeshi Nehru'; 'Dalai Lama melts sunshine' (27 Oct. '98, *The Telegraph*) which means Dalai Lama appeals to pacify the West Bengal government decision to ban Tibetan garments on its roads that suggests a purely tendentious, subjective approach which our readers can absorb like hot cake. Some other examples are "Sonia taunts congress men", "sleep well Mantrij" (suggesting sex scandal) and many more.

The writer's words of affiliation

(a) Global/commercial affiliation

The newspaper readers are no less affected by the liberal commercial and global accessibility of the present time. A common market condition has made all of us know about every product everywhere. The economy of one country is influenced by the other. In such a scenario, the world of advertising and the forum that displays it significantly (the journals and newspapers) take up the task of binding the people commercially just as earlier they used to be united on cultural, social grounds. So people are in search of economy in everything and eye catching words and phrases serve their purpose. The professionals are a growing section in the day of private enterprises, individual company sectors and so on who love a purely functional, practical, need oriented language since the earlier grammatical patterns could not adequately meet up to their expectations.

Also the strictly constructed patterns in English appear dull and pompous to this variety of people who constitute the larger section. And if English has to survive as the most effective language, it must be flexible, volatile and changing in its nature unlike Sanskrit which suffered due to its rigidity. In today's world nothing is static. Purity is a relative term. So English cannot afford to neglect the global move to give rise to separate 'Englishes' within the broad native English.

And the newspapers mostly serve to the purpose of these readers who are constantly in need of the abstractions; yet pragmatic touch of the language.

Apart from the cultural religious affiliation of the readers which are met by special features on them as we find for example in *The Times of India*, 5 Feb. '99 "Dharma and Governance" by Chaturvedi Badrinath where he talks of words like 'Kutil', 'Saral', 'Adharma', 'Prabhav' and many more such issues; the global commercial interest of the readers are met with advertisements especially that use abstractions in language structure deliberately. Britannia advertises (5 Feb. '99, *TOI*):

> "Britannia Khao
> World Cup Jao".

Airtel cellular phone company advertises: "handset koi bhi ho, magic dalo, say hello".

Kawasaki Bajaj advertises for its new brand of motor bike and also names it 'CALIBER'. The purpose is to attract because of the deviation and to make the word 'Calibre' simpler, according to our understanding of the concept of spelling. Again "Caliber: the unshakeable" comes another example. Pepsi advertises: 'The Pepsi Blue-Eyed Boyz (4 Feb.'99, *TOI*); a cold drink advertisement.Words like 'Hindustrial', 'Flexigerator', 'Sexpress', 'Hinglish' are easy entry into our vocabulary of English through newspapers and journals not just due to the subjective, global, commercial affiliation of the writers but are out of an indirect pressure on the writers in order to fulfil the inner desire of the readers for a fresh, new idiom with economy and variety. So it directly owes to the readers' affiliation of certain issues too.The recent controversy on the film *Fire* had made all the people acquainted with the issue which comes below. "The Sunday Review", special report (*TOI*): "Now that Fire has been passed without a single cut, the foreign Dyke-Didis are going gaga over the steamy scenes between Shabana Apa and Nandita Naani. The Dilli billis Gucci gays are in Seventh heaven." This is no doubt due to the readers, affiliation to the global, free, fashionable attitude towards language which is expressed in a language full of deviation and borrowing words from clearly different and differing contexts.The words 'foreignisation' also satisfies our reader's fascination of the imported products everywhere. *The Times of India*, 24 Aug.'98 gives an article on the modern 90's woman with the electronic gadgets all around and coins the structure, "The One black coffee please woman, Does she exist?" Here the 'black coffee woman' suggests her modernity and the readers facilitate such coinage as they well practise such notions in the commercialised liberal market oriented society. 25 Oct.'98 (*TOI*, Abhee K Barman, columnist) writes : "Dollars, Marks and Pounds... flesh" on economy. International Monetary Fund, recession and everything get assimilated into the language. It was earlier pointed out that *The Statesman* projected the title 'Generationext' as a single word on a feature on the music maestros which is also a catchword in different advertisements such as 'Pepsi' which satisfies the readers' interest with such usage. Nikhat Kazmi in *TOI* gives the title "Real-life Heroes in Unreal Showbiz"and uses structures such as ... " origins to the 'down market biradari', 'Punjabiat' (earlier Punjabiyat) ; 'aam Indian', 'proletarianising', 'prototypal mofussil man' which are permissible due to the internal attachment and interest of the mass with these words related to the filmworld, down to earth themes, heroes etc.There are a number of such instances that reflect the orientation of the readers towards a liberal linguistic canon in a liberal, global, commercial world with fashion and entertainment having primary attention.

(b) Regional affiliation

The readers' world is full of notions directly imbibed from regional local codes and so they feel privileged as well as delighted to get their nuances being projected in newspapers which in fact does not ascertain regional bias but vigorously assimilates the local into the mainstream, the unknown into the known.The example of the Keralite concept of 'Wife house' , Oriya way of speaking. 'Odisa', 'Kataka', the Assames stress on a particular vowel in most words as in 'Asom' (stands for Assam) are some examples in this regard. The regional papers heighten such usage and the mainstream papers have also started putting the regional stamp in their respective sections to satisfy the respective readers. A feature on a particular state or region figures out some expressions related to those areas but comes out of the interest of the readers to meet their own words and structures. All those usages of peculiar accent, stress of a region giving rise to the graphological deviation accordingly, directly reflect the readers' own motivation in rationalising and legitimising the tongue he has practised in his day to day life. The words like 'gormint', 'kudi', 'munda', 'balle balle' are popular from this point of view.

(c) Obsessiveness

The innumerable influences that today's man comes under, makes him choose his own decoding system of comprehension of news items. The print media has to fight and withstand the glamour of the electronic media (TV, Internet, Cyber World). So the kind of attraction it has to build is based upon the readers' subjective interest in the words and structures it uses keeping aside the old, stereotyped expressions. *The Telegraph* studies the growing trend of subjective use of the English tongue (5 December '98); "Mind your Language" by Sudipta Basu who says "everyone is busy developing their own slang these days" and cites examples:

> "total enthu se film dekha", "give me some space yaar," etc. of the college students and discusses the possibility and reality of such a pattern that motivate the newspapers to provide those patterns which are popular among our readers. Since the writers and editors are well aware of the fact that today most readers are interested in sections on 'fashion, entertainment, sports and even advertise-ments'; they evolve the new words and structures, strange combination and deviation in word formation, links in these areas. The extra concern and over enthusiasm in these fields pressurize the writers to create the new idiom. *India Today* (14 December, '98) writes, "Career menopause ... But a life on fast forward". The title is on a feature, interview with film actress Rekha. The use of the word 'menopause, regarding the waning of Rekha's film career seems so strange here which the readers absorb as their subjective codes can easily decipher the meanings. Similar is the use of 'Salaam Sonia', 'faultline Sonia' in the same magazine July 7, (*TOI*) writes "Don't genderise the Women's bill." The word 'genderise' is a natural growth out of 'gender' which the readers' licentiousness guarantees.Nikhat Kazmi writes 'Out of closet, off the shelf' on 20 July, '98 (*TOI*) in which she uses the words 'Dilliwallah', 'fizzical', 'muchness' in contexts which seem to have subscribed to the readers' personal day to day modes of conversation.

On 18 July,'98 (*TOI*), columnist Jonathan Freeland also uses the words 'oohed and aahed' being aware of the Indianness of the newspaper addressing honestly to the Indian readers. One columnist uses the word 'museumise' just like 'genderise' quoted earlier which also owes to the readers' subjective requirements. Words like 'Restaurateur' (from Restaurant), Monicagate, Moniclinton, megatainment seem to have come under such compulsions.

"Ms Lewinsky was very accommodating, and would never want to deter gents, particularly, those helpful to her careers"; comes the news in *The Times of India*; also 'Mo Knicker' (23 August '98) which intelligently, humorously talks to the readers' being aware of the stained clothes of Monica which was kept unwashed and 'detergents' being used as two words to suit two meanings in a context. On 3 Feb. '99 *TOI*, article: "Grin it and Beer it"; writes Anupam Srivastav who talks about a kind of Beer which can fight gastric; so the word 'beer' is used as a verb replacing 'bear'. "Talking Turkey" (30 Sept. '98, *TOI*) uses a sentence: "Black is Unbeautiful" (Dipankar Gupta, *The Telegraph*, 29 Sept. '98) which is an ironical remark.Titles like, "Midnight's end" (29 Sept. '98, *The Telegraph*), "Satanic years" and so on speak to an extent the weightage of reader's subjectivity and capacity who have read the respective novels.

The writers/columnists are also serious readers. So the famous figures who otherwise keep record of what is written today and who often are invited to write for noted newspapers give the best interplay of their linguistic and cultural affiliation which motivates the change.

REFERENCES

1. V.K. Gokak, *English in India, Its Present and Future* (Bombay : OUP, 1964).
2. E. Haugen, "Linguistics and language planning", *Sociolinguistics*, ed. W. Brigat (Mouton : The Hague, 1966) 4.
3. J. Spencer, "A Multilingual Commonwealth", *Books* (N.P. : n.p., 1965).
4. J. Spencer, "Language and Independence", *Language in Africa*, ed. J. Spencer (London : Cambrige University Press, 1963) 25.
5. J. Holloway, "I will tell you one thing", *The Hudson Review*, Autumn (1959) 409.
6. R.C. Goffin, "Some Notes on Indian English", *S.P.E. Tract* (N.P. : n.p., 1934).
7. S. Umamaheswari, "The Role of Newspapers in the Present Society", *The Competition Success Review*, March (1994) pp. 13-14.

Chapter - 4

General Morpho-syntactic Processes in English, Words Formed in Deviation and the Predominant Processes

Focus

It is of paramount importance to classify the processes of change going on behind the newly formed words in newspaper English. So first we seek to describe in brief the general morpho-syntactic processes in English. By it we mean the morpho-syntactic methods of word formation that are available. We also enlist the representative words in deviation and the processes that help in their formation and fast growth. Both the new words and the new usage of some existing words are discussed. We also say that such changes are not just accidental but deliberate and follow a pattern of its own. The earlier chapter has already highlighted the socio-cultural factors behind such change. And here we categorise the internal linguistic mechanism at work towards this change. We discuss the processes of word formation under one heading and see their utilisation in the outcome of Indian English.

The Morpho-Syntactic Structure of English

Morphology comes from the term morpheme; that is the smallest grammatical, meaningful unit of the language. It refers to the scientific study of the minimal grammatical units of the language.

The two meaningful units of the word "Friendship" are 'friend' and 'Ship' of which the first one (friend) can stand by itself and is known as a 'free' morpheme. The other one is a 'bound' morpheme. The process of 'affixation' by which different units are added to the 'free' or 'base' morpheme is very common to generate new terms for everyday use.

Examples:

(a) Un + democratic = Undemocratic
(Prefix) (free form)

(b) Global + ise = Globalise + ation = Globalisation
(Free morpheme) (Suffix) (Suffix)

1. Some other new expressions as appear in newspapers can be seen; *The Times of India* titles one news (8 April '99):

   "The art of growing old healthfully." The term 'healthfully' replaces the structure 'full of health' thereby giving economy of expression.

   Health + full = Healthful + ly = Healthfully.

2. A number of times the word 'netizen' has been used in recent writing on newspapers of which one occasion is cited here. The word is formed by another morpho-syntactic process; blend, which is another productive method of word formation.

"Netizens frown on Jaya's moves". Such citizens of the Net are brilliantly termed so which captures both the systems; the concept of a citizen and that of internet. And a minimal interest, awareness in today's pro-technology world would easily make one guess such a new coinage. So change is also sudden in the case of newspaper writing which does not always borrow from the specific linguistic description of the lexical items and structural units. But its in depth study seems to have utilised the Chomskyan notion of 'deep structures' as the surface structure 'Netizen' can be broken into the deep structures; 'Citizen' and 'Net'. Chomsky's idea that "the overt structure (surface) and abstract (underlying) structure are linked by transformations", is utilised here too.

J. Harris[1] says: "...Language change is of interest to the theoretical linguist to the extent that it is a valuable source of date relevant to the formulation of explanatory theories concerning the general properties of human language and, ultimately of human cognitive processes in general. In this respect language change takes its place alongside other sources of data, for example, the study of particular synchronic grammars, language acquisition, language disorders, language play, and so on." It explains the need of processes of change which is there in the morpho-syntactic rules of English. We seek to discuss the processes in detail below.

The Processes of Change in English

We here analyse the distinct processes of morpho-syntactic change in English.

Affixation

An affix is a bound form of the word which can be divided into prefixes, suffixes and infixes. Infixes are not prevalent in the English language.

(a) Prefix

The affix which can be added before a free form (the base form) is called a prefix.

So a word can look like

Bound form	+	Free form	+	Bound form.
BF	+	FF	+	BF

The prefixes may have certain approximate meanings too.

Examples:

anti	—	against	→	antinational
pre	—	before	→	pre meditated
Inter	—	between	→	Intercollege
Intra	—	within	→	Intraclass
Un	—	not	→	unknown

Prefixes also co-exist as in non-cooperative, ex-vice principal.

These prefixes have the capacity of getting added to any noun to produce new forms of words.

(b) Suffix

The affix that follows the base form is called a suffix. Suffixes perform two different functions in a language.

(i) The grammatical requirement; example: 'He goes to school' performs the requirement which the third person singular pressurizes; go-es → goes; which is known as inflectional suffix.

(ii) Derivational suffixes which perform the function of coining new words:
effect+ive→ effective. Just +ify→justify and so on. We discuss both these types in detail below.

1. Grammatical functions

The new words which are formed to meet the grammatical functions are the inflected forms such as

(i) Plural suffixes functioning for the plural cases

Cat	—	Cats
Rose	—	Roses
Book	—	Books
Flower	—	Flowers

(ii) Case suffixes

The nouns in English have inflected case forms like possessive or genitive cases.

Girl's, girls', flowers' or flower's etc.

(iii) Tense

(a)	He looks	(Present tense)	—	s
	He looked	(Past tense)	—	ed
	He teaches	(Present tense)	—	es
	It is created	(Past Participle)	—	ed
	He is going	(Present Continuous)	—	ing

(iv) Vowel change (Modification) :

Man - Men
begin - began - begun etc.

(v) adding 'en'
Speak—Spoken

(vi) Changing final consonant; send—sent

(vii) Changing both vowel and consonant
teach—taught

(viii) Changing vowel and adding 't'—sleep—slept

(ix) Suffixes that show degree in adjectives, adverbs etc.
Strong—Stronger, Strongest. (er, est)

(x) Pronominal inflections—
The pronouns have suffixes like:

One	—	One's
Other	—	others, other's
our	—	ours
her	—	hers etc.

(xi) Suppletion — where no distinct form of the suffix is seen since the new form is entirely different.
Ex. my, we, good, better etc.

(xii) No change — In English certain words do not change in case of plural usage and so on; Furniture — Furniture, Deer — Deer etc.

2. Derivational functions

There are certain suffixes which derive new words from the base. So new nouns, adjectives, verbs are found :

ing	—	writing, interesting (noun, adjective)
fy	—	personify, classify (verb)
less	—	worthless (adjective)
ise	—	minimise (verb)
ous	—	prosperous (adjective)

Diagrammatically we see the division as:

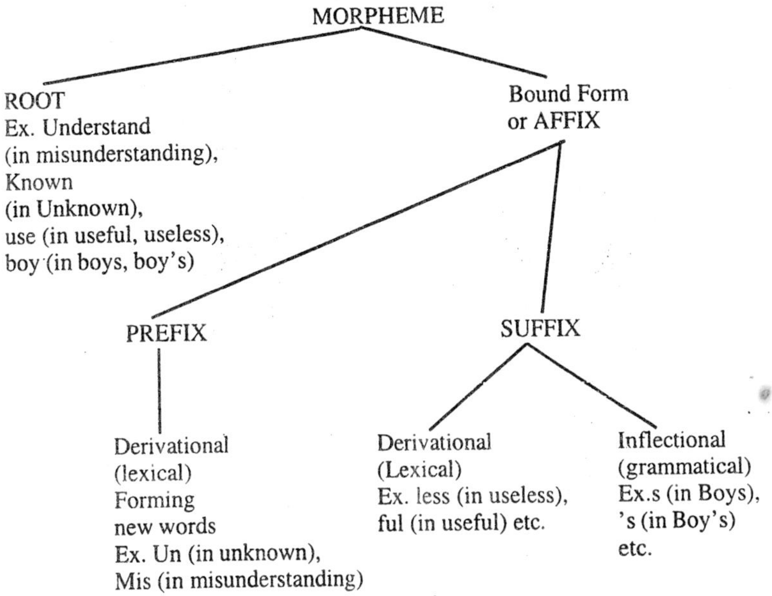

Fig. 1

Morphemic division from T.C. Baruah, *The English Teacher's Handbook* (New Delhi: Sterling Publishers Pvt. Ltd., 1984).

Paradigms and Compounds

Paradigms offer a set of related words to one root word which may be used replacing one.

Example:

Love
Lovely
Lovable
Loving and so on

Compounds are obtained by combining two or more free forms of a morpheme. Certain compounds which are formed by juxtaposing (keeping side by side) the two forms are like :

horse	+	race	→	Horse-race
(N)	+	(N)		(N)
Cat	+	walk	→	Catwalk
(N)	+	(V)		(N)

eye	+	catching	→	eye catching
(N)	+	(V-ing)		(Adj.)
mean	+	minded	→	mean minded
(adjective)	+	(N+ed Suffix)		(Adj.)

The other compounds require certain syntactical arrangement :

farewell	(V	+	adverb)
opening song	(ing v	+	N)

father-in-law (Phrase compounds)

Blends

There are blendings in English word formation such as:

smoke	+	fog	→	smog
motor	+	hotel	→	motel
lion	+	tiger	→	liger
Europe	+	Asia	→	Eurasia etc.
Breakfast	+	lunch	→	(eakfast + l) deleted= Brunch
Tran(sfer)	+	(re)sistor	→	Transistor

Acronyms

Acronyms are formed by joining the initial letters of the words such as NIIT, TV, UNESCO etc.

Some of them are pronounced as words, example :

Radar (Radio detecting and ranging). Acronyms are also called 'alphabetism'.

Conversion

In English we have cases of conversion where the same word is used as different parts of speech.

A verb becomes noun	:	Cheat → Cheat
An adjective becomes noun	:	The dailies and weeklies (Newspapers, Journals)
Affix becomes noun	:	He does not believe in *isms* (Marxism, Nazism etc.).

Clipping

When a long word is made short by omitting a part of it that is known as clipping. Example:

Photo from photograph.
Phone from telephone (Both used as nouns)
'rhino' from 'rhinoceros'
When both sides are eliminated—Influenza—Flu.

Sandhi

Sandhi (the Sanskrit word) is a significant process of word variation and change.

(i) Loss of phoneme: words like 'indirect', 'incorrect' refer to the negative which is done by losing the allomorph/in/and seeing it as a prefix.
This is 'loopasandhi' (Sanskrit). Words like irregular, illogical are formed by it. The allomorph / ir/, /il/ are lost here.

(ii) Addition of phonemes:
Strong + er → Stronger
The silence of the phonemic sound can be observed by the phonetic transcription of the above terms.
This case of addition of suffix is formed as 'aagamasandhi' (Sanskrit).

(iii) Assimilation:
The sound quality and manner of articulation is changed here.
In + complete → incomplete
alveolar + Velar → velar + velar
This is 'aadesha sandhi' in Sanskrit.

(iv) Stress shift :
em'ploy — emplo'yee
'method — metho'dology

Imitation or Onomatopoeia

It is one of the old methods of word formation from the sound that the object suggests : bang, pop, buzz, click, hiss, giggle etc.

Abbreviation

It is a shortening of word which gets into normal usage :

Mathematics	—	Maths
Main examinations	—	Mains
Examination	—	Exam

Syncopation[2]

The process by which a vowel is lost

Ones	—	once
henes	—	hence

Metanalysis

By this process one form of word structure becomes another. Ex. science and arts — science and darts, a flashing eye — a flashing guy; at home — a tome.

Back formation

This process is an important method which is mostly deliberate and most often out of necessity new usages are formed by it. Certain verbs have come out of their usage in the noun forms. For example, verbs like beg, edit, peddle are the back formation of the nouns begging, editing and peddling. 'To beg' is new and formed from the usage of begging. So it is a new formation from the back side. Similarly,

Resurrection	—	to resurrect
subscription	—	to subscribe

Slangs

Words like chap, shabby, coax were taken as slangs and not good English even during the 18th century (Wood, 1969). Slangs are formed depending upon the category and context of speakers.

Words coming from proper names

Utopian, Lilliputian are words that have come under such practices. Most of these processes (cited above) have been analysed by F.T. Wood (1969). We have described the normally used processes of word formation in English here although some of those do not directly relate to the use of new words in newspapers as they give stress to pronunciation as in the case of 'stress shift', 'assimilation' etc. Chiefly we find that affixation and modification (in terms of blend, compounding etc.) describe the whole process of morpho-syntactic change in British English. These processes are also highly utilised for word formation in Indian English. Since we find a perceptible change in many areas between British English and Indian English, we seek to discuss certain parameters that facilitate such differences before analysing the new words and processes.

The Parameters of Change

The parameters of change refers to the areas of change of British English in the context of India on the pages of its English newspapers. The parameters as the axes of change do not prescribe any limit or boundary of changes already made or that could be made, but give a scope for flexibility that work taking roots out of certain perceptible branches of change.

The Formal Parameter

It discusses the grammatical, lexical, orthographical areas of separation of British English (B.E.) and that of Indian Newspaper English (I. N. E.). At this level there is no perceptible new process of change or new pattern prescribed by Indian standards. Here false analogy, adoption of British English rules at unusual contexts give rise to a deviant word. For example, following the British English formula we create new words that we may not find in British English.

Urgency	—	Urgent (existing word)
Emergency	—	Emergent (new word)

But 'Emergent Meeting' is not used in British English (Labru, 1984).

Formally and grammatically we may see the change here:

Grammatical level

At this level of change the source language provides the 'head' morpheme and the recipient language gives pluralisation, noun-adjective derivation etc. When the Indian word 'gherao' is taken into British English usage, the 'head' morpheme 'gherao' remains intact. And the formula of pluralisation of British English (B.E.) is applied to it in case they want to use it plurally. Ex. 'gheraos', past tense — gheraoed.

Indian Word	*British/IndianEnglish*
gherao	gheraos, gheraoed
ghat	ghats
Ashram	Ashrams, Ashramite
Chill	Chillies

But in case of Chhola (an Indian word), the rule of Indian language formula is applied for its pluralisation (chhole).

British English	*Indian English*
Bore	'Boryat' instead of 'Boredom' (orthographical deviation)
Curious	Curiouser. (Lexical deviation) (Editorial, 4 Aug. '99, *TOI*)

Now we consider certain words in Newspaper English that have got their origin, change at the grammatical level. The words that look deviated work in a grammatical context. So both lexical and grammatical axes are taken into consideration. In other words, it gives an account of the lexico-grammatical deviation.

1. Cool comes to the movies — Title of the news item (3 January, '99, Sunday Review, *TOI*) by Sonal Nerurkar. The status of the word cool (which is already there and not a new word) as a noun is a significant drive for change.
2. Another expression like: 'Picnicker of the Year' (3 Jan. '99, 'Sunday Review', *TOI*).

The formula is thus :

a man who goes is a goer
a man who takes is a taker
a person who goes on a picnic is picnicker.

3. Mother in law (BE)→ ma-in-law (IE)
(advertisement of *Femina*, 27Dec.'98 *TOI*, "Sunday Review").
4. 'The art of growing old healthfully (*TOI*, 8 April '99) forms the title of an article 'Healthfully' is not an usual word. The structures like skilfully could be the influence to coin a word like this which means 'full of health'.
5. 'The Unputdownable' (*The Telegraph*, 3 July '99).
The word comes in the category of 'Unsurpassable,' 'Unconquerable' etc. (A phrasal verb like 'putdown' is getting a blend grammatically to form a noun).
6. The sprouting, leafing of branches... (*TOI*,16 Aug '99)
It appears in an article By P.V. Narayana Swamy: "Samsara and the cosmic Aswatha Tree". The term 'leafing' (that is coming of new leaves to a branch) takes its root from a deviated grammatical code.
give → giving
(verb)
Take → taking
(verb)
leaf → leafing
(noun)

The Contextual Semantic Parameter

This section briefly discusses the pressure of the Indian context and Indian semantic scales that act upon creating the change at the lexical level. The pressure of context and semantic scales on structure and meaning difference would be discussed in chapter 4th and 5th. Since the writers, editors of Indian English newspapers work under Indian contexts, some of their created words get validity under this parameter. Examples:

1. Beyond 'achar-papad' syndrome. (Chandrika Mago, *TOI* News Service, 16 Aug. '99).
   The caption above is the title of a news item. We are not concerned here about Hindi or Indian words like 'achaar' and 'papad' in their own rights. Our finding is that, taken together, 'achaar-papad' is one expression, complementary and stands for a particular concept, that is domestic, day-to-day, ordinary livelihood, relating to works that an Indian house wife is supposed to do. So such an expression is new and gets validity as our way of looking at an important behaviour that takes its leap from the native thought. The whole caption is not written in the Hindi language or any Indian language, only the concept has been accommodated into the traditional format of the English language.
2. 'Lakshman Rekha' is the title of an editorial (*The Statesman*, 14 Aug.'99). First of all the very usage of 'Lakshman Rekha' is purely an Indian cultural thrust. It is taken from the *Ramayana* that speaks about a line of warning and limit. Here it not only speaks about that warning but the content reveals that the person concerned; an Ex. M.P. is known as Lakshman Sett who has dealt certain issues in a way that provokes the editor to express his reaction in such a way.
3. "Samsara and the Cosmic Aswatha Tree" (*The Times of India*, 16 Aug. '99, by P.V. Narayan Swamy) is the title of the article. Our point is that 'Samsara' is beyond the English equivalent of life, Universe or Society or World. 'Samsara' speaks of illusiveness of life too, the 'Maya'; the tricky way in which Man is wrapped in worldliness. So the appropriate word to replace any such idea is 'Samsara' though it is put into a British English structure. This is how Indian Contextual appropriateness works and serves its purpose.

The English linguistic structure and Indian socio-cultural structure move hand in hand in the use of English in newspapers here.

The Distinct Processes Operative in Newspaper English in India

We here record and analyse the distinct processes that facilitate the change as seen in the body of Indian English newspapers for formation of new words along with the newly formed words and expressions.

The new terms are the representative ones and have been collected over a period between 1996 and early 2002 by random sampling of data. Although the processes are familiar, the methods of indigenisation are clear in the nature of these new terms. So it can be said, Indian socio-cultural and linguistic experience along with the universal linguistic processes help derive the new entries.

The words and expressions are noted down in the order of their collection along with the respective processes they utilise. It is found that the processes of 'affixation' (addition of prefix and suffix) and 'blend' are used most while forming new words, though all other processes contribute substantially towards it. For easy access of the dominant processes we mention the respective serial numbers cited before the words.

For the process of affixation :

> See item numbers 1, 2, 4, 7, 10, 11, 12, 13, 15, 24, 27, 28, 31, 33, 34, 35, 36, 37, 40, 45, 46, 47, 49, 50, 54, 55, 58, 61, 62, 63, 64, 68, 69, 70, 74, 75, 77, 78, 79, 80, 81, 84, 85, 86, 89, 90, 95, 97, 100, 101, 102, 103, 104, 105, 106, 107, 108, 109, 110, 111, 112, 113, 114, 115, 118, 119, 120, 121, 124, 125, 126, 127, 128, 132, 133, 135 etc.

For the process of blend:

> See item numbers 3, 6, 8, 14, 16, 18, 19, 20, 22, 23, 29, 30, 32, 38, 41, 42, 43, 44, 48, 52, 56, 59, 60, 66, 67, 71, 72, 92, 93, 94, 96, 99, 117, 123, 129, 134 etc.

We mention below a few item numbers for the other processes:

For the process of Sandhi	:	See 131, 139 etc.
For clipping	:	See 84, 170 etc.
For abbreviation	:	See 82, 84, 136, 156 etc.
For code switch/mix	:	Items listed (Page 158 onwards).
For syncopation	:	See 41, 87 etc.
For slang	:	Items listed (Page 168 onwards).
For acronym formation	:	See 9 and 15 for a number of examples.

For words from proper names :	See 9 and 15.
For words from proper names :	See 3, 17 (Page 151 and 154 respectively).
For conversion :	See 25, 35, 128 etc.
For onomatopoeia :	See 224.
For compounding :	See 16, 51, 76 etc.
For metanalysis :	See 21, 39.
For back formation :	See 53, 57.

Apart from these, the Indigenised methods; as utilised can be seen in the last sections.

New words in deviation and the processes involved

	Items	*Sources*
1.	unputdownable	*The Telegraph*, 3 July'99.

Context: The unputdownable.
Process: It first adopts the process of affixation.
Put down — Put downable (suffix—'able')
In such a process the phrasal verb becomes an adjective.
Again the process of affixation (prefixing 'un') is at work for the change.
Put downable (prefixing 'un') → unputdownable
It gives us two words: 'Put downable' and 'unputdownable'.

2.	(i) Marketisation	S.K. Pillai, *Indian Express* 25 June, '99
	(ii) Siachenisation	Rohit Nair, *The Asian Age*, 30 June, '99
	(iii) Customisation	Editorial, *TOI*, 3 Dec.'99
	(iv) Genderise:	

Context: "Don't Genderise the women's Bill".	Editorial, 7 July'98, *The Times of India*

The Process: Affixation
It follows the model of words like 'globalisation', 'commer-cialisation' etc.

		ise(suffix)	*ion(Suffix)*	
Market (N)	—	Marketise (V)	—	Marketisation (N)

	ion(suffix)			
Customise (V)	—	Customisation (N)		
	ise (Suffix)		ion(suffix)	
Siachen a glacier (N)	—	Siachenise (V)	—	Siachenisation (N)
	ise (suffix)			
Gender	—	Genderise (V)	—	also 'genderisation' can come out of it.

So in this double suffixing process we get a number of words to be used both as new verbs and new nouns.

(v) Museumise   Shiv Visvanathan,   *TOI*, 13 Sept. '98

In the same process as above this word is generated. It can also be used as a noun as in 'museumisation'.

Museum (N)	–	Museumise (V)	–	museumisation (N)

3. Manmohanomics — (i) *The Economic Times*, 23 July '96 and frequently quoted in a number of newspapers. (ii) 27 Oct. 98, Interview with Manmohan Singh, *The Times of India*.

Swaminomics (Swaminathan Ankalesh Aiyar, a leading Economist) — A regular column in *The Times of India* frequently used as the column on the economic scenario.

Kargilonomics — Ashim Chatterjee, *The Asian Age*, 30 June '99.

Naidunomics — Editorial, *The Times of India* 18 Oct. '1999.

The Process : Blending.

The active use of all these processes here has the credit of the Indian hands using them for their use and contribution in terms of new vocabulary content.

Manmohan Singh (The Ex.Finance Minister) (N)	His economic policy —————— (+Economics)	Manmohanomics (a particular trend in the Economic Policy)

Swaminathan (Ankalesh Aiyyar) (N)	The column he writes on the economy	(+ Economics)
		Swaminomics (what he says about economy) (N)
Kargil (Place name) (N)	(The economic situation — prevailing due to the war) + Economics because of it	Kargilonomics (N)

There is every possibility of a word like 'Kargilisation' which could set the Indian figurative use of the word to highlight the war scenario.

These words are formed out of proper names. But since in all languages so many words have come from important names, events, places, it is also a fertile area in Indian standard to use the possibility extensively for new words.

4. Words given below characterise Indian assertion of colloquialism. — Editorial column, *The Times of India,* 12 Aug. '99

   Maroing—(suffixing 'ing' to an Indian word)
   Jharoing—(suffixing 'ing' to an Indian word)
   Process: suffixation
   Meaning:
   Maroing means misappropriation of funds.
   Jharoing means giving a jhar (Indian word) —Someone being bashed up.

5. Great Anarch— — *The Times of India,* editorial, 3 Aug. '99

   Process: 'Anarch'(N) comes from 'anarchy' or 'anarchic'.
   (N) (Adj.)
   And it is done by 'back formation'
   It is also influenced by the word 'Monarch'(from Monarchy).
   If 'Monarch'is used, why cannot anarch' ?

6. Kleptocracy
   (i) Srikant Gupta, — *The Times of India* (5 Aug. '99)
   (ii) Sauvik Chakraverti — *TOI*, 22 Sept. '99
   Process :
   The words which are already in use are 'Kleptomania' and 'Democracy'. 'Autocracy' etc.

And the new word comes by blend.
Kleptomania + Democracy = Kleptocracy
The term is again repeated in the same paper by Souvik Chakraverti on 27 May, '01 in an article "Hobbes' Mistake" as 'Kleptocracies'.

7. Curiouser and curiouser *The Times of India* August 4,'99
Suffixation takes place to create the requisite word to meet the growing need.
Curious - er(suffix) = curiouser.
Apart from the title, the news item also uses a sentence like '...the controversy is getting curiouser and curiouser'.

8 (i) Netizen (i) *TOI*, 10 Aug. '99 and used very frequently in all English Dailies.

(ii) "Netizens frown upon Jaya's moves" (ii) *TOI*, 9 April '99.

The process is that of clipping and blend which take place beteween two words :

(a) Net actually has come from internet. It is a case of clipping.
(b) Net and the citizen using Internet → Netizen (N)

A new noun is formed by blending.
(iii) Netizen *The Times of India*, 5 Oct. '99.

9. X Press Engine, *The Times of India*, 13 Aug. '99, LML vespa advertisement, also appears on 26 Aug. '99.

X-treme Thrills *TOI*, 19 Sept. '99, Title of an article by R. Edwin Sudhir.

Steam X Press (Advertisement of Usha Iron), *Film Fare*, July '97).

The process of syncopation [ones→ once], loss of vowel [at home→a tome] comes to active use in these cases and acronym formation also has a role to play here.

10. Suited, booted, tie wearing gentry, *TOI*, 15 Aug. '99.
By suffixation new adjectives and past participles are formed.
Suit -ed (suffix) = Suited
(N)

Boot (N)	-ed (suffix)	=	booted

The writer does not use the word 'tied' but retains 'tie wearing' since such a use may confuse the reader with the usual meaning of the word 'tied'(in chains or thread etc.).

11. (i) Winnability — Editorial, *TOI*, 17 Aug. '99
Context: "Women lack the winnability factor"
(ii) Winnability Trap, → Title of an essay *TOI*, 10. Jan. '98
(iii) Winnable, Fightable → K. Subramanyam, "Linkages and Leverage, Diplomacy in the Nuclear Era", *The Times of India*, 28 Sept. '98.
(iv) Winnability factor — Editorial, *The Times of India*, 13 Oct. '99
(v) Winnability — Ajay Mehra in "Bizarre in Bihar" *The Hindu*. 17 May 2001

The term 'winnable' is also again used by *The Hindu* as discussed ahead.

By suffixation such words are used.

Win	(able) suffix	winnable-(ity) — winnability
Fight	(able) suffix	Fightable.

12. (i) Stop Damming — *The Statesman*, 14 Aug. '99.

The process of suffixation; 'ing' suffix added to the noun 'Dam'; gives a verb in which 'Damming' means constructing a Dam. The Dictionary only talks of the phrasal verb 'Dam up' and not 'damming'.
Example (in dictionary): Dam the river up and 'Dam' as a noun. So Damming is a new usage.

(ii) Electrify and be Dammed — *The Times of India*, 29 Oct. '98. (Interview with Ex-Power Minister, P.R. Kumaramangalam by Lalita Panicker).

13. (i) Talibanise
context:... grave threat centred in Talibanised Pakistan and Afghanistan — Editorial, *The Times of India*, 21 Sept.'99.
Talibanising — *TOI*, 24 Nov.'01/25 Nov.'01.

(ii) Talibanisation
context: ...Talibanisation of Pakistan... — Editorial, *TOI*, 22 Sept. '99

(iii) Talibanised
Process : Affixation. — Dilip Chitre, *The Times of India*, 28 Sept. '99.

By suffixing 'ise' to the terrorist group known as Taliban in contemporary times, a new word is created which can replace or stand for terrorism, gradual growth of insurgency and some such ideas.

14. Adultescent
Screenager — Rasmmeez Z Ahmed, *TOI*, 24. Aug. '98.

The columnist explains that a person (an adult) who is addicted to youth culture is an adultescent and a computer addicted teenager is known to be a screenager.

The Process : (i) Compounding:
Just like Teen + ager → Teenager
Screen + ager → Screenager
(ii) Process: Blend:
Adolescent + Adult→ Adultescent

15. "An acronymed world" — Article by Sudip Ghosh, *TOI*, 31 Aug. '99.

The columnist gives a list of new acronyms which are actually popularised by being projected on a newspaper.

The word 'acronym' itself is used as an adjective in the title.

Acronym (noun)	*Suffixing 'ed'*	acronymed (adjective)

The process of acronym formation gives the following words (Internet and Computers also create new acronyms as can be seen here)

(i) ADN — Any Day Now
AFAIK — As Far As I Know
AFK — Away From Key board.
B4N — Bye For Now
BAK — Back at The Key Board
BRB — Be Right Back
BTA — But Then Again
BTW — By The Way
CU — See You

DIKU	—	Do I Know You
EOM	—	End Of Message
EOT	—	End Of Thread (End of Disucssion)
F2F	—	Face To Face
FAQ	—	Frequently Ask Questions
FISH	—	First In, Still Here
FUD	—	Fear, Uncertainty and Doubt
FYI	—	For Your Information
G	—	Grin
GA	—	Go Ahead
GAL	—	Get a Life
HTH	—	Hope this Helps
IAC	—	In any case
IC	—	I see
IIRC	—	If I recall/remember/recollect correctly
ILY OR ILU	—	I love you
OIC	—	Oh, I see
POOF	—	Goodbye (leaving the room), a case of metanalysis.
THX	—	Thanks (It is a case of shortening, abbreviation of the word).
ARE	—	Acronym - rich Environment

(ii) The acronyms below are listed by an article on *TOI,* 22 Aug.'99 by Vinay Kamat.

ERP	—	Enterprise resource planning
TQM	—	Total Quality Management
SCM	—	Strategic Cost Management
ABC	—	Activity Based Costing
SSS	—	Supply Side Strategy
SPST	—	Same Place, Same Time
ASAP	—	As Soon As Possible

He also says it is the culture of "Lingua Shrunka". like "Lingua - Franca"; 'shrunka' comes from shrinking linguistic trend by new acronyms.

(iii) Saarc

The change is like this :

S.A.A.R.C. — SAARC — Saarc by Acronymisation — *The Statesman* 31 July'98

16. In 'Coin your own, for fun and profit' by William Safire, *The Times of India,* 12 Nov.'98 the terms below appear.

(i) Billygate (Carter's crisis)
(ii) Monicagate (Clinton's crisis)
(iii) Irangate (Reagan's crisis); all take their root from the *Watergate* crisis in America.
So it is the process of blend/compounding.
By the process of sandhi and blend respectively words like
(iv) Workaholic, chocoholic are created.
Initial source word — alcoholic.
(v) Faxathon :
That comes from Fax and Marathon which means an unending stream of faxes (messages by fax); process of blend.
(vi) Sea scape (Original source word is landscape)
Moon scape
city scape
By blending/compounding.
(vii) Like the 'free-lancer' a new creation is 'e-lancer' that means 'a free agent who is electronically linked for specific projects and moves swiftly' when the work is done.
Similar is the case with words like
e-text, e-money, e-bucks, e-commerce, e-generation, e-reader and so on which comeout of the process of 'blending'.
The frequently used word e-mail is used as a single term: 'EMAIL'. — Advertisement, *The Times of India*, 28 Sept.'99
(viii) Curryholic (Somebody who is used to curry favour always); the process of Sandhi. — C.P. Surendran, *TOI*, 11 October '98

17. To Skirt China is to Skirt The Issue. — *The Times of India*, 7 July, '98.
The dictionary talks of the phrasal verb 'Skirt round'.
And the liberal use of the word 'Skirt' as a verb only in the specific sense for which the phrasal verb stands is done by a process of back formation.

18. (i) Linglex:
study of linguistics and lexicography (by blending), an interview with Prof. John Wells, a linguist in English by Ratnottama Sengupta "Downsizing Queen's English", *The Times of India.*
(ii) Hyperlink, multitasking, home page, down loading, down size, number crunching.
By compounding, all these words have come from technological fields and are popularised by the print media.

(iii) Edultainment
Infotainment
Infomercial
Docudrama
The processes:

Education that entertains or entertainment that educates becomes edutainment.The new word is created by blend.

Information about entertaiment— 'Infotainment' by blend.
Commercial information is replaced by 'Infomercial' through blend.
A documentary as a drama is a 'docudrama' by blending.
Also the word 'Infotainment' is used in headlines. *(The Times of India* 10 March 2000 p.10 suggesting inclusion into the stream of vocabulary).

19. Adhocracy (Adhoc democracy) : a case of blend
Downshift: a case of compounding.
Blairism [suffix (ism) added to proper name, Tony Blair, P.M. of U.K.].
The above words appear in "Linguistic Liberalisation" by Rashmee Z. Ahmed, *The Times of India*, 24 Aug. '98.

20. SCITECH
This is a case of blending between the two words Science & Technology to get 'Scitech' for economy of expression.
It appears in *TOI*, October 12 '97, 4 January '98. It is also a regular column in *The Times of India*'s Sunday Review Section on Scince and Technology.

21. HOWZZATT, HOWZZAT
This is a case of metanalysis by which the clause 'How is that' is compressed to one new single word. Also the process of syncopation is at work here. (the vowel being lost).
Source : Pradeep Vijayakar, *The Times of India*, 4 January, '98 and appears frequently on newspaper, sports section etc. 27 March '98, *TOI,* 24 Nov. '01 and so on. A spelling variation is marked too by this.

22. CULTURECRAT
"Sunday Review" of *The Times of India,*14 December, '97.
By the process of blend a new word is formed.
The Bureaucrats who try to grab the autonomy and freedom of artists and cultural aspects are known as 'Culturecrats'. It can also stand for a Bureaucrat or professional who has been endowed with rich artistic cultural faculties.

23. Sexcess
"The Sweet smell of Sexcess", title of an article, *Film Fare,* July '97.
This word is created for economy by using the process of 'blend'. So that it contains the idea of "excess of sex".
Excess + Sex—Sexcess.

24. APTECHITES
(means the students who go for a course in 'Aptech computers Ltd.')

Advertisement on Computer education, *TOI*, 12 Aug. '98
By Suffixation the company name is transformed to meet the requirement of a label for its students.
APTECH- ite(Suffix) — Aptechite.

25. Mobile
(as a noun).
(It is not the usual adjective, but stands for 'Mobile telephone'). By the process of 'conversion' now-a-days the word 'mobile' in the specific context means more than its adjective shape and stands for a noun.
"Italian P.M. speaking on his mobile as he walks on..." *TOI*, 7 Aug. '98 and is very much in current use.

26. I. Day
(Independence Day)
Like Identity card — I. card.
So by the process of acronymisation the short version of the word is popularised.
The Times of India, 11 Aug. '98 and used everywhere in the newspaper.

27. Non-stoppable
The Dictionary talks of 'Non-stop'.
And by suffixing 'able'
The new word to meet such requirement is created.
The process: Suffixation.
Title — "Payoli Express : Nonstoppable". *TOI*, 27 July '98.

28. Robotical,
Robotically
The new adverb 'Robotically' is derived from the existing words; Robotic (adj) and Robot (N) by the process of 'Affixation' (Suffixing 'ally' in this case)
Sudha Umashankar, 'Sunday Review', *TOI*, 26 July '98.

29.(i) 'Moniclinton'
It is a process of blend by which a particular crisis is given shape with a single word. 'Moniclinton' is a new word like 'Monicagate' which refers to a 'scandal'.
"Moniclinton is still oozing out of every media pore..." Bachi J. Karkaria, *TOI*, 23 Aug. '98.

(ii) Acculturated, acculturate
It is a case of 'affixation' by which the words are used.
Culture+prefix 'ac'—acculture+suffix 'ate'—acculturate-'ed' suffix—acculturated.
Source: Same article as referred above. It means somebody unaware of the cultural pursuit.

(iii) Artivist

The process of blend creates the new word that stands for a person who is both an 'artist' and an 'activist' (social activist).

Artist + Activist → Artivist.

Source : Same article as above.

(iv) Sloganeering

It is the process of affixation (suffixing).

Source: Same article as above.

Slogan + er(suffix)—sloganeer + ing(suffix)—sloganeering

It is also influenced by the existing words like engineering, electioneering etc.

(v) Sloganeering *India Today*, 6 Sept. '99

30. Megatainment

It is a process of blend. Advertisement, *TOI,* 6.Sept. '98 for Akai Elecronics.

Mega entertainment is compressed to one word 'Megatainment' by this method.

31. (i) Islamically (adverb) — Edward Zwick, *The Times of India*, 19 Nov. '98.

(ii) Islamised (verb, adjective) — Editorial, *TOI*, 23 Sept. '99

(iii) Islamisation (noun) — Editorial, *TOI*, 23 Sept. '99, report on Osma Bin Laden, *TOI,* 26 Sept. '99.

(iv) Islalmophobia (noun)

It is a process of blend by which a new word emerges along with the words like xenophobia, anglophobia etc. "Letter to editor", *The Times of India*, Sept. 29, '99.

These new usages come from the existing word 'Islam' to meet the requirements of the editor/writers and are derived by 'affixation'.

Islam ise(suffix) → ed suffix → Islamised → ion (suffix)→ Islamisation

Islamic ally(suffix) → Islamically

32. (i) Punjlish

A new word produced by blend, to stand for a mixture of Punjabi and English

Punjabi + English → Punjlish (Gurmukh Singh, *TOI,* 2 Dec. '98)

(ii) Hinglish (*The Times of India* 14 Feb. '99)

Hindi + English → Hinglish

(iii) Hinglishstani, Hinglishstan (Hinglish+Hindustani or Hindustan).

33. Foreignisation

K.R. Malkani talks of allowing the foreign insurance companies in India *TOI*, 8 Dec. '98

It follows the formula of globalisation, commercialisation and so the need for a single word which can replace the idea of rapid growth in the tendency to affiliate with foreign culture.

This is done by 'affixation'; suffixing 'ise', 'ion' to the existing words as seen below:

Foreign + 'ise' suffix Foreignise 'ion'suffix → foreignisation

34. Homing (verb) C.P. Surendran, *TOI* 8 Nov. '98

Process: Affixation

By suffixing 'ing' to the existing noun 'Home' a new usage (that of a verb) is utilised.

Example :.. "the last of the birds were homing"

35 "Police Lathicharge Youth Congress Protestors"

'Lathicharge' as a noun has already been acceptable. *The Times of India*, 1 October '98.

By the process of conversion, a noun is turned to a verb here. And it opens the path of two more new words for use (by suffixation):

Lathicharging,

Lathichargeable and so on.

36. Context:

(i) Government accused of trying to 'Saffronise' broadcasting (*TOI*, 4 Feb. '99)

The process of affixation has created the new word.

Saffron + ise(suffix) → Saffronise

Context:

(ii) Attempts to saffronise Shimla Institute (*TOI*, 20 Feb.'99).

(iii) Out-Saffronise (Surendra Kumar and D.R. Goyal, "Culture of the Insecure", *Politics India*, vol. IV, no. 2-3, Aug./Sept. '99).

(iv) Saffronite

(v) Saffronism

Context : Indivisuals wedded to saffronism. (Editorial, *TOI*, 23 Nov. '99)

37. Unbeautiful Dipankar Gupta, *The Telegraph*, 29 Sept. '99

By 'affixation' a new word that serves the purpose of economy is formed

un + beautiful → Unbeautiful

(Prefix)

38. 'Sexpress yourself' *Femina*, 15 Dec. '96

'Sexpress' is a new word coming out of 'blend' that stands for the idea of 'expressing sexually.

39. Valyou.
"Valyou for money" — Advertisement of CIELO car, *The Telegraph*, 20 Feb. '98

By blending the two parts of the words and choosing the parts according to the pronunciation level the word 'Valyou' comes to the forefront which can be an alternative, substitute or stay side by side with the existing word 'value'. This is also a case of metanalysis.

40. (i) Yadavisation
(ii) Mandalisation — (i) Ratan Manilal, *The Times of India*, 2 March '98

Process : Affixation

By suffixing 'ise' and 'ion', new words as above are used which are directly related and a big requirement for the contemporary political, social structure of India.

(iii) Mandalised India — (ii) Editorial, *TOI*, 3 Dec. '99.

Yadav	*ise*	Yadavise	ion	Yadavisation
Mandal		Mandalise		Mandalisation
(N)		(V)		(N)

41. Power'nergy — *The Times of India*, 25 March '98
'Focus on Power'nergy'

This is blending by which the two words come together as they are usually associable words. Also syncopation works here (loss of vowel).

The next step is: Power'nergy — Powernergy

42. Hindustrial — Jug Suraiya, *The Times of India*, 5 April'98

Context :"Lotus and Robot in Hindustrial India". The blending of 'Hindu' and 'Industrial' meets the requirement of a single word to express the Hindu way of industrialising India in the present context.

43. Flexigerator

The word comes out of the advertisement for Whirlpool Company for its product which creates a new word. The process of blend between 'Flexible' and 'Refrigerator'(A refrigerator that has a flexible door) is advertised as

'Flexigerator'. A television with a flexible price can also be termed as 'Flexivision' and so on.

44. Walkoutathons (Editorial title), *The New Indian Express* (BBSR edition) 12 June '98

Just like the term Faxathon (already quoted in this chapter) which stands for an unending series of fax calls, this new word is formed from a phrasal verb (walk out) by blending it with the term 'Marathon' since the context talks of members of AIADMK walking out of the Parliament (the majority of members).

45. Utterly Butterly Kurien — Interview with Dr. Verghese Kurien, the man behind National Dairy Development Board (NDDB) for Amul, *The Times of India,* 28 Oct. '98.

Utterly Delicious (Butter)

Utterly Butterly Delicious — *TOI,* 13 Nov. '99 Advertisement for Amul butter.

The word Butterly comes from:

Butter (N)	suffixing 'ly'—	Butterly (adjective)

So the process is 'affixation'.

46. Bankable — Interview with Manoj Bajpai (actor) by Nikhat Kazmi, *The Times of India*, 8 Oct.'98.

Affixation is the process by which this word is utilised to meet the requirement. It also opens the path for words like 'cashable', 'mannable' 'actable' and so on.

Bank able(Suffix) Bankable

47. (i) Congressized
Context: "Congressized India"

(i) Rashmee Z. Ahmed "In Reel life Too, It's Jinnah vs Gandhi", *The Times of India,* 28 Sept. '98

(ii) Congressisation, Congressised.
By the process of affixation (by suffixes):

(ii) Swami S. Aiyar, *The Times of India* 10 Oct. '99

Congress ize(suffix)ise Congressize(ise) ed(suffix) Congressized(sed)
an organisation
noun → verb → adjective

These two words are formed for their respective utilization.

48. Autarchic
Context: 'Autarchic Policy'
By blend:
Auto + Anarchic → Autarchic
A new adjective to explain the requisite term is formed.

Editorial, *The Times of India,* 26 Oct. '98

49. Securitisation
Context: 'Securitisation in vogue'
A case of Affixation
Security _ise(suffix)_ Securitise _ion(suffix)_ Securitisation
(noun) (verb) (noun)
Two words are formed by the process.

The Economic Times, 28 Oct. '98.

50. Illiquidity
Process : Affixation
Liquidity Prefix 'Il' Illiquidity

The Economic Times, 26 Oct. '98

Context : "Illiquidity hurts".
By this process the word that negates the meaning of the existing word is formed with economy.

51. Childwise
Context : "On becoming Childwise"
By the process of compounding this word is formed as an alternative for 'childlike'.

The Telegraph, 27 Oct.'98

52. Oxbridge
By the process of blend between 'Oxford' and 'Cambridge' a new word which can stand for Somebody's association with both the premier institutions is formed.

Jug Suraiya, *The Times of India,* 25 Oct.'98

53. 'Nu-Power'
It is a process of 'back formation' (also by abbreviating the term).
Nuclear — (backformed into) — Nu
Title, Susan Davis, *The Times of India*, 23 Oct. '98

54. Monickergate
Bachi J. Karkaria, *The Times of India*, 20 Sept.'98
By the process of affixation:
Suffixing 'er' to Monica → Monicker and compounding it with the term associated with other crises like 'Iran gate' and 'water gate', the new term 'Monickergate' is formed and used.

55. Casteing
"Casteing votes"
Sreedhar Pillai, *Sunday*, 29 Aug— 4 Sept. '99
Process: Affixation.
(By using the 'ing' suffix)
The noun 'Caste' in the process plays the role of a verb for its semantic necessity.

56. Brickmanship
Editorial, *The Times of India*. 25 Sept. '99
The word is formed from the existing word 'brickbat' by dropping one element (so by blending the word a bit) and then compounding it with 'manship' as it happens in workmanship, workmanlike etc.

Brickbat (original)	drops the element 'bat'	brick →	Compounds with → manship'	Brickmanship, the outcome of a noun.

57. FemPower
FemPower to her
Interview, *The Times of India* 16 March, '99
By the process of 'backformation' and abbreviating the word 'Feminist', the new item 'Fem' is derived.
(Feminist Power) → FemPower

58. "The art of growing old healthfully".
The Times of India, 8 April '99
Like 'skilfully', 'skilful', 'healthfully' and 'healthful' are new words created by compounding and suffixing 'ly'. Healthy has been the existing word.

59. Cyberabad
Context: No Cinema please, — *The Times of India,* 1 Feb. '99
We're Cyberabad.
Cyber + Hyderabad
(use of cyber technology extensively)→ Cyberabad
(a case of blend). (a new name coined for Hyderabad).

60. Jocoserious — A regular column of *The Assam Tribune* on Cartoons.
The process of blend
The term 'Jocular' twists itself
to 'Joco'.

61. Staffer
Manipur varsity *Staffers* — *The Assam Tribune* 30 Sept. '99.
Stage pen-down strike".
Suffixing 'er'
staff is twisted into
'staffer' which is a
new entry.

62. 'Bifocal' — *India Today*, 6 Sept. '99
(a person focusing on two
points at a time,
in a speech or so.)
Process : Affixation
Prefixing 'bi' the new term is created

63. Policing — *India Today* 6 Sept. '99
Context : "Policing the Polls".
The word is derived from
policy (noun) by affixation.
Here suffixing 'ing' the
new word (verb) is formed.

64. Kisser, kissee — Jug Suraiya, *The Times of India*, 30 Oct.'99
Process: Affixation
Kiss —er(suffix)— Kisser
Kiss —ee(suffix)— Kissee
(Like Addresser—Addressee).

65. Webward — *The Times of India*, 6 Oct.'99, advertisement of website training.
Context : 'Move webward'
Process : Like 'forward'
'backward'
which refers to direction 'web'
is joined with 'ward' and forms

a compound. So it is done by compounding.

66. Celebripolitician
It comes by blend between
Celebrity + Politician→ Celebripolitician
(a reputed, celebrated politician).
The Assam Tribune, 5 Oct. '99

67. Netiquette
Net — etiquette → Netiquette
The word is created by blend between the two source words which means the requisite norms of using the Internet.
The Times of India 5 Oct. '99

68. Proletarianising
Suffixing and blending processes are at work here (dropping one element uses the process of blend).
Nikhat Kazmi, *The Times of India.*

69. Majoritarian
Majority *-ian(suffix)-* majoritarian
By affixation, the new adjective comes up
Swami S. Aiyar, *The Times of India*, 10 Oct '99

70. Internatians
(from Internet, Internet users), by suffixation.
The Times of India, 26 Oct '98

71. Madventure
Mad + adventure
(It is a case of Sandhi).
Jug Suraiya, *The Times of India*, 17 October '99.

72. Coupgemony
The word comes out of a blend between 'coup'and 'hegemony'.
K. Subrahmanyam quotes Zulfikar Ali Bhutto and gives it Prime importance by writing it in capital and popularising it *The Times of India*, 18 Oct. '99 .

73. Cybersquatter
It is case of compounding which means important persons' privacy being illegally exploited by the internet (their picture, details), since 'squatter' refers to such illegal occupation.
The Times of India, 18 Oct. '99

74. Citified
Citify (verb) is also generated by this process.
Raveena Tondon in an Interview with *The Times of India*, 22 Oct. '99.

Context : "Citified housewife"
(adjective phrase),
a case of affixation.

75. Accessorise — Samita Bhatia, *The Telegraph* magazine, 24 October '99.
Context: You can accessorise your table tops. By suffixing 'ise' to the noun 'accessory' a new verb is placed. A case of affixation.

76. Wifehouse — *The Times of India,* 4 Nov. '98
Process: Compounding
(a term known in Kerala and so an Indian concept). The husband visits the wife's house after marriage, where she stays.

77. Hyphenated — *The Times of India,* 28 Oct. '99
By suffixation (Past-ed) to the term hyphen.
Context : "With a hyphenated surname".

78. Victimology — Editorial, *The Times of India,* 28 Oct. '99.
Process: Suffixing 'logy' to the stem, the word is created.
Context: "to go beyond the victimology".

79. (i) Crudified — Praful Bidwai, Political commentator, *The Times of India*, 31 October, '99.

A case of affixation which turns the adjective (Crude–fy–crudify–ed–crudified) to a verbal.

(ii) Churchianity — *The Times of India,* 31 Oct. '99 by B.P. Singhal, MP, Rajya Sabha.
Church + Christianity

It is a case of blend which represents the section that strongly believes in the christianhood and conversion; the Church fraternity.

80. Compactification — Title of a news, *The Statesman,* 1 Nov. '99
By the process of affixation; here suffixing 'ify' to 'compact' we get the verb 'compactify'. Further by

suffixing to it 'cation' and plural 's' we get the word (noun) mentioned above.

81. Digitised. — *The Times of India*, 5 November '99
Context:
"Smells to be digitised on the net".
The process of Suffixation.
(Digit–ise–Digitise –ed–Digitised)
It can generate the term 'digitalised' too. The writer intends to make use of the verb and adjective form here.

82. Celeb/Celebs — *The Times of India*, 5 Nov. '99.
This is a process of abbreviation formation, by which the word celebrity, celebrities are compressed so for economy.
Context: "British celebs light up millennium Diwali bash".

83. ad — *The Times of India*, 5 Nov. '99 and frequent such usage.
(stands for advertisement).
Context: "to form World's 4th largest ad agency". It comes by the process of abbreviation.

84. Okaying — *The Times of India*, 5 Nov. '99
Context: "before okaying the match".
(It is on Madhuri Dixit's marriage),
by suffixation we get the orthographical deviation. O.K. okay - (ing)-- okaying (verb).
It is the opposite of acronymisation.

84. (i) Gen-next — *India Today*, 8 Nov.'99
It is the process of clipping/abbreviation by which 'generation' turns 'Gen' and with 'next' forms an expression by compounding.
(ii) Generationext (by blend) — *The Statesman*, 18 July '98.

85. Learnable — *The Times of India*, 13 November, '99
Context: 'Perfect pitch might be learnable'
(by Suffixation).

86. Cyberian — *The Telegraph*, 15 Nov. '99
A person who uses the cyber space and is in touch with it
(Suffixation).

87. Trilogue
Context: "Indo-Pak-US Trilogue" — V. Sudarshan, main article, *The Times of India,* 19 Nov. '99
It follows the term Dialogue but here the alphabet 'a' is missing. (dropping a vowel).
A case of syncopation.

88. Fest (Stands for festival)
Context:
(i) new millennium winter fest — (i) *TOI*, 22 Nov. '99
(ii) Calcutta film fest — (ii) *Telegraph*, 20 Nov.'99
(iii) No takers for heritage fests (in plural) — (iii) *TOI*, 21 Nov. '99
It is a case of clipping and abbreviation that is at work for economy

89. (i) Savviest
Used as a superlative — The *Times of India*, 21 Nov.'99
Context: "Who is the Savviest of them all?" on a few Chief Ministers who have taken up Information Technology (IT) to the forefront (a case of suffixation).
(ii) Newbie — *The Times of India,* 21 Nov. '99
Context: "She's a newbie". Written referring to Delhi Chief Minister Shiela Dixit relating to the use of Information Technology.

90. Filmic
Context: "Filmic imperialism" — Siddhartha Varadarajan, *TOI*, 28 Nov. '99.
A case of suffixation, 'ic' attached to 'film'

91. Genderquake — Nikhat Kazmi, *TOI*, 28 Nov. '99
Earlier we noted 'Genderise'; now it is 'Genderquake' like 'earthquake'; a noun. A case of compunding both Gender and quake.

92. Cycoon

(i) Title— "Triumph of the 'Cycoon' " The process of formation of this word is also described in the article too :

Cyber + Tycoon = Cycoon

The process of Sandhi, says the writer. But it is actually a blend.

Editorial Title, *TOI,* also used three times in the article with emphasis on its origin 4 December, '99

(ii) Future cycoons. —do—

(iii) Mumbai's Cycoons —do—

(iv) Cycoons Editorial, *The Times of India* 12 Dec. '99

93. Funterprise

Editorial title, *The Times of India,* 12 Dec. '99

It is a case of blend. The editorial also explains that it is the seamless merging between 'fun' and 'enterprise'. And this is a growing tendency in the Information Technology (IT) age.

It also says:

"The universal acceptability of the many faces of India should now be used profitably to project India as Funterprise Inc., a place where profits and pleasure go together". The idea in fact fuses fun, entertainment in the field of Beauty queens, Sportsmen, Cinestars of India marketing India outside.

94. Matrimoney

Editorial, *TOI*, 11 Dec. '99.

Context: "Holy matrimoney"

It is by the process of blend that the conventional idea of 'matrimony' is changed to 'matrimoney in order to emphasize the factor of economy and

role of money in every marriage.
This is liberty of use of the language to mean the desired idea.

95. Nuclearise — Praful Bidwai, *The Times of India*, 13 May 2000
Denuclearise
Nuclearism
Reference :
"The high costs of nuclearism."
This a case of suffixation and prefixation.

96. Global + Local →Glocal — *The Telegraph,* 13 April 2000
(on consumerism trends)
It is a case of blend.

97. Scurrylous claim — Editorial, *The Times of India* 8 Dec. '99
The word 'Scurrylous' is not in the dictionary and it is not here used as 'Scurrilous' (indecent) but by the process of suffixation the writer has used it in the sense of scurry (hurry).

98. Provogue — Advertisement on Dress *India Today,* 13 Dec. '99
(pro fashion)
A case of compounding.

99. Globo Indian — Swapan Dasgupta *India Today*, 13 Dec. '99
(means the new Indian of globalised world, on free trade).
Process: compounding/blend.

100. Weaponisation — *The Times of India*, 14 Dec. '99 *Frontline,* 18 Feb. 2000, p.4

The dictionary only speaks of 'weapon' and 'weaponry.'
It is a case of suffixation by which a new noun is made ready for our use.

101. Unseat — *Frontline*, 18 Feb. 2000. p.42
Context: "To Unseat a government" (throw). By prefixation.

102. (i) Unkindest — *The Economic Times*, 8-14, March 2000.

By both using a superlative mode and prefixation of such an usage is made.
Context : "Unkindest Cut of all" — *The Telegraph* (editorial), April 2000

(ii) "Unkindest cut" (Like 'unbeautiful' as cited before)

103. Valuing a dot com is an art. — *The Outlook*, Feb. 21, 2000 p. 56
Process: Suffixation and syncopation.

104. (i) Arty — (i) *The Outlook*, 21 Feb. 2000, p.78
Art-Arty. An adjective is framed by adding the suffix 'y' to the existing noun 'art'.
Context: Arty Facts
(ii) Arty Kapoor (on Karishma Kapoor-filmstar) — (ii) *TOI*, 20 March, 2000

105. Shapeliness — Editorial, *TOI*, 10 March 2000, p.14
Process: Suffixation

106. Unchested — Editorial, *TOI*, 19 March 2000, p.14
It is a case of affixation.
chest → ed (suffix) → chested
(N) (adjective)
Un + chested → Unchested
This word speaks about the frequent showing of open chest as brawn symbol in Hindi films which requires such a word to be expressed (by prefixation).

107. Scentuous — *The Outlook*, 13 March, 2000, advertisement of Park Avenue perfume.
Context: "Scentuously male"

The word follows the method :
Sense → Sensuous
Scent → Scentuous-ly-(suffix) → scentuously.

108. Songster (the singer) — *TOI*, 1 April 2000, p. 6
It also follows the word 'youngster' (suffixation).

109. Editorialised Process: Suffixaton	Editorial, *TOI*, 9.Feb. 2000
110. Duplicitousness (from Duplicity) Process: Suffixation	*TOI*, Feb. 2000
111. Biker (a person riding a bike) Bike → 'r' (suffixation)→ Biker	*The Telegraph* advertises for Hero Honda, 10 Feb. 2000, p. 7.
112. Wirelesser Process: Suffixation (any person using a mobile phone or wireless).	Editorial, *TOI*, Feb. 10, 2000
113. Inferiorise (verb) Inferiorises (verb) From 'Inferior' (by suffixation).	*TOI*, 10 Feb. 2000, p.12
114. Patriotisity Just like Religion—Religiosity Patriotic—Patrioticity By suffixation the new noun is formed.	Editorial, *TOI*, 11 Feb. 2000.
115. Neighbourliness By suffixation the noun is formed.	Editorial, *TOI*, 11 Feb. 2000.
116. Juiciest One can also use 'juicious' Process: By suffixation.	Editorial, *TOI*, 14 Feb. 2000.
117. Mobocracy, Hidutvist Mob + (Demo)cracy → Mobocracy (auto) by blend. Hindu + Artivist → Hindutvist A case of blend. Sandhi Mobocracy refers to 'gundaism', criminal activities by people. And by Hindutvist he means Hindu fanatic.	Manishankar Aiyar, *TOI*, 13 Feb. 2000, p.14.
118. Dollarise Context: "To dollarise the economy", by suffixation the term dollar	*The Frontline*, 18 Feb. 2000, p.112.

creates a new concept,
a new trend and a new verb.
Function: The verb—For linguistic purpose
The trend—Globalisation
The concept—Dependence
(metaphoric, affective use).

119. 'Mumbikar' and 'Bombayites'; both used by the same article by suffixation. (The people of Bombay). (These terms are also discussed under a separate column ahead). — *Telegraph* (weekend section), 26 Feb. 2000, p.3.

120. Commonality (The common interest), by suffixation. — K. Subrahmanyam, *TOI*, 13 April 2000.

121. Rightsizing "Rightsizing the government is imperative". It has become a verb just like 'downsize' and by suffixation it is formed. It refers to curtailing the jumbo cabinets. From such usage the term 'righted' (right → righted) can be formed. Like wrong →wronged. — H.D. Shourie, *TOI*, 7 April 2000.

122. Hawzaatt (cited before too), a case of syncopation and metanalysis (stands for 'How is that'). — 8 April, 2000, *TOI*.

123. Educrat Just like 'Democrat', 'Bureaucrat'; Education + crat a case of blend. It means educationists with a bureaucratic mindset, used in a derogatory manner. — Sauvik Chakraverti, *TOI*, 12 April 2000

124. Thirtyish (adjective) Like style—Stylish Thirty—Thrityish context :"His thirtyish daughter" (by suffixation). — *TOI* (Sunday Review), 23 April 2000

125. Attitudinised Context: "He attitudinised behind his — *TOI*, Kishore Bhimani, 28 April 2000

sunglasses" on Hrithik Roshan's impact on Cinelovers, youngsters (suffixation).

126. Imagineers — Poonam Barua, *India Today*, 27 March 2000

Like Engine—Engineer
Imagine—Imagineer
Here a new noun is formed which is quite essential in several social and literary contexts. By the process of suffixation the term is coined.

127. Jihadisation of state (on Pakistan). — M.D. Nalapat, *TOI*, 27 April 2000
Suffixation is the process by which a new trend of Islamic fundamentalism is reflected.

128. Straitjacketed — M.D. Nalapat, *TOI*, 14 March 2000.
Context: "India cannot be straitjacketed."
This is a case of conversion by which a new verb is created.
The process of suffixation works also.

129. Femillennium — Editorial, *TOI*, 9 March 2000
Feminine + millennium = Femillennium
A case of blend.

130. Wordy — Editorial, *TOI*, 9 March 2000
Just like 'arty' (cited before), 'wordy' comes to play.
word — wordy
(N) (Adj.)
A case of suffixation.
Context: "Wordy cause".

131. Westoxication — Dipankar Gupta, *TOI*, 8 Jan. 2000, p.14.
The writer uses and defines the term and differentiates it with 'westernization'. He explains;
Westernisation—universalisation of humanistic, scientific, rational norms (good).
Westoxication—consumeristic, superficial display of commodities

produced by the west (pejorative).
By blend.

132. Unbeknown — Editorial, *TOI*, 4 March 2000.
Prefixation is the process to create such a word.

133. Chatterati — *The New Indian Express*, 31 May, 2000.
The chatting group
chatter + ati (suffixation).

134. Guesstimates — Shreekant Sambrani *The New Indian Express*, 29 May 2000.
(Guess + estimates)
(weather forecasts)
Process: Blend

135. Diaggregated
Process: Prefixation and verb formation by suffixing 'ed'.

136. Sis — Kaveree Bamzai, *TOI*, 19 June 2000.
Example: "It's bliss to be Sis"
(Sis stands for Sister).
A case of abbreviation.

136. Cross windz at Music Word — *TOI*, 19 June 2000.
(The plural pronunciation is reflected in the graphic expression).Winds -'s' substituted by 'z' (suffixation).

137. Technopolis — B.R. Srikanth, *Outlook*, 7 Feb. 2000.
Process: Blend.
From Metropolis
the idea of 'Technopolis'(big cities providing technological excellence) is created.

138. Spotlighted — *TOI*, 15 Dec. 2000.
Context: "Up elections has spotlighted the emergence of a newly made over politician."
Process: making a noun transform into a verb through affixation.

139. Happenstance — Editorial, *TOI*, 14 Nov. 2001.
Context: "This is pure happenstance"
(means happening for instance, for once); a case of Sandhi.

140. Oustees — *The Hindu*, 16 March. 2001.
(The noun is formed from the verb oust by suffixation)

141. Unwisdom
Prefixation is the process here to form such a word from its base 'wisdom'.
Editorial, *The Hindu*, 17 March 2001.

142. Inferiorised
The Hindu, 20 March 2001
The *TOI* has used it too (discussed before). This term has been used in the article "The secular conceit" by Prof. M.S.S. Pandian.

Inferior (Adjective) Suffixation ise inferiorise (verb) –ed–inferiorised

143. Hinduise
A case of suffixation.
By Asghar Ali Engineer in *The Hindu*, 24 March 2001.

144. Deicing
Prefixing 'de' to 'ice' and adding suffix 'ing' to it.
Example: Here it is used in the context of the rivers shedding the ice for water in the Himalayas.
Editorial, *The Hindu*, 22 March 2001.

145. Retiree (a retired person).
The noun is formed like that of addressee, examinee, trainee etc. by the process of suffixation.
The Hindu, 27 March 2001

146. 'Shamed'
Shame --ed-- Shamed
(suffix)
The past tense form creates a verb out of the noun.
Context: "Shamed and Crippled" (Title—cover page)
India Today, 26 March 2001.

147. averaging
From average—averaging by suffixation
It is used in the context of Cricket run rate average.
The Hindu, 28 March 2001.

148. Demutualisation
Case of affixation.
The Hindu, 31 March, 2001

Prefix suffix suffix demutualisation
de ---- mutual ---- ise ---- ation ---- (N)

149. Winnability — *The Hindu*, 30 March, 2001 (also cited in *TOI* before)

150. Subcontinentality — Farrukh Dondy, *TOI*, 2 April, 2001 (Editorial).
This term comes out of suffixation.

151. Short-Termism — *The Hindu*, 2 April 2001.
The expression comes from 'Short-term' which is made a noun like any other 'ism' (Marxism, Fascism etc.) through suffixation.

152. Traffication — Editorial, *The Hindu*, 2 April 2001.

suffixation

From traffic +ation traffication

153. Strategising — "Sunday Review", *TOI*, 25 March 2001, p.5

Strategy—(Suffixation)—strategise *ing* (Adj.)
N V

154. Supremacists — Editorial, *The Hindu*, 24 May, 01
Context: "Jewish Military Supremacists"
(suffixation). Supremacy *ist* (suffix).

155. Right-sizing, wrong-sizing — *TOI*, 25 June, 2001 (also used before and analysed, *TOI*).

156. Undergrats — *TOI*, 26 June 2001.
(for under graduates)
Context: "Undergats head overseas". This is formed by the process of abbreviation.
Example: Congratulation—congrats (in spoken English).

157. Trade-unionised — *The Hindu*, 28 June 2001.
(suffixation)
Union → *ise* unionise *ed* unionised.

158. Scamster — *TOI*, 1 July 2001.
(like gangster, youngster etc.)
Harshad Mehta (the stock broker) is termed so (suffixation).

159. Batter (The term is formed from 'bat' by adding the suffix 'er'). The dictionary says the term is used in Baseball. But here the columnist uses it in cricket. — V. Srivatsa, *TOI*, 1 July 2001.

160. Candidacy from 'Candidature' or candidate By suffixation. — Editorial, *The Telegraph*, 27 Aug. 2000, p.10

161. Hybridity from 'hybrid' by suffixation. — 27 Aug. 2000, p.8 by Rukun Advani, Weekly magazine, *The Hindu*.

162. Filmi This is done by giving a functional touch to the term, by suffixation. — Lakshmi Balakrishnan, *The Hindu*, 27 Aug. 2000.

163. Thievery It comes from the word 'thief' by suffixation. thief-thieves-thievery (the act of stealing). — "Hobbes' Mistake" (article) by Souvik Chakraverti, *TOI*, 27 May 2001

164. Anarcho-Capitalism This is a case of blend. Anarchy + Capitalism It means a liberal capitalist society where the individual fights for self-benefit. — "Hobbes' Mistake" (an article by Souvik Chakraverti, *TOI*, 27 May 2001).

165. Oomphomaniacs Context: "Tennis ? It is all about Oomph." (about lot of sex appeal among the lady Tennis players and the term is influenced by 'nymphomaniac') — Vinay Kamat, *TOI*, July 2, 2001.

Oomph--mania (suffix)—Oomphomania—plural suffix—Oomphomaniacs

A case of blend.

166. E-messaging (like e-mail, e-ticket, — *The Hindu*, 17 May 2001

e-bucks and so on)
A new verb influenced
by the new
infotech revolution
Innovation as well as
application of earlier
coinage (e-mail) is there
in creating it.
A case of acronymisation.

167. Fancysome — *Femina,* 1 May, 2001, p.136
(like handsome,
written about
fashion design)
a case of suffixation and blend.

168. Bearding — *Femina,* 1 May, 2001, p.118
(from beard).
a case of suffixation forming a verb.
Context: "Bearding the lions".

169. Xpert — Title of an article, *Femina,*1May,2001, p.16
Context: "The xpert files."
The pronunciation is given
weightage in this process
which is related to the
process of acronym formation.
We have also recorded words like
'xpress' in this chapter.

170. Celebspeak — *The New Woman,* Aug. 2000, p. 99
[like webspeak, Skipperspeak (column
by team's skipper in a newspaper)]
The word comes by the
process of blend between the
words 'celebrity' and 'speak'.
This is also a case of clipping (celeb).

171. Teargass (as a verb) — *The Times of India* (p.4) October 10, 2001.
Context: "Protesters
teargassed in Srinagar"
(from the noun,
'teargas' we get the
verb by suffixation).

172. Itemise — *The New Indian Express,* 25 Nov. '01

Item	ise	Itemise
	suffix	
(N)		(V)

173. Talkathon — An advertisement of a Cellphone by Essar. *TOI,* 26 Nov. '01
Talk + marathon
(unlimited
times it refers to,
or long talk by phone).
By blend this word is
formed.

174. Talibanana — Sastri Rama Chandran, *TOI,* 27 Nov. '02.
(Taliban + Banana democracy)
Context: "Talibanana State"
This is a case of blend.

175. Sis in law — *TOI*, 5 Dec. 2001.
(Instead of sister in law) This is
a case of abbreviating.
The terms given below are taken
from an article by Hasan Surror
(A fizzy touch to new English) in
The Hindu on 24 July, 2000 (p.7)
where the columnist explains their
meaning (No.176 to 181) :

176. Alcopop (a sweet fizzy drink with a dash of alcohol) By the process of blend the term is coined.

177. Phone rage/trolley rage/store rage are less hazardous equivalents of the road rage.
A case of compounding.
Example: Anyone irritated at a shop, store is under 'store rage' and so on.

178. Vanilla Version (an unvarnished account of an event)
A case of compounding.

179. Infommercials (long-winded commercials containing far more

information than one
can take in at one go)
This is a case of Sandhi.
Information + Commercial—Infommercial.

180. (i) Web master (who runs the show on website)
(ii) Hot-desking (related to computer functioning).
The first one is a case of compounding whereas the second is of both compounding and suffixation.

181. Commonalities — K.K. Katyal, *The Hindu*, 21 Aug. 2000. Also cited before (*TOI*).
From 'common' by suffixing we get 'commonality' Which is again pluralised by the same process.

182. (i) Debureaucratisation — S. Krishna Kumar (former Union Minister), *The Hindu*, 15 Aug. 2000.
(by both prefixing 'de' and Suffixing 'isation' to the 'bureaucrat')
(ii) Epochal — In the same article quoted above; "Liberalisation and the Gandhi Test". *The Hindu*, 20 Aug. 2000, p. 2.
Context: "epochal life".
Epoch-suffixation-epochal
'epochal' appears again in

183. Speechify, speechifying — R. Natararajan, *The Hindu*, 15 Aug. 2000.
Speech (by suffixation) speechify
(N) (V)

184. Absenteeism — Vimala Rama Chandran, *The Hindu*, 13 Aug. 2000
Absent—suffixation—Absentee—
(adjective) (Noun)
suffixation —absenteeism
(Noun)
(as a trait).

185. Finessing — *The Hindu*, 24 Aug. 2000.
(the word 'finesse' is there in dictionary which is made a verb

by suffixation).
The news item is "Finessing their differences on CTBT"

186. Assly — *The New Indian Express.*
(for Assembly)
Context: "Assly Session Begins today".
This is a case of abbreviating the terms.

187. (i) Kargilized — Harish Khare, *The Hindu*, 26 July 2000, p. 10.
(From Kargil, a place where India fought with Pakistani infiltrators).
Since the place became famous, a verb got validity out of it through suffixation which is used here in a pejorative sense to mean a 'false show of nationalisation'.
Title: "Kargil candle in the Mumbai Wind."

(ii) Triumphalism

Triumph	suffixation	Triumphalism
(N)		(N)
		(a quality)

188. Customised — *The Hindu*, 26 July 2000, p. 2.

Custom + ise	*customise*+ ed	= customised
(N)	(V)	adjective

The process of suffixation.

189. Righting — By Neera Chandhoke *The Hindu*, 27 July 2000.

(From, Right	→	Righting)
adj.		(V)

'Righting historical Wrongs'
in "Memory and narcissism"
(suffixation).

190. (i) Judicature — V.R. Krishna, *The Hindu*, 3 August. 2000, p. 8.
(caricature involving the Judiciary).
By blend.

(ii) Fiduciary
As used in the context:
"Judiciary is a fiduciary for the public".

191 Daredevilry — *TOI,* 15 Aug. 2000, p. 10.
(a case of suffixation)
from daredevil(N) to daredevilry (N) (a quality).

192. Securitization — *The Hindustan Times,* 23 June 2000
Security *suffixation* Securitization.
(a new noun is formed
out of it).

193. Orphan (as a verb) — *The Hindustan Times,* 23 June 2000
Context: "An orphan that
orphans a million"
(on a Christian Priest's death).

194 Peoplisation — K.N. Govindacharya, *India Today, 17* July 2000, p.27.
People *suffix* peoplisation
(On populist methods)

195. Trendz (the plural form) — *The Hindu*, 12 July 2000. ('windz' has been cited before).
'trends' is actually pronounced
as 'trendz'.
So the spoken usage is reflected
in the written.
This is done by replacing one
phoneme for another (suffixation).

196. Congrats — *The Hindu,* 14 July 2000.
(Just like 'Undergrats'
as referred earlier)
The term is compressed
by the process of abbreviation.

The terms below come from an article by Nikhat Kazmi and Vandana Agarwal; "WWF has given the new lingo for boy rage", on 10 April 2000, *The Times of India.* They say the World Wrestling Foundation (WWF) has given the new lingo which the *Fight Club Dictionary of Slangs* has given validity. But here in fact the majority of people come to know about them from our newspaper that popularises it through its column No.197 to 203:

197. Stunner
(Jam the neck of the opponent
in your arm, jump and sit down).

198. Rock Bottom (Throw the opponent on the ring
by holding his arms and swinging him around).

199. Blocobuster (Leap on the
opponent and get his head
between your legs).

200. Low blow (A solid blow the belt fisticuff)
201. Pedegree (Get his head between your legs, hold up his hands and sit down on the ground).
202. Choke Slam (hold him by the neck and fling him on the ground).
203. Tombstone (Lift the opponent with his legs and fling him, face downwards).
The columnists say the words above are often used by many 'under-13' group of boys.
204. Wannabe, wannabes (means 'want to be'). This is an American usage which is pluralised by suffixation. Context: "The wannabes of '97" (written about celebrated litterateurs, artists, sportsmen and cultural, political heads). — "The Sunday Review", *The Times of India,* 28 Dec. '97.
205. Deutsche Wilkommen
It is a German expression as the article is about the German Chancellor designate Gerhard Schroeder's policies and gaining power in German politics. — Editorial, *The Times of India,* 28 Oct. '98.
206. Boyar
Context: "A suitable boyar" (A Russian word is used here on Russian choice of Primakov as Prime Minister. — Editorial, *The Times of India,* 5 Sept. '98.
207. Fundas
(from 'fundamentals; it has become a colloquialism by the process of abbreviation/clipping). — *The Times of India* 20 Feb. '99.
208. Mathematicising
Mathematicise
The Subject 'Mathematics' is suffixed to make a verb out of it. — T. Kashinath, 'Maths and Theology—In search of God' *The Times of India* 24 Nov. '99.

This is also a process of conversion since
a noun is changed into a verb.

209. Thatcherism — L.K.Sharma, *TOI*, 10. Oct. '99.
Context : "Reinvented Thatcherism"
(the use of such an expression is done by suffixing 'ism' to the ex-Prime Minister of U.K., Margaret Thatcher.
It talks about her policy.

210. Speakeasy — *India Today*, 5 July '99,
Authorspeak — *India Today*, 14 June '99,
Cricket crazy — *India Today*, 19 June '99,
(We have already discussed terms like 'celebspeak','skipperspeak', 'plainspeak','new age speak'). — *The Telegraph*, 16 Nov. '98, *The Telegraph*, 28 May, '96.

The above terms result due to the process of compounding.

211. Muchness — Nikhat Kazmi, *The Times of India*, 20 July '98
by the process of suffixation

212. (i) baddie — (i) *The Times of India*, 11 January '98.
(ii) baddies — (ii) *The Sunday Times of India*, 14 Nov. '99.
(iii) baddies — (iii) Swapan Dasgupta, *India Today*, 29 Nov '99.

(The word is derived from 'bad' by inflectional suffixation to make a noun, to address someone of bad character and for plural use).

213. Waterrelief — *The Statesman*, 18 July '98
(advertisement of Cello water bottle)
a single word formed by compounding/metanalysis.

214. biggies — *The Times of India*, 6 Dec. '98
(just like goodies, baddie etc.)
Here it means
the two big political parties,

The BJP and the Congress. (By suffixation). big—biggy—biggies.	
215. Also the Congress still has a longish way to go long—longish (by suffixation)	*The Times of India,* 6 Dec. '98.
216. Mostest "Kiran Kher is television's hostess with the mostest *Queen of chat*". It is done by suffixation and asserts the writer's autonomy in using such a term.	'Graphiti', *The Telegraph,* 18 July '99.
217. baddest (e.g. "the baddest guy of Indian writing"...) on a novelist.	*The Times of India,* 5 January, '98.
218. Bestest Context: "My Teacher, the bestest".	Advertisement of greeting card, *The Times of India,* 30 Aug.'99.
219. Tensest [The most (only) tense situation] Context: "The tensest situation". By suffixation the above three words are created.	*Indian Express,* 3 June '99.
220. Thingy (adjective) (thing-thingy). By the process of suffixation a noun becomes an adjective here. Similar verbs by the process of conversion are: Parent, impact rocket, knee(kicking), string, stall.	"New Age speak", *The Telegraph,* 28 May. '96 by Punita G. Singh.
221. Impacted By suffixation and conversion the new verb is formed.	C. Uday Bhaskar, *TOI,* 3 Dec. '99, p. 10.
222. Busness as usual. Context: 'Bus' has become an image here. (a) In contemporary field, the Bus travel (amity)	Editorial, *The Times of India* 1 March '99

between Delhi and Lahore
is hinted.

(b) The role of bus (while organising meetings, agitations etc.); a number of bus full of people gathering together and so on. From there the idea of busness comes which stands for the meaning; a good rapport. It is formed by compounding.

223. T-zone — Ghazala Wahab, "Graphiti", *The Telegraph*

This is used as a figure of speech (metaphor) which comes from the 'T-shirt' culture and here it means the whole informal attitude of contemporary life, the rough and tough fashion, typical urbanite culture. By acronymisation it is formed.

224. Tom Tamming — *India Today,* 6 Sept. '99.

Context: "EC goes Tom Tamming". It is an expression which comes from the sound of the drum and so Onomatopoeia gives rise to such an expression. (The news of election being circulated by drum play in some villages by the Election Commission).

225. Pinko — "Sunday Review", *The Times of India,* 25 Oct. '98

It has come from 'Pink' which stands for 'capitalists' whereas 'Red' stands for leftists (suffixation).

226. Botel (these are variants of 'hotel') — The editorial, *TOI*, 3 Dec. '99

Flotel/Botel' is a water borne accommodation.'Flotel' provides floating facilities for workers on oil rigs, says, the editor. Similarly

the editor opines, journalistic inventiveness could go a bit far with words like 'Skotel' and 'Spotel'.
Skotel — airborne hotel
Spotel — a commercial accommodation in space where space walk is possible and observation of the planet earth is undertaken. It is a case of blend.

227. Cyberia — Editorial, *TOI*, 18 Feb. 2000.
Context : "Southern cyberia" (a place). Here also 'Cyberia' refers to a place in the wake of IT revolution. Here it refers to Bangalore and Hyderabad which experienced 'Cyber revolution'. 'Southern' refers to Indian southern parts. A case of suffixation. We have noted 'Cyberabad' before.

228. e-lancing — Geeta Sharma, *The Telegraph*, 19 Feb. 2000
It is used like 'free-lancing' (also cited earlier). Abbreviation of 'electronic' is taken into account. A case of acronym formation.

229. "Survival of the *freest*" — Ashok Mitra *The Telegraph*, 16 Feb. '2000
Free—Freest (the most free) serves for economy and is created by the conscious exercise of suffixation by the writer.

230. Naiduvian flavour — *TOI*, 19 Feb, 2000
Refers to progressiveness, development theory now, as the person stands for that (The Chief Minister of Andhra Pradesh). Suffixation.

231. Himbo — Nikhat Kazmi, *TOI*, 8 March 2000, 12 March 2000 and 26 March 2000
The existing word has been 'bimbo' that refers to girls

who pose as sex symbols.
On that line 'Himbo' (with 'him' referring to the male) is created that means the guys who represent the new image of fashion, love and strength. This is created by the process of blend.

232. Guys and Gals — *TOI,* 19 March 2000

These terms that refer more to the pronunciation than the exact spelling are valid as they are used more often, be it Americanised or Indianised as seen in a number of occasions. Also there is a dress company by this name. The process of metanalysis (Girls-Gals) is utilised here.

233. Prez — *TOI,* 20 March 2000 and repeated very often; used in the wake of Clinton's visit and then has become normal in usage.

Just as the previous items(trendz,windz) this also refers to the plural form of 'Press' as in pronunciation.
This is a case of metanalysis.

234. Automated — Editorial, *TOI*, 20 Jan. 2000

The word 'automatic' is suffixed for its past participle form.

235. Excitability — Editorial *TOI*, 20 Jan. 2000

Excite	—	*Excitable*	—	Excitability
(V)		(adj.)		(N)

By the process of suffixation and conversion.

236. Messaging — *TOI*, 24 Jan. 2000

Out of 'message' by suffixation.
The writer makes the noun a verb (conversion).

message	—	messaging
(N)		(verb)

237. 4 XPMS do not add up to a 3rd front. — *The Times of India* (Head line) 16 April 2000

The use of numericals as well as the substitution of 'ex' by 'x' which as an 'alphabet' create such a word XPM (like Xpert, Xpress). A case of acronymisation.

238. Veggie — *TOI,* 24 April 2000.
Context : "Patna goes Veggie".
Refers to growing vegetarians in Patna.
Vegetarian—Veg—veggie
Clipping + Suffixation.

239. Absurdest — Rahul Singh, Editor in→ Chief of *Indian Readers Digest* and *Sunday Observer* writes in *TOI*, 12 March 2000.
Absurd + est→ absurdest, a case of suffixation.
Context : "Making Amritsar dry is the *absurdest* of all".

240. Jargonistically — Moy Roy (ad personnel) is quoted by Sudipta Basu in "Mind your Language", *The Telegraph,* 5 Dec. '98.
Jargon *'istic'* Jargonistic (Noun) Suffixation (adjective) then suffixing 'ally'—Jargonistically (adverb)(a process of multiple suffixation).

241. Puppeteer — Editorial, *TOI,* 24 Nov. 2001
(Puppet *suffixation* Puppeteer)

242. Guesstimate — Jitesh Pillai, *TOI,* 9 Dec. 2000
Blend between two words; 'guess' and 'estimate' results in a new word. Earlier the verb form of the word (Guesstimates) has been also noted.

243. (a) Jehadify, Jehadification Jehadified dejehadified — Rahul Shivshankar, "Advantage : No one Misplaced Hopes of Moderate Pakistan", *TOI,* 11 Dec. 2001
Suffixation and prefixation result in multiple variation of the term 'Jehad' which has been

very popular in the world today.
That stands for 'holy war' that the
terrorists declare against others.
The words form a paradigm.

(b) denazification
(Nazi—Nazification—denazification)
Nazism, Fascism
have been different
regimes and schools
of thought. Similar is
Marxism, Capitalism etc.
The examples above may trigger new
terms like 'demarxified'; 'decapitalified'
and so on.

244. Complementarities — Editorial, *TOI*, 11 Dec. 2001
Complementary — Complementarity — Complimentarities.
(adj.) (N) (N)

245. Courting Disinvestment — Editorial, *TOI*, 12 Dec. 2001
Court *suffixation* courting
(N) (V)

246. Readies
CBI readies to chargesheet Jagir — *TOI*, 15 Dec. 2000
By suffixation the first term is
generated.
Chargesheet is used as a verb too.

247 Xtra, xciting — *TOI*. 25 Dec. 01, p.2.
Context: "An xtra xciting x-mass"
A case of syncopation. It also
abbreviates and metanalyses
the term.

248. Vigilantism — Editorial, *TOI*, 27 Dec.2001
The word comes from 'vigilant'
by suffixation

249. Multiplexes — *TOI*, 27 Dec. 2001, p. 4
Multiple complexes.
A case of blend.

250. Factored — Editorial, *TOI,* 8 Jan. 2002
(comes from factor)
The dictionary talks of the word 'factorise' only.
A case of suffixation (inflectional suffix).

251. Religionists — Rafiq Zakaria, *TOI,* 8 Jan. 2002
A case of suffixation (inflectional).

252. Extraditing — Editorial *TOI,* 8 Jan. 2002
A case of suffixation creates the adjective. The dictionary mentions the words 'extradite', 'extradition' only.

253. Disenabled — Editorial, *TOI,* 9 Jan. 2002
Context: "Disenabled people".
A case of prefixation creates the word which mimmicks the policy for the disabled.

254. Younglish — Vinay Kamat, *TOI,* 2 Sept. 2001
The kind of English used by the young. A case of blend (Young English).

255. VJ-ing — *TOI,* 15 Jan. 2002
(V)
by suffixation the word comes from VJ (channel V music), the album makers.

256. Truckers — *TOI,* 14 Jan. 2002
Suffixation

257. Meritocracy — Infosys CEO, Narayana Murthy, *TOI,* 15 Jan. 2002
Merit + democracy
It means a democratisation of merit. A case of blend.

258. Softie — Dileep Padgaonkar, *TOI,*13 Jan. '02
By suffixation to the word 'soft' it becomes a noun.
(other terms: good—goodie, bad—baddie)

259. Context: — *Cricket Talk*, 7 Oct. 2000, p.42
"Indian Captain Saurav Ganguly

is a *huge* Amitabh Bachchan fan".
The use of the word *huge* marks
an increase in the degree of
idealisation which is not normally
used. 'Huge' is otherwise used in
case of quantitative measures.
This is innovative use of the word.
It also offers a new collocation.

260. R-Day (like I-day) — *TOI*, 25 Jan. 2002
Stands for 'Republic Day'.
A case of syncopation.

261. Anecdotally — "Kashmiris Abroad", Rashmee Z Ahmed, *TOI*, 29 Jan. 2002.
The dictionary mentions about
its noun and adjective form only.
It is an adverb here.

262. b'day — *TOI*, 28 Jan. 2002.
(I-day, I-card etc. are cited before).
It stands for 'birth day'.

263. No-balled — *TOI*, 8 Feb. 2002.
From 'no-ball'(N), the verb
(used in Cricket) is formed by suffixation.

Words in deviation, the processes involved along with certain distinct traits of Indigenisation

Here under this column we cite a list of certain words that have been used by the newspapers and magazines which very often retain some Indian notions; in the form of Indian proper names being altered, twisted to suit to the need, utilisation of the bilingual nature, Indian national, regional mode of pronunciation governing the English words, other names such as Indian food, articles, place names, the context of India, Indian words, Indian slang, colloquialism and so on. We record the words and expressions of Indian origin only to display how they trigger the rapid inclusion of many other such words and open up the way to treat them as part of the English language in India.

1. *Chow Biz* — *Outlook*, 26 Jan. '98
Context: "No Biz like — Chow Biz"
Such a term comes out of replacing

'Show' (ShowBiz) by 'Chow' having onomatopoeic usage. Cinema stars owning 'Chow Restaurants' throw such a term into usage.

2. *Net biz* (here 'biz' stands for business as above) (Net business of the present time). — *The Times of India*, 3 Oct. '99.

3. *Shot gun* — *The Asian Age*, 20 Feb. '98
The word has been popular by frequent use by a number of newspapers and magazines which comes from a proper name (that of actor Shatrughan Sinha). By the process of twisting the proper names which is a very fertile area of change. The process of syncopation and metanalysis contribute to it.

4. Shatrughan — *Shot gun.* — *The Asian Age*, 10 March'98
Tondulkar
Tendulkar — Ton dul kar
By the same process as above; metanalysis. The new twisted form of the word, throws the idea of a 'ton' (in case of this a good score in cricket) by the batsman.

5. *Sonia phant* — *The Times of India*, 11 April '98.
It uses the proper name and blends it with a part of the British English word 'Sycophant' and the result is an Indian English word (the process of blend), referring to the sycophants of Sonia Gandhi, leader of the Congress party now.

6. *Sunnyish* — Nikhat Kazmi, *The Times of India*, 27 April '98
Context: "Social Realism, Sunnyish style".
It fuses the proper name of an actor, Sunny Deol with 'ish' (suffixing) and

	creates a new word for Indian English. The people who are famous role models, evoke such response from the writers that of creating new words.	
7.	*Guwahatians* People of Guwahati represented so. Suffixation results in such a word.	*The Assam Tribune*, 21 Oct. '98
8.	*Mumbikar* Earlier the word 'Bombayite', 'Mumbaite' used to be cited for a person staying in Bombay (Mumbai). So the new word is a new entry by such twist. Here it suffixes another term, 'kar'.	Darryl D'Monte, The *Times of India*, 24, Sept. '99.
9.	*Lucknowites* By the suffixation of 'ite' the proper name (of a city) is utilised regarding its people.	*The Times of India*, 24 Sept.'99
10.	(a) *Upiyat* (b) *Punjabiyat* In case of (a) it is an abbreviated term twisted into a new word. (Uttar Pradesh—UP). By suffixation. In case of (b) it is just a twist of the state name Punjab adding the suffix to it.Those terms refer to the quality of an Upite, Punjabite.	*The Times of India*, 24 Sept.'99
11.	*Dilliwallah* The process of twisting the name of the city (as it is pronounced in India as *Dilli*) with an Indian word from Hindi to create such a term. A case of compounding. Also a case of code mixing.	Nikhat Kazmi, *TOI*, 20 July '98
12.	*Jugular* It comes from the name	*The Sunday Times of India* (regular column)

Jug Suraiya, a journalist following the model of Joke — Jocular, his column is termed so; Jugular as it is humorous. This is a process of blend.

by the journalist Jug Suraiya

13. (a) Still so *Sunny*
In sports column Indian readers easily get the idea that it talks of Sunil Gavaskar (Cricketer) who is popularly known as 'Sunny' and who has also written the book *Sunny Days.*
(b) *Future Sunnies*
The same article uses it which means future good cricketers like S.M. Gavaskar.

Gautam Bhattacharya, *The Times of India,* 22 Nov. '98.

14. *Don Bradman*
Don Bradman (Cricketer) was great and here the contrast in usage highlights the contrast in quality too (that of a corrupt politician) The process of metanalysis comes to use.

Vir Sangvi, *The Telegraph,* 15 Nov. '98, on a corrupt politician who is branded that way.

15. *Bangalorean*
The people of Bangalore are addressed Bangaloreans. Suffixation is used.

Editorial, *The Times of India,* 9 Oct. '98

16. *Nanny, Nannies*
Such use (the plural version also) refers to a popular relationship in family circles in Indian context (suffixation).

Editorial, *The Times of India,* 8 Oct '98.

17. *Sonne*
(Sonia Gandhi is addressed so here which means 'zero' as defined by the column), 'that of being Zero in politics'.

India Today, 6 Sept. '99

18. *Kolkatta* (new coinage)
'Kolkata' comes on the line of Pune, Mumbai, Chennai, Katak, Odisa and so on.

(i) All Newspapers,
(ii) *TOI,* 30 Sept. '99.

19. A *Saeed* way to go. — *Outlook,* 30 Aug. '99.
    On Saeed Jaffrey, film actor
    (the name used as an adjective).
20. *Kisswant* Singh — Jug Suraiya, *The Times of India,* 30 Oct.'99
    (in place of Khuswant)
    It refers to the contemporary event that of Khuswant Singh (writer) kissing a girl. A case of Onomatopoeia.
21. Train to *Peckistan* — Jug Suraiya, *The Times of India,* 30 Oct.'99
    (Pakistan — Peckistan)
    It is termed so by exaggeration and due to the subject related to it contemporarily.
    Context: The author of *Train to Pakistan* has pecked a Pakistani girl which raised controversy).
    Blend comes into use here.
22. *Cal* — Jug Suraiya, *TOI,* 25 Oct.'98
    (Calcutta is referred so)
    clipping is the process, also abbreviation.
23. *Calcuttans* — *TOI*, 17 Oct.'99
    Context: "*Calcuttans* believe in suffering in silence".
    Process : suffixation.
24. *Dravidanadu* — Shastri Ramachandran, *The Times of India,* 22 Sept. '98
    Tamilnadu is twisted by dropping 'Tamil' and adding 'Dravida' which represents the ancient race there. It is like a paradigm and by the process of blend the new term is formed.
25. *Cherra* — Nirmalya Banerjee, *The Times of India*, 25 Oct. '98
    (It is used instead of Cherrapunjee)
    "The last of old Cherra".
    (Process: Clipping)
26. *Momma T* — Jug Suraiya, *TOI,* 25 Oct. '98.
    (Mother Teressa)
    T-Teressa, by acronym formation.

Here we can draw the conclusion that proper names, places offer a fertile area of change which the journalistic community exploits. The autonomy of the writers is reflected in the way they handle the new figurative, suggestive coinage. It opens up a vast domain of such practices which can contribute for a parallel learning of English usage other than the chaste, pure English of text books. So this is a big source of influence for further such coinage which is on a fast move in all newspapers and magazines.

27. *Citibank* — *The Times of India*, 4 April '98
The spelling change gives it the status of a new entry and very often used in an advertisement.

28. Raw *Dadaism* (on Shiv Sena activists) — Editorial, *The Times of India*, 1 May '98.
The Indian word undergoing affixation creates a new term.

29. *Moronism* — *The Telegraph*, 30 Oct. '98
Context: "Affordable *Moronism*", written about Indian popmusic. The word 'modernism' is replaced by 'Moronism' which reflects the pronunciation of the common, the mass. Process: Metanalysis.

30. *Womantra* — Kanchan Apte, *TOI*, 1 May 2000.
Woman + mantra (a Sanskrit word; stands for hymn). By the process of Sandhi. And here it refers to Women Priests.

31. *Laloonomics* — *TOI*, 30 March 2000
(Refers to Laloo Prasad Yadav) (Ex- C.M. of Bihar and his economic policy). Here it is pejorative as his policy is condemned. A case of blend. Laloo's economics—Laloonomics. (This has a message which is well understood by an Indian).

32. Senate *Okays* Presidential waiver of economic sanctions for one year. — *The Times of India*, 18 July, '98.
Okaying can be another term for use. Process: Suffixation Also cited before.

33. (i) *Fizzical* (for Physical) — Nikhat Kazmi, (i) *TOI*, 20 July, '98.

(ii) All *fizz*, more *fizz* (this is the base word) — (ii) *The Times of India*, 3 Dec.'99, p. 2.

Such coinages are obtained deliberately by a spelling change to give us more options. This is done by clipping and abbreviation.

34. *Delhites* (discussed before too). The people of Delhi it refers to (by suffixation). — *The Hindu*, 4 March, 2000

35. *Patnaites* (The people of Patna) By suffixation. — *TOI*, 24 April, 2000

36. *Kashmiriyat* (The question of the status of Kashmir, its speciality). By suffixation. Other examples: Punjabiyat, UPiyat etc. — *TOI*, 11 Feb. 2000, p.14.

37. Poll *Punditry* Punditry (N) comes from Pundit (N) who is a famous name in India, a Brahmin, a knowledgeable person. Here it means an analyst of clection results. By the process of suffixation we get the word here. — *India Today*, 6 Sept.'99

38. *Gormint* The typical Bihari way of pronunciation of 'Government'. Context: "Rabri Stamp gormint". It is like 'Moronism'. — Jug Suraiya, *The Times of India*, 27 Sept. '98

39. *Missis* (as 'Mrs' is pronounced locally). — Jug Suraiya, *TOI*, 23, Feb. '98.

40. *Stoopid* (The new spelling — *The Times of India*, 15 Nov. '98

characterises the writer's individual autonomy and usage).

41. *Phillum* — *The Times of India*, 3 Jan, '99
Context: "Hindi Phillums were about as cool..." (It again gives weightage to the local pronunciation (Film : Filim or Fillum).

42. *Amma* — Editorial, *TOI*, 5 Dec. 2001.
Context: "Amma's day" (Refers to J. Jayalalitha, Ex-C.M. of Tamilnadu as she is popularly known so there).

43. *Dilli* — Lakshmi Balakrishnan, *The Hindu*, 27 Aug. 2000.
This is the presentation of the native pronunciation of the city of 'Delhi'. This is done by simplification in the spelling rule.

The process of code switching / code mixing and the entry of new words

Another significant area which covers the processes of code switch/ code mix is of ample use and seem to be the predominant Indian process of creating an alternative text, alternative English in the Indian context to influence the readers.

Code Switch/Code Mix[3] : This is a process by which the words in Indian languages, especially in Hindi and some other regional languages are used normally and in the process get the affiliation of the readers since they are used to such expressions. This comes from a language context situation and is utilized heavily in conversation. Here though the English equivalents of the words in the native language are available, the writer uses them deliberately. Such a mixture of two or more codes of different languages refers to code mixing. The above processes create profound space for autonomy of the writers to completely switch over or mix other codes of other languages and by doing so make Indian English a distinct variety, flexible and worth noticing in the international field and open it for further research in this field.

We here list certain words that have flooded into the newspaper columns in recent times due to code switching/code mixing.

1. Chalaak — clever
Yaar — old boy or buddy
Tarmuj (Watermelon) that stands for a deceptive person (green outside, red inside), bhaat (with a hard 't'), bakwaas — rubbish, nonsense. It justifies the entry of such words into *The Oxford English Dictionary*.
"Brave new words", editorial, *The Times of India,* 12 Aug.'99
2. "Heady mix of *dharma* and *rajniti*". — Smita Gupta, *The Times of India,* 24 Sept.'99
3. "Atalji will make the mandir possiblc". — *The Times of India,* 23 March '98
4. "Mehta duo enthrals audience with qalaams". (The ghazal singers above can be explained by the use of the Urdu word). — *The Times of India,* 10 April '98
5. The *Parivar*
Context: (*The Janata Parivar*) — *The Times of India,* 10 April '98
6. Chhupa Rustum
Context: "Privacy, Chhupa Rustum and Holidays" (on Narsimha Rao's book *Insider*). — *The Times of India,* 10 April '98
7. "Richard Gere : In Quest, of Improving *Karmas*." — Manmohan, *The Times of India,* 26 April '98.
8. "No *Chai Cauphee* on the Konkan Railway". — Jerry Pinto, *The Times of India,* 26 April '98
9. "*Artha,* not *Dharma* Propels the BJP". The article also uses terms like 'mantra', ' maryada' 'Purushottam' etc. — Taufiq Subhan, *The Times of India,* 24 May '98
10. "A nuclear lesson, from *Bhasmasura*." — Sidhartha Varadarajan, *The Times of India,* 29 May '98
11. In the article, "Figures of thought" these words and concepts are discussed and explained with its cultural significance in India and in the process, make the outsider grasp the special meaning that these Indian terms retain without the English equivalents.
The Times of India, 20 May '98

	Tamas, Shakti, Nirgun, Brahma, Vikaras, Tattvas, Sattva, Shabdabrahman, Purusha, Prakriti, Tantrashutras, Sahasra, Padma, Kundalini, Pralaya, Shaktirupa and so on. The article also clarifies its purpose to be that of explaining the philosophical, cultural roots of words and ideas in current use.	
12.	"Swadeshi talk Videshi thought".	Siddhartha Varadarajan, *The Times of India,* 6 June '98
13.	Guru Dakshina	*The Times of India,* 9 June '98
14.	Karamachari Frequently used in the news items. (The Sanskritised *Karmachari* is not used but the local, colloquial use of the word as written above).	*The Times of India,* 10 June '98
15.	"Awakening the *Kundalini*". (On Pokhran nuclear test)	Cover page caption of the journal *Politics India,* Vol-II, No.12, June '98
16.	natak, masiha, dehati Context: (i) Let us understand what all this natak is about. (ii) Laloo is the masiha of the down trodden. (iii) This remarkable dehati woman.	Pritish Nandy, "The enemy at the gate", *The Assam Tribune*, 21 Oct. '98.
17.	bhanti, bhaity (Assamese terms for brother and sister quite popular in the North East).	*The Assam Tribune,* 25 Oct. '98.
18.	Mandap, Pandit, Mummy, Papa, Nanaji, Taoji, Buaji,	Bachi, J. Karkaria, *The Times of India,* 15 Nov. '98.

Barhi-Mummy, Mehndi, Sangeet, Jalebi, Churi, Masi, Chacha, Chachi, Pishi-ma, Masi-ma, Balle balle, Rabdi, Rabba Rabba and so on.	
19. "How will the economy escape from the *Chakravahyu?*" The word is popularly used in India, known to Indians as an ancient war policy/strategy.	*The Times of India* July 14, '98.
20. dekko, topee, veranda, Charpoy, Sepoy	An interview with Prof. John Wells (author of Longman's *Pronunciation Dictionary*) by Ratnottama Sengupta, *The Times of India.*
21. Dhaba (So popular in India as a road side restaurant) Context : "*Dhaba* owner found murdered" (title of a news item).	*The Times of India,* 10. Jan.'98
22. (i) dishum dishum (popular sound out of film fighting)	(i) *The Times of India* 14 Dec. '97
(ii) *dishum dishum*	(ii) *TOI,* 21 Dec.'97
23. Stylebhai (A male fashion designer is addressed so by the writer).	*The Times of India* 16 Aug, '98
24. Samadhi Context: "Youth damages Gandhi's *Samadhi*"	*The Times of India,* 26 July, '98.
25. River Sutra	Editorial, *The Times of India,* 26 July, '98.
26. (i) "Meaning of *Moksha*"' (renunciation) (ii) "Path to freedom from *Tamas*" Tamas—darkness	Chaturvedi Badrinath, *The Times of India,* 26 July, '98.
27. Yoni Yeti Context : "From *Yoni* to *Yeti*"	Bachi J. Karkaria *The Times of India,* 27 July, '98.
28. ghoos (bribe) Sifarish	Madhu Kishwar, "Making a home of hell",

Context: "a *ghoos* from below or a sifarish from above." — *The Times of India,* 2 Aug. '98.

29. gaddi — *The Times of India,* 6 Dec. '98
    Context: "... to seize again the *gaddi..*"
    (Although it has already been recognised by *The Oxford Dictionary's* "Indian supplement", it is the use which makes it popular and newspapers make that reach the people for further application).
30. Bhakti, Puja, Archana — Editorial, *The Times of India,* 12 Nov. '98.
    Context: "Language of *Bhakti*".
31. Bahu — Sashtri Ramachandran, *The Times of India,* 13 Nov. '98.
    "Basu and Bahu"
32. Behan — V. Radhika, *The Week,* 22 Nov, 99.
    Context: "Madam *versus* Behan" (Title of the article).
33. Tamashewali — *The Sunday Times of India,* 13 Dec. '98.
    "My mother, the tamashewali". (an article), on a doctor's private life.
34. abhinaya — Sudhamahi Raghunathan, *The Times of India,* 1 Nov. '98.
35. Saab — *The Times of India* 1 Nov. '99.
    Saheb - Sahib - Saab (more informal)
36. Akhara — *The Times of India,* 4 Nov. '98.
    (Wrestler's gymnasium)
37. Swadhin Asom — *The Assam Tribune,* 2 Nov. '98.
    (Assam is pronounced so).
38. Swadeshi, — Farrokh K.R. Mehta, *The Times of India,* 7 Nov. '98
    Deṣi, dum (strength) havaldar, lungi, chowkey, Dekho, aarey, magajin, phoren (The last two refer to a code switch in pronunciation

	patterns in Indian colloquial situation).	
39.	Junta (Janata) Context: "Backdoor *Junta*"	Editorial, *The Times of India,* 8 Oct. '98.
40.	(i) Kumar Purnima (a festival in Orissa, title of a news item).	*The Times of India,* 8 Oct. '98.
	(ii) *Diwali's* for the birds.	*The Times of India,* 15 Oct. '98
41.	Jungle *Jammin*	*The Statesman,* 15 Oct. '98.
42.	Sampattikar (Property tax) Samasya (problem) Samadhan (solution)	Advertisement by property tax department, Municipal Corporation of Delhi, *TOI.*
43.	(i) Makar Sankranti sky (14th January every year) 'A thousand kites move through *Makar Sankranti* sky (It is like Western Christian festivals and dates. People learning British English are supposed to know their festivals. So is the case with Indian English at the backdrop of Indian culture.'	*The Times of India,* 23 Oct.'98.
	(ii) a *mithaiwalla's* stall	*The Times of India,* 23 Oct.'98.
	(iii) "...they don't have the *Pehchaan.*"	
44.	darshan, Shivling Context: "...one of their deepest dresires is to go to Mecca, for a *darshan* of a *shivling.*"	*The Times of India,* 25 Oct. '98.
45.	"Complacency is *Hara-kiri*".	Ravi Shastri, *The Times of India,* 25 Oct.'98.
46.	(i) biskoot Context: "Amartya takes the *biskoot*" (repeatedly used so here) (This is how 'biscuit' is pronounced in Indian languages).	Jug Suraiya, *The Times of India,* 25 Oct.'98

(ii) bongs (Bengalis) (iii) Hon-bongs(Honourable Bengalis) (iv) Bongdom (like kingdom) refers to Bengali dominance. Context: "Bongdom everywhere". (v) Rabindro sangeet (vi) Bongness (vii) Amartya da	This is a satiric approach on Bengali fundamentalism as perceived after Amartya Sen was honoured with the Nobel Prize.
47. Annadata (King is addressed so in India) Yajna (Sacrifice) daasi (maid)	Section : "The speaking Tree", *The Times of India* 26 Oct. '98
48. Mantri Mantriji	Jerry Pinto, *The Times of India* 20 Sept.'98.
49. Phatphati (auto rickshaw driven by Bullet Engine in metros)	*The Times of India* 27 Sept. '98
50. Bhelpuri ("Life has become bhelpuri"). mast masti Phaltu bakwaas	*The Times of India,* 20 Feb, '99 Also dealt in the section for slogans, colloquialism.
51. Senapati (Like Mantri)	*TOI,* 15 Feb., '99
52. Natarani (Danseuse Mrinalini Sarabhai)	Ravi Jha, *TOI,* 13 Feb. '99.
53. Chukchukgari (Stands for a Train in India).	*TOI,* March 7, '99
54. avatar (incarnation);	Rakhee Gupta, *The Assam Tribune,*

	a new role in the present	6 Dec. '98.
	context: that of a politician.	
55.	Klesha	Michael McGhee,
	Dukkha	*The Times of India,*
	Shraddha	5 Dec. '98.
56.	Mulk	Miriam D'Souza,
	Dil	*TOI,* 18 March, '99
57.	Rathyatra	*The Sunday,* 10-16 January, '99.
	Pracharak	
	Shila Pujan	
	Samaj	
	Shilanyas	
	Vatan	
	Sants	
58.	Puttar	*TOI*, 3 Jan. '99.
59.	biradari	Nikhat Kazmi,
	aam	*The Times of India*
	Mofussil	
	Namaste	
	Balle balle	
60.	Shringara rasa	Editorial, *The Times of India,*
	Yaksha	23 April '98
	Vairagya	
61.	Durbar	D.E. Nizamuddin,
	Dilli	*The Asian Age.*
62.	Agni Pariksha	K. Subramanyam
		The Times of India
		10 April '98.
63.	Hanuman	Section:
	Siddhi	"The Speaking Tree",
	bhakti-marga	Devdutt Pattanaik
	(School of devotion)	*The Times of India*
	Mahavira	2 April '98.
	Mahabali	
	Purushottam	
	maryada	
	Jivatma	
	Paramatma	
	Ahamkara	
	Brahmacharya	

64. Kutniti	Editorial: *TOI*, 26 March '98.
65. Suradhyaksha Arthashastra.	*TOI*, 23 March '98.
66. Sattvic, desi, haldi, burra, shukto, macher jhol, paratha, Sandesh, Kebab Sabji-roti	"Movable feasts", Dileep Padgaonkar, *TOI*, 25 Feb. '98.
67. Arrc yaar, baqwash hangama, Dilli, azadi, dhanda, Sutra	Jug Suraiya, *TOI*, 23 Feb. '98.
68. Abbajaan Nani-ma	Bachi J. Karkaria, *TOI*, 23 Feb. '98
69. Basmati	Swami A. Aiyar *TOI*, 23 Feb. '98
70. Pratinidhi mantripad	Editorial, *TOI*, 25 March '98
71. "*Vedacharya* from the west", refers to a learned person on *The Vedas* (our ancient scripture in India).	*TOI*, 30 March 2000
72. "Police to welcome *Poila Baisakh in Bangla*". It refers to the use of Bengali in message delivered by the Police in West Bengal.	*TOI*, 1 April 2000
73. "Rabri balances *ghar* (house) and *bahar* (govt.)".	*TOI*, 9 March 2000
74. Arth Moksha Context: "The Best of Arth and Moksha". (also cited before).	Interview with S.P. Hinduja, *The Times of India*, 13 Oct. '99 by L.K. Sharma.
75. Ragas (Classical Musical pattern Raga) Context: "Healing *Ragas*."	Editorial, *The Times of India*, 13 Oct. '99
76. Poshak (The commonly used and	*The Times of India*, 4 Dec.'99, p.1.

	accepted (generic) word for any kind of dress in India) Title: "Getting Posh, about *Poshak*".	
77.	(i) Josh (as an adjective) "Acquire *josh* status"	(i) Ford Icon advertisement, *The Economic Times,* 8—14 March 2000.
	(ii)"Be seen in *josh* circles"	(ii) Same advt. on 10 March 2000
78.	Humko Tumko	The title of the editorial, *TOI,* 1 April 2000
79.	"Will *Vidhayakji* be *Vidushakji* too", refers to the people's representatives becoming magicians in doing all developmental work.	*TOI,* 10 April 2000
80.	biradari (cited before too).	"Kashmiris Abroad", Rashmee Z. Ahmed, *TOI*, 29 Jan. 2002.

Indian slangs, colloquialism and the processes of change

The focus here is to categorise the number of slangs, colloquial expressions, informal chat which give a separate lingo. The contemporary situation, need, fashion give rise to it. The formation of such terms also distinctly authenticate a deliberate process of creativity responsible in bringing such expressions to the forefront for wider public notice, application and the normalization of an alternative text of language learning in English. We seek to mention a few words and a theoretical standing to them.

Sudipta Basu[4] says in his article about the authentication of Indian slang, college students' chat, professional level communication. He also records the statements of certain important people in this regard. First he quotes a few lines from such an informal chat :

"*Fandu* concept *tha be*.Total *enthu* se film *dekha. Pur ladki kya* Powder *thi, yaar...*" The expression is about a girl making powder of their brains and ears. Next he quotes from one such conversation :

"Give me some space *yaar,* the run around is too tight here".This is what Basu says the 'Private lingo' and this is 'reinventing the English language'. Again he says, "Indians writing in English have invented a new idiom and the Veejays on television have made Hinglish fashionable. Never mind if the academic world is yet to gather this phenomenon within its fold."

He also quotes Yasmeen Lookmani, head of the department of English, University of Bombay: "Language is expressive of a culture and enormous cultural changes are taking place which are being reflected in language". He again quotes Sunil Gangopadhyay, noted litterateur: "this is a growing need to interact and innovatively experiment and resorting to Pidgin English". ('Pidgin' is the language that emerges out of contact between the two sections who use the same language differently).

One student of Presidency College is quoted to be saying "this is one great way to unwind, shed inhibitions and touch base with others". Another student says "speaking the Queen's language is an archaic concept. The only way to gain acceptance and relate to others and have others relate to you, is to use a form of communication that's unique yet distinct and sets you apart from the rest". Prof. Eunice D'Souza of St. Xavier's College, Mumbai also agrees for a modification of the language on a creative line. Tushar Uchil, a student is quoted to have said that "slang develops in Colleges where there is a tradition of hanging out, although the nature of the jargon will differ from campus to campus". The students feel, "to fill the gap a new lingo must enter immediately". Bharat Dhabolkar, playwright, is quoted so: "why should one get stuck with searching for the right words in English, when there are ready expressions to fit in from vernacular languages?"Ashok Banker, writer is quoted:

"There is no language called English any more. Language in fiction is a reflection of what is randomly used otherwise by everyone in real life. English has a lot more influence of Asian languages. We are definitely moving towards a world language. Basu then quotes from advertisement personnel Moy Roy of Mass Communications, Calcutta: "Speaking jargonistically is a short-cut for making polite conversation. Being metaphorically in your thought and language structure means that one tends to develop one's own lingo, following one's own distinct style". Lookmani is also quoted as saying:

> "this trend has to be studied and observed academically", and "it encourages popular culture and language becomes aggressive which may lead to the establishment of an entirely different value system". Basu also quotes Dhabolkar to be saying that if in

England in the use of English language, the Yorkshire, Cockney, Irish accents are acceptable, in India also there must be variety rather than a uniform English language imposed upon us. Indirectly he is justifying the role of local accents, slangs, private colloquial expressions in enriching our English Basu gives a list of such new slangs on the page of the newspaper as cited below. He terms them *Dictionary of New Words*. We also cite the source of origin of these words and their context specific meanings.

1. Sentu (B.E.) — Sentimental
2. genu (B.E.) — genuine
3. Jamachhe (Hindi) — Under control
4. Booty trap (B.E.) — well-endowed woman
5. Manchester (B.E.) — Flat chested woman
6. Chipku (Hindi) — free advice
7. Ghees mara (Hindi) — Scrape through an exam
8. Chota (Hindi) — Chits of paper used for copying
9. Jhaddimara (Hindi) — lech
10. Thhek (Hindi) — hang out
11. Heavy (B.E.) — terrific
12. Intu Pintu (Mixture, onomatopoeia) — affair on the sky
13. Half soul (B.E.) — jilted lover
14. Liquor (B.E.) — tea

He also uses the word 'hazaar'. We give a list of some other such expressions that contribute in this regard abundantly.

15. Maramari (Hindi)

Jug Suraiya, *TOI*, 23 Feb. '98

16.	Flipping (B.E.) *e.g.* Flipping dad (in spoken form) Flipping cold (in spoken form)	Interview with John Wells (Professor) by Ratnottama Sengupta *The Times of India.*
17.	Car bra (B.E.)	Rashmee Z. Ahmed "Linguistic Liberalism" *The Times of India,*
18.	Pani-Puri (Hindi, Oriya etc.)	24 Aug. '98.
19.	Cuppa (Punjabi accent of English) Ex. Cuppa cha cuppa coffee (English)	Jug Suraiya, *The Times of India,* 25 Oct.'98
20.	gormint (English)	Jug Suraiya, *TOI*, 27 Sept.'98.
21.	Phaltu	
22.	bakwaas	*The Times of India,*
23.	fundas	14 Feb.'99
24.	mast	
25.	masti	

Source : 21 to 25 (Hindi).

A list below contains the list of a few other usage of slang developed by the street language of Mumbai and the local,Indianised meanings attached to them.

Sl No. contd.	*Terms*	*Local meanings*	*Source*
26.	Chikna (M) chikni (F)	Stands for any good looking fellow, smooth	Shabnam Minwalla, "Of cutting and Kauva", *TOI,* 14 Nov.'99
27.	Keeda	An absolute pest	
28.	Bevada		
29.	Gutter		
30.	Taankee	A drunk person	
31.	Batli		
32.	Johnny Walker		
33.	Tapri	A road side shop	
34.	Chotay Chottays	Any kid working in a shop	
35.	Manikchand	A person who chews gutka	
36.	Dhoop Chaav	Refers to road side barber shops which just have a hole-ridden rag for the chaav.	

(Contd....)

37.	Mahim-Matunga	A term used
38.	Vasai-Virar	For squint eyed individuals.
39.	Cutting	Half a cup of tea is called so; venders also say so.
40.	Kauvaa	Underworld phrase for a mobile phone.
41.	Chidiyaa	Underworld phrase for a pager.

Source : 26 to 28 (Hindi); 30 to 31, 33 to 38, 40 to 41 (Hindi); 29, 32, 39 (English).

Summary

The triggering processes that facilitate such coinage come out of teen age fascination with broken, half-English as a part of fashion and modernity. For most of the students, the chaste, matter of fact English becomes drab and formal. So their usage in the extra-classroom context is that of an exaggerated variety, often arbitrary and transformational in nature but follows a common code for comprehension by a specified circle. The college, University campus is one such circle where a common (with few exceptions that vary from one campus to the other) code goes on well.The other aspects confine to a sort of regionalising, colloquialising process in the body of the Queen's English, market friendly economy in expression (enthu, chikna etc.) and a cultural shift (replacing one's own cultural traits in the form of language) that is clearly evident in the body of newspaper English. Having classified the available new entries, change in lexical coinage, we seek to establish such a change of structural variety as available in the next chapter.

REFERENCES

1. J.W. Harris, "Diphthongization, monophthongization and metaphony revisited", *Diachronic Studies in Romance Linguistics*, eds. M. Saltarelli and D. Wanner (Mouton : The Hague,1975) 537.
2. F.T. Wood, "The growth of vocabulary", *An Outline History of the English Language*, 1941 (MacMillan India Ltd.,1969).
3. S.V. Parasher, "Communication Styles in Indian English", *Language Matters*, ed. K.V. Tirumalesh (Hyderabad: Allied Publishers,'99).
4. Sudipta Basu, "Mind your language", *Telegraph* 5 December '98.

Chapter - 5

General Syntactic Processes in English, Syntactic Deviation and Underlying Processes Involved in It

Focus

The previous chapter discusses the morpho-syntactic deviation and the processes making room for the change. The morphemic variation leads to syntactic change. Syntax is the scientific study of the sentence. A sentence is a combination of words, phrases, clauses and so gives enough opportunity for change in its structure. Our focus here is to briefly discuss the nature of the syntactic structure in English, record the different instances of structural change along with new structures and assess the predominant factors and processes behind such change. We will take into account the change in phrase, clause, idioms, figures of speech and the recurring patterns of a poetic, alliterative structure as appear in the journalistic register.

The Syntactic Structure of English

The way of arrangement of words to form larger units is called Syntax. Although words carry meanings of their own, they convey complete meaning only when they are in structures. So comes the question of the syntactic structure of the language. Syntax offers words in their proper linguistic contexts; in other words, syntax is word arrangement in a sentence structure. If we take two forms like this:

(i) Girl one one boy love in fell and,
(ii) One boy and one girl fell in love; we find the second structure meaningful.

So syntax tells us the rules behind the arrangement which make the sentence meaningful.

In English, infinite number of sentences which are used have come from the finite set of structures which may be called the basic structures of a fixed order.

(i) I go (S V type) = Subject - Verb

(ii) That is there (SVC type)

	s	v	c	
(iii)	She is sorry (Subject verb complement)			
	s	v	c	
(iv)	He	killed	a tiger.	
	subject	verb	object	
	s	v	o	
(v)	He	kept	the mirror	on the shelf
	s	v	o	place
(vi)	We	made	him	angry
	subject	verb	object	complement
(vii)	She	gave	me	a fruit
	s	v	o	o

In the context of performing syntactic functions, words can be divided into 'Content words' or 'Full words' such as:

(i) nouns (ii) adjectives (iii) verbs

(iv) full adverbs, having recognisable meanings, and 'structure words' or 'function words' without distinct meaning such as

(i) Prepositions—at, in, of, for etc.

(ii) Determiners—the, a, an, my, both

(iii) Auxiliaries—be, do, have, shall

(iv) Pronouns—I, She

(v) Adverb parts—up, down

(vi) Relatives—who, when, what

(vii) Interrogatives—when, how, where

(viii) Subordinators—because, since, then

(ix) Conjunctions—and, so, neither, nor

(x) Connectors—therefore, however

Structure word occur more than the content word as they

function as the joining links between the content words and are more meaningful in the syntactic sense.

We cite the different groups of word order here[1].

TheNominal group (where a noun pronoun or noun equivalent heads the structure with or without the modifiers). Example - Asim (Nominal only)

- She
- Water

- the water (determine + noun) or (modifier + noun)
- hot water (adjective + noun)
- College students (N + N)
- Ellora's book (Genitive + Noun)
- moving train (ing from + Noun)
- twisted word (past participle + Noun)
- one girl (numeral agent + Noun)

Similarly modifiers can follow the noun as in

- a magazine with pictures (N + Prepositional phrase)
- a picture to see (N + to-infinitive)
- the photo that I gave you (N + Clause)
- the camera containing photographs (N + ing form)
- Lesson III (N + Numeral)
- the lesson there (N + adverb)

Where noun equivalents head the group (the relevant nps have been underlined):

- *to err* is human
- *Talking nonsense* is what he does
- *The lovely* is precious on the earth.

The verbal group (where a verb is the head added to the modifiers).

- make
- is making (Be + Head, ing form)
- had made (Have + Head)
- is made (Be + Head), Past participle

- was being made (Be + being + Head)
- had been made (have + been + head) and so on.

These groups also could be preceded by modals.

- modal + head—will make
- modal + be + head (ing form)—shall be making
- modal + have + head—may have made
- modal + have + been + head (ing form)—would have been making
- modal + be+ being + head—may be being made
- modal + be + head—may be made
- modal + have + been + being + head—should have been being made.

The Adjectival Group (where the adjective form takes the role of the head and may be added to modifiers).

- Blue Sky
- Black Suit

Modifiers or intensifiers which precede the adjective head can be shown as below :

Determiner	*Adjectival group*		*Noun*
	Intensifier	*Head*	
a	very rather pretty	modest good beautiful	proposal

The modifier that follows the adjective head is often termed as complement as in :

- She was angry *with me*
- I am worth *this job*

The Adverbial Group (where the adverb heads the group).

- Quietly (Head)
- Very soon (Intensifier + Head).

Example : Quietly he left
Very soon I will reach Bhubaneswar.

Some of the groups as discussed above can be seen in unison as below:

Nominal group	*Verbal group*	*Nominal group*	*Adjectival group*	*Adverbial group*
She	Sings	Songs	Very	Softly

(a) ***Idioms***

There are idioms, phrasal verbs (the peculiar usage of certain words to mean something specific to the language and culture).

Examples : Tooth and nail, Black and white, Black and blue, Cats and dogs, Catch fire, Turn down, Make out and so on.

(b) ***The Passive Voice***

In case of the passive voice the SVO order is reversed.

He ate Rice → Rice was eaten by him
S V O

The syntactic structure of English can be shown diagrammatically as under:

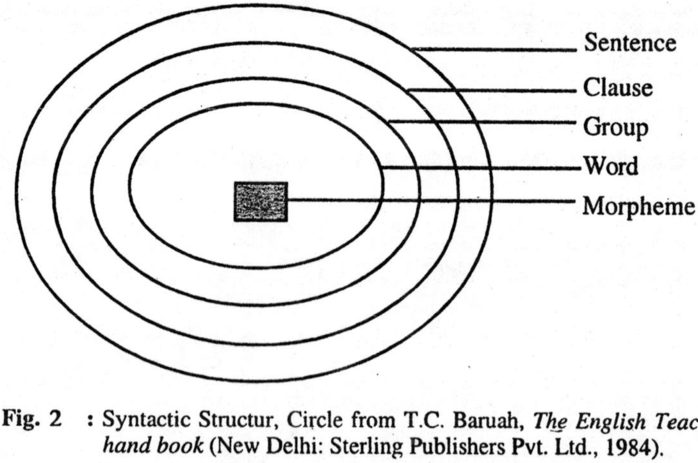

Fig. 2 : Syntactic Structur, Circle from T.C. Baruah, *The English Teacher's hand book* (New Delhi: Sterling Publishers Pvt. Ltd., 1984).

So we can say the syntactic structure is a big structure containing other small structures and the English syntax has a rigid word order.

Phrase Structure Rule

The phrase structure (PS) rules give the idea that the sentence (S) is the highest order element, the immediate constituents of which are the noun phrase (NP), the verb phrase (VP). The VP in turn may have constituents, NP and V.

Each NP may have an article (A) and Noun (N) which can be shown by a tree diagram below:

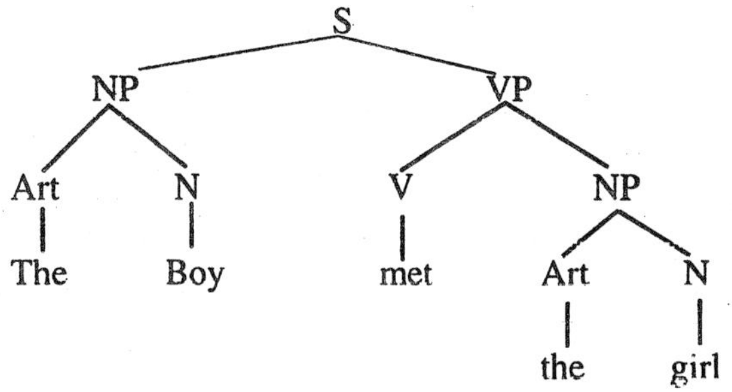

Fig. 3 : Tree Diagram of the sentence with its constituents, from T.C. Baruah, *The English Teachers Hand book* (New Delhi: Sterling Publishers Pvt. Ltd., 1984).

Another example :

The man loved the woman.

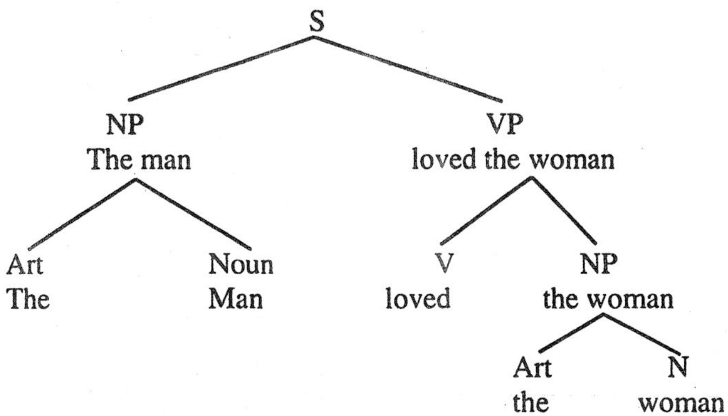

Fig. 4. : Syntactic relation, from T.C. Baruah, *The English Teachers Handbook* (New Delhi: Sterling Publishers Pvt. Ltd., 1984).

But this is not the only sentence structure in English as can be seen ahead.

When we think of the auxiliary, the tense element and the base form of the verb; the structure can be changed slightly :

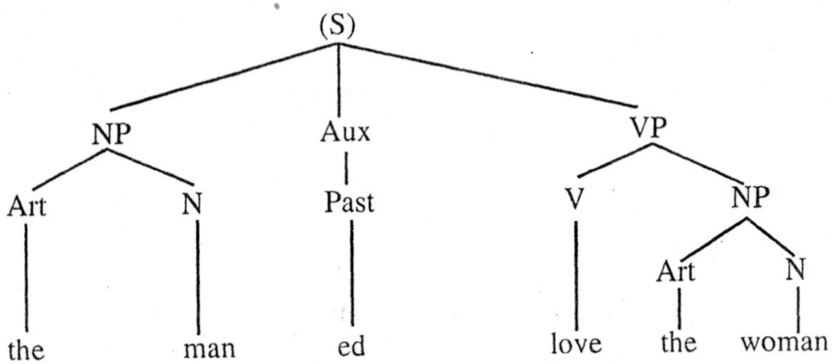

Fig. 5 : Syntactic relation, from T.C. Baruah, *The English Teachers Hand book* (New Delhi: Sterling Publishers Pvt. Ltd., 1984).

So the previous rule

S → NP + VP

is amended to

S → NP + Aux + VP

The above tree diagram comes under the heading "Syntactic relation" (since it is a relation of different parts of the sentence).

The Formal Axis and Processes of Change

The formal level sees the erratic use of articles, rank reduction (sentence rank variation), idiomatic changes, interrogative, active passive, prepositional deviations and so on which will be seen here:

For example in British English, a 'verb + adverb' structure is more common which is just the opposite in Indian English because of the influence of the mother tongue.

In British English the common type is :

He ran away	quickly
(v)	(adv)

In Indian English equivalent :

(i) He quickly (adv) ran away (v)

In Hindi : Woh jaldi daauda

(ii) In IE : One should first work hard (adv) (v)

instead of: One should work hard first (BE).

In Indian English usage, the use of article is restricted since it is not there in Indian languages.

Example in Hindi : Log Sarkar banatc hain
Example in English : People make *the* Government.

Similarly, new idioms, collocations, figurative use of the language according to either the mother tongue or the deliberate creative notions of the writers with strong socio-cultural pressures are getting dominance in newspaper English now-a-days.

CATEGORIES, EXAMPLES AND PROCESSES OF CHANGE

Articles

The most dominant area of deviation in syntactic patterns in newspaper English is the approach to articles.

(a) The diminishing role of articles, deliberate dropping of the articles happen due to the communicative approach (which believes in passing the message and fulfilling the purpose) and economy.
(b) It influences the learners, students, writers, professionals, academicians and other such users of the English language in India.
(c) It facilitates the use of an informal, diary language with full freedom.

Although it happens in newspapers abroad too, here our learners are influenced by it for academic/professional interest; so it forms a part of our English. We here give the list of a number of such usage from the contemporary Indian English newspapers and journals taken by random sampling. The loss of article has been mostly evident.The missing article position is marked by a dash and the usual article is noted down.

Sl.No.	*Data*	*Missing articles*	*Sources*
1.	Varsity senate members elected unopposed	(the)	Title news, *The Times of India* 6 Aug. '99
2.	Fake mark sheet gang busted in city.	(a)	*TOI*, 6 Aug. '99
3.	Examine impact of globalisation	(the)	*TOI*, 21 Sept. '99
4.	(i) Kapil Dev is_ new coach (ii) Kapil Dev appointed_ coach for two years	(the)	*TOI*, 22 Sept. '99
5.	Harshad held guilty of_ Maruti funds misuse	(the)	*TOI*, 28 Sept. '99
6.	BJP is unable to contain_ damage in U.P.	(the)	Seema Guha, *TOI*, 29 Sept '99
7.	_Congress decimated in Orissa	(the)	*TOI*, 13 Oct. '99
8.	_Europeans live good life that Americans find no time for	(the)	*TOI*, 13 Oct. '99
9.	_CPM sponsored the strike to teach_ city a lesson	(the)	*TOI*, 12 Oct. '99
10.	Blow to Clinton as_ Senate rejects CTBT	(the)	*TOI*, 15 Oct. '99
11.	Allott likely to join_ squad	(the)	*The Telegraph*, 14 Oct.'99
12.	Mayurbhanj villagers oppose_ plant	(the)	*The Statesman*, 14 Oct. '99
13.	_Assembly Postponement draws_ flak	(the and a)	*The New Indian Express*, 3 Dec. 99
14.	_House Passes insurance Bill amid_ walk-out	(the and a)	*The New Indian Express* 3 Dec. '99
15.	_Bihar parties harp on _Jharkhand issue	(the)	*The Hindu*, 4 March 2000
16.	Concern over_ lack of security for_ poor	(a and the)	Same as above
17.	_Protest against _constitution review panel	(a and the)	Same as above.

It can well motivate the young learners to adopt the practice in their writing skills.

Alliteration/Poetic Structure

Most of the captions, titles of news items and especially the editorial heading, are found to be deliberately alliterative, containing a specific patterning, rhyming sound between the words. This poetic use of the words in news papers is certainly fulfilling the purpose of an alternative text which can be best manipulated to teach the methods of poetry and music. The factual register of newspapers as it is supposed to be is not so in practice which is exploiting a subjective, poetic syntax that influences the readers from all spheres of life.Though the usages do not hint at completely new structures, it is observed that such deliberate musical pattern reflects Indianness as Indians have been more kin on music, melody. Our Vedas, Upanishads, Purans and Scriptures have been musical and follow a poetic structure. The English newspapers in India retain that medium and tone which in return teaches certain poetic, alliterative modes of English.

We here note down (by random sampling) a number of such usage in our newspapers:

Sl. No.	*Items*	*Sources*
1.	No Deal for wheel	Editorial, *TOI,* 17 Aug. '99
2.	BJP Springs Sushma on Sonia in Bellary	*TOI*, 19 Aug. '99.
3.	Sushma Surprise to Sonia Suspense (N+N+N+N).	*The Telegraph,* 19 Aug.'99
4.	Poll Panel Props PM Press Party Class: N N N N N N	*The Telegraph*, 19 Aug.'99
5.	Song of the shirt	Editorial, *TOI,* 19 Aug.'99
6.	On the Bomb with Aplomb	*TOI*, 19 Aug. '99
7.	Kareena too has got the Karisma	*TOI*, 20 Aug. '99
8.	Sense and Censorship	Editorial, *TOI* 27 Aug. '99
9.	Policing the Police	*TOI*, 27 Aug. '99
10.	(i) *P*oll and *P*ush	Editorial, *TOI,* 24 Aug. '99
	(ii) *C*op in *c*lover	Same as above
	(iii) *S*ony *S*hine Days in India	Same as above
11.	*C*yber *s*pice	Editorial, *TOI* 6 Aug. '99
12.	*G*ingrich *G*rounded	Editorial, *TOI,* 26 Jan. '97
13.	*M*use and *M*achine	Editorial, *TOI,* 25 Jan. '97

14.	*F*rightening *F*igures	Editorial, *TOI,* 24 Jan. '97
15.	(i) *S*entinel to *S*aviour	Editorial, *TOI,* Dec. '96
	(ii) *R*aj to *R*iches	Editorial, *TOI,* Dec. '96
16.	(i) Oi*l*'s not wel*l*	Editorial, *TOI,* 17 Jan. '97
	(ii) Star cross'd *s*tory	Editorial, *TOI,* 17 Jan. '97
17.	(i) Bad *v*ibes from *v*irar	Editorial, *TOI,* 15 Jan. '97
	(ii) Mid*dl*e Did*dl*e	Editorial, *TOI,* 15 Jan. '97
18.	(i) Fear of Flying	Editorial, *TOI,* 14 Jan. '97
	(ii) Carry on, Clio	Editorial, *TOI,* 14 Jan. '97.
19.	Jamboree in Zail	Editorial, *TOI,* 2 Feb. '97
20.	Trying Times	Editorial, *TOI,* 1 Feb. '97
21.	(i) Misguided Move	Editorial, *TOI,* 30 Jan. '97
	(ii) Advantage Akalis	Editorial, *TOI,* 30 Jan. '97
	N N	
22.	Lament Literature	Editorial, *TOI,* 29 Jan. '97
	N N	
23.	Gift of Greeks	Editorial, *TOI,* 1 Jan. '97
24.	Azza Razzmatazz	Editorial, *TOI,* 31 Dec. '96
25.	Frozen for future	Editorial, *TOI,* 27 Jan. '96
26.	(i) Catch the Crooks	Editorial, *TOI,* Dec. '96
	(ii) In water writ	Editorial, *TOI,* Dec. '96
27.	Person and Persona	Editorial, *TOI,* 15 Dec. '96
28.	(i) Odd man out	Editorial, *TOI,* Dec. '96
	(ii) Eating out	Editorial, *TOI,* Dec. '96
29.	Gowda vs Gowda	Editorial, *TOI,* 30 Jan. '97
30.	(i) Jaya in Jail	Editorial,*TOI,* Dec. '96
	(ii) Pope and Pop	Editorial, *TOI,* Dec. '96
31.	Beauty and the Best	Editorial, *TOI,* 30 Nov. '96
32.	Pacific chic	Editorial, *TOI,* Nov. '96
33.	Calcutta crawling	*TOI,* Nov. '96
34.	(i) Liquor in Quicker	Editorial, *TOI,* 26 Nov. '99
	(ii) Battle of Britain (both columns of it)	Editorial, *TOI,* 26 Nov. '99
35.	Boot for Boutros	Editorial, *TOI,* Nov. '96
36.	(i) Beauty and the Bench	Editorial, *TOI,* 22 Nov. '96
	(ii) Gender Mender (both columns)	Editorial, *TOI,* 22 Nov. '96
37.	Plato and Pop	Editorial, *TOI,* 20 Nov. '96
38.	Critique of critics	Editorial, *TOI,* Nov. '96
39.	Doctored Degrees Luckless Laloo Pop goes Politics (all three columns)	Editorial, *TOI,* 17 Nov. '96
40.	Paying a price capital costs Bulls and Bears (all three columns)	Editorial, *TOI,* 5 Feb. '97
41.	Downhill from Davos	Editorial, *TOI,* 6 Feb. '97

42.	Leading in Letters	Editorial, *TOI,* 7 Feb. '97
43.	Dil Does Dhak Dhak for Madhuri (with code mix)	Interview with Madhuri Dixit (film actress), Editorial, *TOI,* 29 Dec. '98
44.	Dance with the Dragon	V.V. Paranjpe, Editorial, *TOI,* 5 Feb. '99
45.	Pawar Play	Editorial,*TOI,* 10 Aug '99

It is observed that in all the cases above, the process of alliteration formation is clearly visible.The title, caption sound interesting and poetic because mid-February '97) in a period of four months, almost everyday a leading daily like *The Times of India* in all its editorial columns (the three columns) has used the practice of such alternative pattern and occasional code switching to pattern it with the alliterative mode. This practice was observed for a period of time continuously to find out that this alliterative usage is an established, fossilized process today in most of the newspapers which record their impression of it in influencing the readers, opening it for further use and that it is on a fast move. It was again observed at a period between August and October '99 to have been amply used. Some of those along with certain other cases from different journals can be seen here.

Examples :

57.	Nawaz's Nemesis	Editorial, *TOI,* 14 Oct. '99
58.	Troubling Tamasha	Editorial, *TOI,* 16 Oct. '99
59.	Sonia Still on shaky ground	*The Statesman,* 14 Oct. '99
60.	Mystique Masala	*TOI*, news item, 14 Oct. '99, p. 8
61.	Trial by Terror	Editorial, *TOI,* 12 Oct. '98
62.	Basu and Bahu	*TOI,* 13 Nov '98
63.	Kumble's Kraft	*The Statesman*, 5 Nov. '98
64.	Ode to the Onion	Tanushree Podder, *TOI*, 6 Nov. '98
65.	Viva Viagra	*TOI,* 24 Sept. '98

The three column titles of the same day paper:

66.	(i) Holi High (ii) Healing Touch (iii) Wine and water	Editorial Column, *TOI,* 28 Feb. '99
67.	Courting Controversy	Cover story, *India Today*, 25 Jan. '99

68. Legal Eagles	*The Telegraph*, 18 April 28 Feb.'99
69. Music Meri Mohabbat	Ratnottama Sengupta, *TOI*, 22 Aug '99
70. (i) Golden Goose	Anupama Chopra, *India Today*, 1 Nov. '99
(ii) Preaching Papas	Nandita Choudhury *India Today*, 1 Nov. '99
71. Brief case Babus	Nitin Gokhale, *Outlook*, 1 Nov. '99
72. Hooked on Toons	'Saturday Times', *The Times of India*, 29 Nov. '97
73. Azza Maza	Editorial, *The Times of India*, 6 Jan. '98.
74. The blame game	"Saturday Review", *TOI*, 29 Aug. '98
75. Still so sunny (On Sunil Gavaskar)	*The Times of India*, 22 Nov. '98
76. Kya Karega Qazi	Interview with Pakistan High Commissioner, Asraf Jahangir Qazi by Janak Singh, *The Times of India*, 7 Dec. '98.
77. Kuch kuch kyon Hota Hai	*The Times of India*, 7 Dec. '98.
78. Jacks in Pack	Editorial, *The Telegraph*, 23 Nov. '99

Certain specific advertisements teach the imperative usage which are catchy, poetic and provide a non-canonical, alternative text rather than subscribing to the strict teaching of grammaticality, accuracy and conformity.

S.No.	*Items*	*Companies*
1.	The Time Keeper of the Nation	HMT Watches
2.	The Milkman of the Country	Amul
3.	Take home the leader	Videocon
4.	Get a king with his two princess (one big Computer with two small ones)	Computer advertisement
5.	Take it easy	Limca
6.	Taste the Thunder	Thums up
7.	Brought to you by Baron	Aiwa
8.	Buy now or wait for the next thousand years	Samsung *TOI*, 29 Oct. '99
9.	Flatter then the flattest flat	*The Telegraph*, Sony TV, 28 Oct. '99

10. Neighbour's envy, Owner's pride Neighbour's envy, World's pride (an example of Antithesis).	Onida
11. Made for each other	Wills Filter Cigarette
12. "We innovate, you benefit." "It is a steal anyway." "We will forgive you for mobbing the nearest Akai dealer."	Akai TV, *TOI*, 5 Nov. '99
13. Better than the best	Ad, Sansui TV, *TOI*, 5 March 2000
14. Switch on reality	Ad, Panasonic TV, *TOI*, 5 Nov. '99
15. Eat Cricket, Sleep Cricket, Drink Pepsi Here a collocational variation is also evident.	Pepsi soft drinks (All Newspapers)

Apart from the deliberate coinage of alternative expressions to form the bold titles, captions, it is also observed that the newspaper writing comes loaded with such alternative, proverbial, poetic expressions within the content of the articles, news items. It draws the conclusion that the writing mode of the writers is set to such expressions, it is fossilized in their mind which is of fast growth.

1. Don't be a bunder grow to the taste of thunder	Advertisement of Thums Up, *The Hindustan Times*, 19 March '98 and all newspaper.
2. Aap ki Bari Atal Behari	*TOI*, 23 March, '98 (a special report).
3. MITI or Mitti (MITI — Ministry of International Trade and Industry).	Swami Aiyar, *TOI*, 30 March '98
4. Stree Shakti It refers to the bargaining of J.Jayalalitha and Mamata Banerjee(politicians) as political partners.	Editorial, *TOI*, 28 May '98
5. (i) Will stable Atal now be Able (ii) Awesome Twosome Mayawati; (On Mulayam Singh and two politicians).	Cover story, *India Today* 18 Oct. '99
6. Your home is your pride with Hawkins by your side	Advertisement of Hawkins Pressure cooker, *TOI*, 26 Oct. '99

7.	Those boot-button eyes have melted many hearts	'Saturday Times', *The Times of India*, 29 Nov. '97
8.	Maha trouble in Malaysia ('Maha' comes from Mahathir Mohammed, politician from Malaysia).	Abheek Barman, *TOI*, 6 Sept. '98
9.	Waste NOT, want NOT	Sudha Palit, *The Statesman*, 20 Nov. '98
10.	Dyke Didis Dilli Billis Gucci guys (The above structures have been put into the normal sentences which project a rhythmic, deliberately patterned discourse).	Special report, *TOI*, 22 Nov. '98
11.	Bargain Bazaar	Advertisement of a Cyberspace unit, *TOI* 29, Oct. '99
12.	Gyan and Vigyan (On India's nuclear test)	Editorial, *TOI*, 23 May '98
13.	Homeless, hungry Orissa on hair trigger	*The Telegraph*, 2 Nov. '99
14.	Highway to hope littered with hell holes	*The Times of India*
15.	Dhak Dhak Dixit ties the knot ('Dhakdhak ...' is a song picturised on Madhuri Dixit, the actress)	*TOI*, 5 Nov. '99
16.	'Should you worry? Atal Behari?'	Jug Suraiya, *TOI*, 27 July '98
17.	Causes of conversion	M.D. Nalapat, *TOI*, 29 Sept. '99
18.	Platitudes are no substitute for Paani	K.C.Shivaramakrishnan, *TOI*, 29 Sept. '99
19.	Greeting Grooms	V.N. Kakar, *TOI*, 29 Sept. '99
20.	Pretty woman, Prettier man Picture imperfect	Nikhat Kazmi, *TOI*, 10 Oct. '99
21.	Dal loser in Atal balancing act. The writer says that in Atal Behari Vajpayee's expansion of his Ministry, Ramakrishna Hegde, a Janata Dal (United) member is not included and so is a loser. But deliberately to suit to 'Atal' the term 'Dal' is chosen rather than 'Janata Dal' or 'United' or the name of Hegde.	*The Telegraph*, 23 Nov. '99
22.	Start an e-bizness with Lee and Nee	Advertisement, *The Telegraph*, 21 Feb. 2000

23.	Wedding Belles: Mira Ki Ayegi Baraat The code mix as well as Indian proverbial statement "Raja (refers to the groom in general) Ki ayegi Baraat' and change in spelling (Bells - Belles) is because of the reference to French, as Mira Nair, film director was awarded by the French body; all these make an interesting mixture in the syntactic structure.	*TOI*, 24 Nov. 2001 on Mira Nair's famous award winning film *'Monsoon Wedding'*.
24.	Drinking and driving don't mix There is also a conversion of the structure "Don't mix drinking and driving" (as it is an imperative, instruction).	Advertisement by Delhi Traffic, *TOI*, 24 Nov. 2001
25.	The Magical Powers of Mumbai Masala (alliterative and code mixing)	*TOI*, 25 Nov. 2001
26.	Aby's baby Pips Papa to the Post This is alliterative in the linguistic sense. It is done to attract, so eye catching for the readers. And it speaks of the famous cine star in Indian context, Amitabh Bachhan popularly known as AB, Big B, Aby and it also refers to his son Abhishek Bachhan. It speaks about both their films and the box office equation between them.	*The Times of India*, 25 June 2001

We find that the mode of expression in our English dailies has resorted to such a tendentious appeal. The factors that influence such discourse have been already discussed in Chapter-3 of this study. Now since the usage points out a flexible, less strict poetic medium, we can say that such a mental make up (both of the writers and the editors which also influences the readers) has contributed enough for the possibility of a specialised Indian way of structural change. And apart from the alternative expression we may observe a lot of code mixing independently getting incorporated into the structure to mark the autonomy of the author as can be best seen here:

It's all kiss-met for Parizaad The message: Parizaad is a recent	*TOI*, 24 Nov. 2001

film actress. 'Kiss-met' refers to her 'Kismat' (fortune in films) and her kissing scenes.

Next, we intend to see how far the corpus given below ensures a wrong adjustment between subject-verb, plural-singular notions and other such anomaly between the parts of the sentence. We also list other areas like preposition variation, dropping of subject or implied subject, deviation in punctuation marks, transitive-intransitive verbs, dropping of possessive case, auxiliary verb and so on.It is observed that the body of newspaper columns have adopted the method of subject dropping, ignoring punctuation marks and so on for economy of expression. By doing so they do not pose a threat to the communicative function of a language. Since this technique does not make one binding or accountable to the strict textual, grammatical notions of the language, it becomes a more suitable language, accessible and adoptable for thc professionals, students and teachers, easy to comprehend and express. They pursue this kind of a diary language through their different modes of usage. So no doubt this deviation has been in the positive interest of our English using community, contributing a lot to the kind of English we get comfortable with and has become an alternatively easy way of teaching English to the learners going in the direction of an anti-canonial system of language acquisition. Learners get acquainted with different Englishes all around them rather than being confined to the rigid grammatical patterns of their curriculum.

We again observe that such usage is not new in its origin as all newspapers worldwide follow the same pattern. But we are concerned about the benefits and applicability of it in the Indian context, giving Indian English the freedom to use it for flexibility in language learning system (to establish the user friendly situation).

Missing Verbs

1. Sonia's foreign origin a major issue — *TOI,* 13 Sept. '99
2. Elections a dreaded time for vehicle owners — *TOI,* 30 Sept. '99
   Dropping of auxiliary and punctuation mark.
3. RELIGION NO BAR
   This is a clause without any verb. — Editorial, *The Telegraph* 6 Oct. '99
4. 'Earth' India's entry for Oscars — *TOI,* 30 Oct. '99

(Either there could be an auxiliary verb or a punctuation mark to avoid the ambiguity or the film 'Earth' could have been italicized in normal usage).

5.	Hongkong now playground of Mickey and Adam Smith	*TOI,* 5 Nov. '99
6.	(i) Fighting on in Chechnya (ii) Sonia still on shaky ground	*The Statesman,* 14 Oct. '99
7.	Rebels Delhi bound to see Gamang ouster. It has dropped the *auxiliary* and *genitive*	*The Statesman,* 16 Oct. '99
8.	Trade Unionism the most profitable business in West Bengal.	*TOI,* 21 Nov. '99
9.	Yukta another icon for Calcuttans	*TOI,* 10 Dec. '99, p.9
10.	More welfare schemes need of the hour	*The Hindustan Times,* 12. Dec. '99
11.	Ramesh not averse to becoming cup captain (Loss of auxiliary and article)	*TOI,* 13 Oct. '99
12.	Restraint the key It looks like an imperative without an auxiliary or punctuation mark.	Editorial, *The Times of India,* 8 Feb. 2000
13.	Basu bill, Naidu benevolence for Orissa There is a deviation that does not speak about Basu's bill and Naidu's benevolence and gives the pattern of N+N+N+N	*The Telegraph.* 17 Feb. 2000
14.	Culture curfew in Kanpur N + N + Prep. + N	*The Telegraph* 16 Feb. 2000
15.	States' demand Just Here conversion of the structure takes place. The structure : 'States just demand' would have been conventionally appropriate.	G. Thimmaiah, *The Hindu,* p.21

The position of adjective is changed. But in Sanskrit the change in position of parts of speech makes no difference and is appropriate.

16. Congress charge of NE neglect baseless — *The Times of India*, 28 Sept. '99
The structure above has multiple deviations like:
   (i) Congress charge → It results in ambiguity. Whether it is 'the charge of Congress' or 'Congress in charge of North East', create a confusion.
   There is a dropping of the possessive (genitive case),
   (ii) and dropping of the main verb.
   Example: N-E neglect is baseless.
   (iii) 'North East neglect' could be written as 'The neglect of North East'. It is done so by translation of the mother tongue structure.
17. Atal breather in Clinton blow (The caption does not put a verb) — *The Telegraph*, 15 Oct. '99
18. Credit where due (the clause replaces the position of elements) — Editorial, *The Telegraph*, 1 Nov. '99
19. Water ban brigade at Advani door — *The Telegraph*, 4 March 2000
   N N N (Prep.) N N
20. Sonia mercy plea for Mother Nalini (Loss of the possessive case) — *The Telegraph*, 19 Nov. '99
21. Yadavs meeting to demand larger share of OBC quota — *TOI*, 12 Dec. '99, p.10
22. Salim one up on deerson Salman (Main verb is lacking) — *The Telegraph*, 17 Oct. '98
23. Our father who *art* in heaven (This archaic, poetic use (replacing 'are' is deliberate). — *The Telegraph*, 24 Nov. '99

Singular-plural anomaly

1. President of CII (Confederation of Indian Industry) says in an interview to *The Times of India:* — *TOI*, 18 Feb. 2002

"To the Indian mindset, services means software. We are saying that services are much more than just software". Here the same word is used as singular and plural. • Also the present continuous form of the verb 'say' is used.

In sports register, the country that plays is represented as plural but in other fields it is not so. The team members' individual contribution in totality is taken into consideration. This is a S-V anomaly.

Examples:

2.	Delhi consolidate their position (Cricket)	Title news, *TOI*, 26 Oct. '99
3.	India don't stand a chance	*Telegraph*, 24 Oct. '99
4.	India restrict Zimbabwe to 221: India win over Aussies	*TOI*, 8 Oct. '98
5.	Tata Sons buys Tisco, Telco shares (In Corporate sector it happens the other way round)	*The Economic Times* 28 Oct. '98
6.	India were out batted	*Sportstar*, 12 Feb. 2000
7.	India must accept their cricket is in trouble and do something about it (no punctuation as well as plural-singular anomaly).	*Sportstar*, 12 Feb. 2000
8.	(i) Hyderabad take lead (ii) Rajasthan enter quarter finals (iii) Indian start with a win	*The Times of India*, 8 Jan. 2000 p. 22

Subject dropping

1. Doesn't Add up — Editorial, *The Times of India*, 23 Aug. '99

   (i) The title doesn't have a subject and it also doesn't take the shape of an interrogative sentence.

   (ii) The news content contains a sentence like this:

	"a delicious irony of these elections". It is a deviation from the normal collocational norm relating to the word 'delicious' (delicious food) that offers a flexibility to use it and some such words with utmost liberty in sentences by any learner.	
2.	'Who bares Wins'	*India Today,* 11 Oct. '99
3.	Don't have to prove I am fit (loss of subject, nominal group) It quotes from Tendulkar's statement	*The Telegraph,* 14 Oct. '99
4.	Time to review the statute (loss of a subject, nominal group)	*The Statesman,* 14 Oct. '99
5.	Not for those who like to stay late in the office	Advertisement of computers, *TOI,* 26 Oct. '99
6.	Think Computer pride Inc.!!! Start an-e-bizness with Lee and Nee	*The Telegraph*, 21 Feb. 2000
7.	Wasn't sure Sachin's Physique would last (quoted from Kapil Dev's statement)	*The Telegraph,* 16 Nov. '99
8.	Ever wished you could get more done in a day?	"Sunday Review", Times Bank advertisement *TOI*, 21 Nov. '99
9.	Think your intelligent to know ur country...	Advertisement, *TOI,* 21 Nov. '99, p.16
10.	Can't buy me their love.	*The Telegraph,* 24 Nov. '99
11.	Dare to take the challenge?	"Ascent", *TOI*, 8.Feb. 2002
12.	Don't have a valentine?	Advertisement of a gift shop *TOI*, p.20, 13 Feb. 2000

Missing Auxiliary

1.	India willing to send soldiers to East Timor	*The Times of India,* 17 Sept. '99
2.	Watchdogs keeping tabs on sound parties	*TOI*, 13 Sept. '99
3.	India rushing MEA officials to Paris	*TOI*, 17 Sept. '99
4.	Fernandes lying, says Poll Panel	*TOI*, 21 Sept. '99
5.	Third Front Support a must for stable Govt.	*TOI,* 21 Sept. '99

6. No excess ballot papers printed for Bihar — *TOI*, 21 Sept. '99
7. Fake mark sheet gang busted in city — *TOI*, 6 Aug. '99
8. Kapil Dev appointed coach for two years — *TOI*, 22 Sept. '99
9. Harshad held guilty of Maruti funds misuse — *TOI*, 28 Sept. '99
10. Jeweller jailed for duping customer — *The Assam Tribune*, 30 Sept. '99
11. Sonia unfazed by risk to life — *The Times of India*, 28 Sept. '99
12. North Korea aiding Pakistan nuclear missile Plans — *TOI*, 30 Sept. '99
13. Harshad convicted of divesting Rs. 39 crore of Maruti funds. — *The Economic Times*, 28 Sept. '99
    Either there should have been an auxiliary verb or a punctuation mark to separate the subject in normal usage. Yet communication is not interrupted.
14. Calamity call Politically motivated — *The New Indian Express*, 3 Dec.'99, p.3
15. Rail link restored — *The New Indian Express*, 3 Dec '99.
16. Congress decimated in Orissa (Loss of both auxiliary and article, echoes the expression in mother tongue) — *TOI* 13 Oct. '99
17. Everybody doing his best in Orissa. — *TOI*, 22 Nov. '99
18. Ramesh not averse to becoming cup captain (loss of auxiliary and article) — *TOI*, 13 Oct. '99
19. Nitis Kumar Sworn in CM — *The Hindu*, 4 March 2000, p.1
    A case of auxiliary dropping and adverb (as) dropping.
20. They Done It — *India Today*, 13 Aug. 2001, p.36
    This is the title of a news story. The grammatical deviation (missing of 'have', or auxiliary dropping) is ignored keeping the message intact. That means the structure word seems to have less importance.

21.	North Korea aiding Pakistan nuclear, missile plans. It would have been "Pakistan's nuclear, missile Plans" in the normal, canonical English.	*TOI*, 30 Sept. '99
22.	BJP making inroads in many Assam areas The structure does not have the auxiliary verb required for strict canonical English, *e.g.* 'many areas of Assam' is changed to 'many Assam Areas'.	Seema Guha, *TOI*, 29 Sept. '99
23.	Sunita clinches third gold; Dalvir Shocked (on athletics)	*TOI*, 30 Sept. '99
24.	Yadavs meeting to demand larger share of OBC quota	*TOI*, 12 Dec. '99, p.10
25.	Policy statements outside House not a Privilege issue.	*TOI*, 10 Dec. '99, p.1

Anomaly in Preposition

1.	Switch to Context: "*Switch to* an LG Air Conditioner."	Advertisement of LG machine, *TOI*, April 2000 and frequently appearing in other newspapers.
2.	Clinton, Vajpayee discuss Pakistan over telephone. (Here the statement drops the preposition before 'Pakistan' although it is used before 'telephone').	*TOI*, 16 Oct. '99

Loss of Possessive

1.	Kargil blame on Army and RAW	*The Telegraph,* 10 Feb. 2000
2.	Basu bill, Naidu benevolence for Orissa There is a deviation that does not speak about Basu's bill and Naidu's benevolence and gives the pattern of N + N + N + N	*The Telegraph,* 17 Feb. 2000
3.	Sharif wife fails to rouse Protesters N + N (possessive case is dropped)	*The Telegraph,* 6 April 2000

4. Rabri Minister resigns — *TOI*, 21 Sept. '99
   Here, 'Rabri Devi's would have been the strict grammarian's structure.
5. Sharif case — *The Times of India*, 25 Nov. '99, *The Telegraph*, 25 Nov. '99 and so on.
   Dropping of the 'genitive'. This kind of dropping of the 'genitive' case is that of translation of the mother tongue structure.
6. Congress charge of NE neglect baseless — *The Times of India*, 28 Sept. '99
   The structure above has multiple deviations like:
   (i) Congress charge → It results in ambiguity. Whether it is the charge of Congress or Congress in charge of North East.
   There is a dropping of the possessive (genitive case).
   (ii) And dropping of the main verb; e.g. N-E neglect (is) baseless.
   (iii) 'North East neglect' could be written as 'The neglect of North East'. It is done so by translation of the mother tongue structure.
7. Atal breather in Clinton blow — *The Telegraph*, 15 Oct. '99
   (The caption does not put a verb).
8. Rabri rage after Governor's age axe — *The Telegraph*, 17 Nov. '99
   Loss of genitive in the first part, but in the second part it is intact. (Such anomaly may be reflected in the freedom of writing elsewhere).
9. Chasm in Sangh Parivar over Pope visit (no genitive) — *TOI*, 28 Oct. '99
10. Sonia mercy plea for Mother Nalini (loss of the possessive case) — *The Telegraph*, 19 Nov. '99
11. Nawaj Sharif defence team threatens to boycott case. — *TOI*, 9 Dec. '99, p.16
12. North Korea aiding Pakistan nuclear, missile plans. — *TOI*, 30 Sept. '99

It would have been "Pakistan's nuclear, missile Plans" in the normal, canonical English.

Loss of Conjunction/Punctuation

1. Nitis Kumar Sworn in CM (dropping 'as' and required punctuation) — *The Hindu*, 4 March 2000, p.1
2. Akai makes you an offer, you cannot refuse ! The exclamatory mark does not seem appropriate here and there is the need of a conjunction ('that' or 'which') for usual sentence structure. — *TOI*, 11 Oct. '99
3. Trade Unionism the most profitable business in West Bengal — *TOI*, 21 Nov. '99
4. If you have a passion for cars an exciting opportunity awaits you !! (also wrong use of the exclamatcry mark) — "Ascent", *TOI*, 27 Oct. '99

Redundance

At times wrong repetitions are used: — Front page news, *TOI*, 28 Feb. 2002

1. Karsevaks were returning back after a tow day stay in Ayodhya. It is redundant.

Interrogative structure

1. Suppose you have a headache ? (The interrogative form is not used so normally). — *The Telegraph*, 10 Oct. '99
2. Ever Seen TV like this ? (Imitates the interrogative structure in the mother tongue) — Advertisement of ONIDA TV, *TOI*, 5 Nov. '99

	Example	Source
3.	Don't have a valentine ? Lucky you	Advertisement of a gift shop *TOI*, 13 Feb. 2000, p.20
4.	Want to be a part of US based IT Company?	*The Telegraph*, 21 Feb. 2000
5.	Think e-profits?	*The Telegraph*, 21 Feb. 2000
6.	Think e-training?	*The Telegraph*, 21 Feb. 2000
7.	No takers for heritage fests ? (The verb phrase in the beginning is lacking)	*TOI*, 21 Nov. '99
8.	Can't take part in such breath taking excursion in real life?	Advertisement of Internet, *India Today*, 29 Nov. '99
9.	Life is beautiful? (echoes the mother tongue structure and so a deviation)	*TOI*, 27 Nov. '99

Use of Adjective and Noun

	Example	Source
1.	(i) The Good ol'days	*The Telegraph*, 29 Nov.'98
	(ii) The ol'E-mail (used in a trendy manner)	*The Times of India*, 24 Jan. 2000
2.	The rights and wrongs of bandhs	*TOI*, 5 Jan. '98
3.	The Hows and Whys of Korea's crisis.	Sidharth Varadarajan *TOI*
4.	India gets ministry Pakistan military The first part means 'Ministry formation of Indian Union'. The second one is not complete (the adjective phrase).	*The Statesmen*, 14 Oct. '99
5.	Captain courageous n adj This inversion is poetic (used in poetry, not in objective report of a newspaper)	Caption, *TOI*, 10 March 2000 (about Saurav Ganguly, the Indian Cricket Captain)

Compressed structures

	Example	Source
1.	Kashmiris' meeting with a difference (the meeting of Kashmiris)	*The Hindustan Times*, 12. Dec.'99
2.	UN-fair and Dangerous It refers to the United Nations and the unfair tendency it had towards	Editorial, *The Times of India* 7 Jan. '99

Sudan's plea. By syntactically deviating to coin an eye catching notion the title creates a strange structure to express both the things with economy.

3. PAN Masala — Editorial, *The Times of India* 7 Jan. '99
   It is also the same as its predecessor. 'Pan Masala' is an Indian coinage whereas the above structure using the popular collocation deviates linguistically as the content shows that it stands for Permanent Account Number. Acronymisation being the process it collocates with the native word.
4. NAM by - Pamby Reflex — Editorial, *TOI,* 5 Sept. '98
   The structure namby — pamby is exploited for another structure. That of the 'Non Aligned Movement' and the reaction of India critically towards the UN Secretary General's use of 'Kashmir' factor in its forum. Acronymisation works here too.
5. UN diplomatic Annan — Editorial, *TOI,* 30 Sept. '99
   By substitution, both 'United Nations', its Secretary General's 'undiplomatic quality' are associated, expressed through one deviated structure. The graphological deviation in all the similar cases cited can be treated as a syntactic deviation since it also results in a deviant structure of the language.
6. EU-phoric. — Editorial, *TOI*, 18 March '99
   Context: Not EU-phoric.
   It is exactly similar to the previous entrises. EU serves for both 'European Union' and a part of the world; 'Euphoric', 'Euphoria'.
7. Am-Bushed Again — Editorial, *TOI*, 1 Feb. 2002
   Refers to America (Am), ambushed by G.W. Bush (its President).
8. CATCH'EM YOUNG — *TOI*, 13 Dec. '99, p. 1
   (A reduced structure by metanalysis).

9.	A Misa-ppraisal [In fact the structure of the word 'misappraisal' is deviated and gives space to fit a proper name (Misa) in to it (that of Rabri Devi's daughter) to speak about the extravaganza and lavishness of her marriage]	N.R. Mohanty, *TOI*, 12. Dec. '99

Transitive/Intransitive

1.	'Who bares Wins' ('bare' is transitive but used otherwise).	*India Today*, 11 Oct. '99
2.	India win over Aussies ('win' also takes an object usually)	*TOI*, 8 Oct. '98

Change in word order

1.	It's politics stupid ! This is a case of conversion seen in the adjective phrase. "It's Stupid politics" would have been the normal expression.	*India Today*, 5 March 2001
2.	Do you know what the national anthem of Pakistan is ? The change of position of the verb 'is' (in the subordinate clause) makes the difference.	*TOI*, 25 June 2001
3.	Two-year term for sensitive posts ? 'The interrogative form is used in an unconventional sense to give freedom to the language user.	*TOI*, 25 June 2001
4.	Aussie Victory soured by Bevan Can attack The second line, 'Bevan can attack' becomes ambiguous which will be discussed in the next chapter. Structurally it would have been 'can attack to Bevan' in normal usage (a player hit by beer can)	*TOI*, 26 June 2001

Example	Source
5. "Rights violation" by chemical Industries (violation of rights).	*The New Indian Express,* 3 Dec. '99
6. It is a rights course. Written on 'Human rights', the structure could have been 'a course of rights' instead.	*The Telegraph* 29 Nov. '99
7. Congress charge of NE neglect baseless The structure above has multiple deviations like— (i) Congress charge → It results in ambiguity. Whether it is the 'charge of Congress' or 'Congress in charge of North East' create a confusion. There is a dropping of the possessive (genitive case), as cited before. (ii) And dropping of the main verb, *e.g.* 'N-E neglect is baseless'. (iii) 'North East neglect' could be written as 'The neglect of North East'. It is done so by translation of the mother tongue structure.	*The Times of India,* 28 Sept. '99
8. Like moths to their flames (It is a title, a subordinate clause which is incomplete in its address)	*Outlook,* 6 Sept. '99
9. Fly you to Singapore for instance (a deviation at the clause level, dropping a subject)	Ford Icon (car) advertisement *TOI,* 11 Oct. '99
10. IMF refuses aid till democracy restoration (means restoration of democracy)	*The Telegraph,* 14 Oct. '99
11. Credit where due (the clause replaces the position of elements)	Editorial, *The Telegraph,* 1 Nov. '99
12. Picnic no drives girl to death It replaces the structure; 'a no to picnic' Context : A girl, denied to go to Picnic, committed suicide.	*The Telegraph,* 14 Nov. '99
13. Lucky you Adjective + Pronoun	Advertisement of a gift shop *TOI,* p.20, 13 Feb. 2000

14.	How is Naveen *any different* from Sonia, ask Oriyas.	Prakas Nanda, *TOI*, 19 Feb. 2000
15.	Maurya it is for Clinton The structure 'It is Maurya for Clinton' is the usual one. ('Maurya' is the hotel where Clinton stayed)	*The Times of India*, 4 March 2000
16.	Policy statements outside House not a Privilege issue.	*TOI*, 10 Dec. '99, p.1
17.	Kashmiris' meeting with a difference (instead of 'meeting of Kashmiris')	*The Hindustan Times*, 12.Dec. '99
18.	'The Write Bureaucrats' It replaces the unambiguous structure; 'The Bureaucrats who write or the writer Bureaucrats' for economy.	*The Statesman*, 11 July '98
19.	The write police (like the above case)	Editorial, *TOI*, 25 Nov. '98
20.	Salmans run amok in MP	*The Telegraph*, 17 Oct. '98
21.	It sure is Ajay Devgan's year The reversal of the normal rule can be very well seen here. (for 'It is surely Ajay Devgan's year').	*TOI*, Feb. '98
22.	Mega Star, Philanthropist and hotelier he is This is a case of inversion of the subject and verb altering the normal order of the sentence.	*TOI*, 4 April 2000
23.	If you do fly on the wall thingy in a college canteen The normal structure is violated due to a change of noun into an adjective (thing-thingy).	*TOI*, 20 April 2002

The formal parameter ascertains a shift towards rapid Indianisation of the old British English structures and manifests it through the circulated English dailies of India.

The contextual semantic parameter (which is taken into account in the previous chapter and will be taken up in CH-6) examines the changes in meaning and certain structural changes if any that these newspapers have taken up to generate an Indian variety of idiomatic English. The impact is well perceived in the new figures of speech, replacement of old metaphoric, idiomatic, collocational terms by a set of new items. This is noted down in the next column.

New Figures of Speech and Proverbial Nature of Structures

The contextual semantic factor (discussed in the previous chapter) plays a dominant role in developing a new series of metaphors, collocations, idioms and phrases that look fresh, user friendly and suitable to the occasion. We may say, the strong socio-cultural pressures bring in such a change. New proverbs are generated by substituting words other than the existing ones. Code switching/mixing and personal creative experiment of the writer take the lead role in playing with the language. Structures are used whimsically, in an informal manner without any strong grammatical standing always. It has resulted in proverbialising the structure of newspaper English.

Items	*Source*
1. (i) go-getter (a person who is trendy)	(i) An advertisement of a professional company, *The Times of India*, 18 August '99.
(ii) The go-getters (successful) Context: "If you are a *go-getter...*"	(ii) *The Telegraph*, 21 Nov. '99
	(iii) *Cineblitz*, July 2001, p-49
2. "Differently-abled get awards" (Here in fact 'differently-abled' is used in substitution of 'disabled' when one gets into the context).	*The Times of India*, 19 Aug. '99.
3. Sense and Censorship The usual structure (known) *Sense and Sensibility*, a famous classic in English literature. To suit to the occasion 'Censorship' has substituted 'sensibility'.	Editorial, *The Times of India*, 27 Aug. '99
4. Saffron Sainiks don army berets The noun phrase 'Shiv Sainiks' is substituted by 'Saffron Sainiks'	*The Times of India*, 27 Aug. '99

5.	(i) More Error than Trial (Usually — 'Trial and Error') (ii) Not Black and white (Usually — Black and white) (iii) Uncivil Aviation (the normal use is 'Civil Aviation') All these cases are that of substitution to suit to the occasion.	*TOI*, 4 Feb. '97
6.	Dance with the Dragon (Since the Dragon stands for a particular religious symbol in China it is used as a proverb) This is a case of creating new proverb for the news about a particular country.	V.V. Paranjpe, *TOI*, 11 Aug. '99
7.	'Setting water, on Fire' (It is a new phrasal verb like 'setting fire') Set fire → set water	*The Times of India*, 13 Sept. '99
8.	'Phenk na jaldi phenk' Title of a news item. This is a case of code switch that results in a native language structure.	*TOI*, 26 Sept. '99
9.	'To the Aurangzebs' It is an Indian figure of speech, Aurangzeb being the metaphor for the conservative personality (against any form of art). So anyone who hates artistic pursuit is an Aurangzeb in India.	S. Kalidas, *India Today*, 6 Sept. '99
10.	Code of non-conduct (The usual expression is 'code of conduct'). It is done by the process of prefixation to validate another term.	*India Today*, 6 Sept. '99
11.	Kaamke Aadme Context: Vote for *Kaamke Aadme* (by code switch)	*TOI*, 4 Oct. '99
12.	Alice in Blunderland (The usual story is famous as 'Alice in Wonderland'). The process of compounding, substitution.	*TOI*, 4 Oct. '99

13. Find-outers — Meera Srivastava, *TOI*, 4 Oct. '99
    Context: 'The five find-outers'
    A phrasal verb (find out) is
    changed to a verb phrase.
    By suffixation it is generated.
14. Netbiz — *TOI*, 30 Oct. '99
    (like Showbiz),
    a new noun phrase (net business)
    comes up.
15. Reins of Power — *TOI*, 10 Oct. '99
    (also it can be rein to power)
    This is a metaphor of the horse trading
    in politics which by using the word
    'rein' suitably creates a new idiom.
    Other such metaphoric, specialised
    meanings are with the words:
    'ayes', 'neighs'
    Context: — *The Sunday Times*, 10 Oct. '99
    'Checkout the *ayes* and *neighs*'
    So *ayes and neighs* becomes another
    metaphor for the pros and cons
    of horse trading.
16. *Lucking out* — Editorial, *TOI*, 11 Oct. '99
    (It is a new phrasal verb
    standing for a chance of lucky
    guess, for politician,
    celebrities etc.)
17. Healing Ragas — Editorial, *TOI*, 13 Oct '99
    (a new verb phrase using both the
    codes, the British as well as the Indian).
18. The best of *Artha and Moksha* — *The Times of India*, 13 Oct. '99
    The above clause forms a
    composite structure, takes
    two words from different
    codes (Hindi) to form a
    separate noun phrase.
19. Line the pocket — Uttam Sengupta, *The Times of India*, 2 March '98
    Context: 'You line my pockets,
    I will stuff yours'.
    It is a new idiom for taking bribes.
20. 'Alliance air' — *TOI*, 8 March '98
    (This is a new coinage,
    that of a new idiom to stand for
    the political alliance in India today).

Example	Source
21. *Monkey around* *Monkeying around* (a new phrasal verb to mean worthlessly moving and gossiping around).	Advertisement, Thums up, *The Hindustan Times*, 19 March '98
22. Hype Hype Hurray instead of 'Hip Hip Hurray'	*TOI*, (editorial), 26 March '98
23. 'Silvery Tea' The writer also uses 'Silvery Welcome' (use of the idiom in an innovative way). Thus a new adjective phrase is generated.	*The Asian Age*, 31 March and 1 April '98
24. Ram Rajya (The ideal government and political system as famous in the Indian psyche).	*The Times of India*, 9 June '98
25. Milking Democracy (pejorative use, means making people fool by false shows)	Editorial, *The Times of India*, 27 Oct. '98
26. The write Bureaucrats The above instance can be utilised as an adjective phrase/verbal phrase It is also discussed before. Instead of writing 'Writer bureaucrat', the writer uses such a structure.	*The Statesman*, 11 July, '98
27. Melody in its own write On a lyricist's poetry. This is also a similar use of the verbal.	*The New Indian Express*, 20 June '99
28. (i) Gill's eye view	(i) Editorial, *The Assam Tribune*, 23 Oct '98
(ii) Child's eye view The original idiom Bird's eye view is altered to suit to other occasions which is a liberal use.	(ii) *The Economic Times*, (special review), 17-23 Nov. '99
29. Zara yaad karo lyricist Ko bhi A total code switch of the structure.	Headlines, *The Times of India*, 13 July '98

30.	Prime Minister ban gaya President (code mix) Here the term 'bangaya' takes the role of a verb to suit to the SVO structure.	Title of a special report, *The Times of India,* 6 July '98
31.	Ho gayi Balle balle Here the cultural ethos (Punjabi) is reflected in the structure.	Sunday Review, *The Times of India,* 19 July '98
32.	Cook in Used as a new phrasal verb This is a regular column too in the newspaper.	*The Times of India*, 3 Jan. '98
33.	Survival of the hippest (on the Disco world) A case of substitution of the old proverbial structure, 'Survival of the fittest'. And 'hippest' comes from 'hippy' by suffixation.	Sunday Review, *TOI,* 4 Jan. '98
34.	Dressing Down (The structure, a phrasal verb stands for nudity), 'stripping off' is usually used for the same.	*The Times of India,* 29 Nov. '98
35.	In a Deep Blue mood also a 'deep blue technology' The adjective phrase is strange and new.	*The Times of India,* 12 October '97
36.	Dilli Door Ast (Code switch)	Editorial, *TOI,* 4 January '98
37.	Hair we go (on hair and louse problem of school children), sounds strange but assertive.	*TOI,* 14 Dec. '97
38.	Sab ka Kalyan (Code switch of the medium)	Editorial, *The Times of India,* 10 Nov. '99
39.	(i) Saffron halo (new phrase that means the rise of a political wing)	(i) *The Times of India,* 25 Oct. '98
	(ii) Saffron Sweep (new phrase that stands for	(ii) *The Telegraph,* 6 Oct. '99

the sweep of the same
political wing)
(iii) Saffron brigade — (iii) *TOI,* 12 Oct. '99

40. The details man — *India Today,* 8 Nov. '99

41. (i) bore Karna
accent marna
line lagana
service karna
(Phrasal Verbs that are created by mixing verb roots of one language with the operators from another language).
Also he speaks about 'maroed', 'gappoing', 'bajaoing' (new verb forms) that comc by suffixation.
— Puneet G. Singh, New Age Speak, *The Telegraph,* 28 May '96

(ii) Fielding Karna
It means waiting for the victim to arrive, obviously a phrase from the underworld (code mix) and
Game Bajana
(it is an underworld lingo too for killing someone).
— Shabnam Minwalla, "of cutting and kauva", *The Sunday Times of India,* 14 Nov. '99

The writer says the above phrases have come from the street talk in Mumbai and is so frequent and popular there that they create a mode, a medium of their own.

42. (i) Pressure cooker politics
(A catchy phrase in recent times) — (i) *The Times of India,* Editorial, 12 Aug. '98
(ii) Pressure cooker world. — (ii) An interview with Bernard Kalb by Rachna Barman, *The Times of India,* 15 March '99

43. Trial by Terror
By a process of substitution, the old proverb 'Trial and error' is replaced. Alliteration tempts for such a change in the expression to suit to the specific need.
— *The Times of India,* 12 August '98

44. Our *mai baap* Sarkar understands only two codes — Madhu Kiswar, *The Times of India,* 2 Aug. '98
This usage is purely Indian and very popular which is a title like the British English 'His Excellency'. This epithet is new to our Indian English canon.

45. (i) De after De — (i) *The Times of India,* 30 August '98
(ii) Children's De — (ii) *Sunday Times of India,* 14 Nov. '99
(iii) Memorial De — (iii) Jug Suraiya, *TOI*, 4 Oct. '98
It is a deliberate replacement of the term 'day' in order to hint at the writer Shobha De who is associated with the news items.

46. UN-fair and Dangerous — Editorial, *The Times of India,* 7 Jan. '99
It refers to the United Nations and the unfair tendency it had towards Sudan's plea. By syntactically deviating to coin an eye catching notion the title creates a strange structure to express both the things with economy.

47. PAN Masala — Editorial, *The Times of India,* 7 Jan. '99
It is also the same as its predecessor. 'Pan Masala' is an Indian coinage whereas the above structure using the popular collocation deviates linguistically as the content shows that it stands for Permanent Account Number. Acronymisation being the process it collocates with the native word.

48. NAM by — Pamby Reflex — Editorial, *TOI* 5 Sept.'98
The structure 'namby-pamby' is exploited for another structure. That of the 'Non Aligned Movement' and the reaction of India critically towards the UN Secretary General's use of 'Kashmir factor, in its forum. Acronymisation works here too.

49. *Tels of Terror* — Jug Suraiya, *TOI,* 6. Sept. 98
It is suggestive of 'tales of terror'. In fact it combines the usual structure as above and the word 'Tel' to hint at the oil crisis then.

50. (i) Garibi hatao hataoed Garib The first one is a common structure used by politicians in this country, popularly used since the time of Mrs. Indira Gandhi, our late Prime Minister. The second one is its parodied version today (expelling the poor from all spheres of public life).	Jug Suraiya, *TOI,* 6. Sept. 98
51. (i) No asha ki kiran (title news) (ii) bachchon ka jail (code mix) In the structure 'asha ki kiran', 'asha' collocates with 'kiran' which is popularly known to Indians.	*TOI*, 30 August '98
52. Will the Censors Zakhm Puja Bhatt? The sentence deviates from the pattern by using an Indian word all of a sudden (the role of a verb here), hinting at the title of her film *Zakhm*. A case of code mix.	*The Telegraph,* 8 Nov. '98
53. The Dhamaka season The adjective phrase uses both the Indian and British codes here. A case of code mix where Dhamaka stands for sound of crackers in Deewali.	Seema Bassi, *TOI*, 1 Sept. '98
54. On your Marx Get set Go? This is a structural change of the old stereotype proverb 'On your March, Get set, go'. Here the content is on the leftist (Marxist) notions across thc world, its status today. It substitutes new proverbial elements.	*The Times of India*, 25 Oct. '98
55. Excess of sorrow laughs It seems to be a new proverb.	Susan Davis *The Times of India,* 23 Oct. '98
56. Playing Santa Clause to the market It is a new usage of the old idea on 'Santa Clause to the globalised market situation.'	*The Economic Times*, 26 Oct. '98
57. DAM IT, MIX IT, FIX IT It is an advertisement where the stress is just on the proverbial looking structure echoing the other old advertisement of Hero Honda; 'Fill it, Shut it, Forget it'.	*The Times of India,* 26 Oct. '98

58. Polls Do Pyaza
Such a structure is appropriately constructed by the editor to hint at the idea of politicians making food of certain issues for the polls and other vested interests. So a food metaphor is manipulated into such a structure like that of 'Chicken Do Pyaza'.
Editorial, *The Times of India*, 26 Oct. '98

59. (i) Cook in
A regular feature in *The Sunday Times of India* (already noted before)
(ii) What is cooking in Brunei
Title news, *The Times of India*, 21 Sept. '98

In this case the user again solves two things together. He talks about Robin Cook, Foreign Secretary, U.K. and his negotiation in Brunei on political matters.
But the use of the phrasal verb is new. 'Cook up' has been an usual expression. 'Cook in' is a new coinage.

60. Viva viagra (it echoes Viva-voce)
A case of substitution that creates a new expression.
The *Times of India*, 24 Sept. '98

61. (i) Sahib, Biwi aur Ghulam
Now it can be used as a popular Indian proverb getting proper weightage in English.
Names can be changed but the proverb remains the same.
R.K. Laxman, *The Times of India*, 27 Sept. '98
Here he refers to Laloo Yadav (Ex-C.M. of Bihar), present C.M. Rabri Devi, and the government they run.
(ii) Sahib, Biwi, Ghulam
It refers to
Sahib Singh Verma (Ex-C.M. of Delhi), Sushma Swaraj (C.M. of Delhi after Sahib Singh was dethroned).

62. Et Tu Ranga
A case of substitution that fits into a different name (Power Minister Rangarajan Kumaramangalam) in the place of 'Brutus' in *Julius Ceasar* and the famous remark : 'Et tu Brute'.
This is how Indianisation of British English proverb takes place.
Editorial, *The Times of India*, 4 Oct. '98

63.	In search of Zamin and Aasman Actually 'Zamin Aasman' is a catch phrase in Indian context used popularly to suggest totality of existence, contradictions in life etc. This is a case of code mix. ('Zamin' stands for reality, 'Aasman' for dreams. 'Zamin' for one end, 'Aasman' for the other end).	*TOI*, 1 March, '99, an interview with the Urdu poet Nida Fazli
64.	"Kill-kill, bang-bang and the baba log" It sounds proverbial on violence. Appropriate collocational terms come together (on violence and criminalisation).	Nikhat Kazmi, *TOI*, 5 Dec. '98
65.	Do Mulk, Ek Dil Code switch takes place, which speaks on Indo-Pak relation. It is an expansion of the catchy slogans into the English media in the original, local, Indian version.	Miriam D'Souza, *TOI*, 18 March '99
66.	Zoom in on Home in on Homing in on Such phrasal verbs are a case of substitution, applying the formula from 'bank in on', 'Cash in on' etc.	Ratnottama Sengupta, *TOI*, 24 Oct. '99
67.	Tie in knot Digvijay Singh *ties* himself in *knots* Here 'ties the knot' refers to 'dealing in troubles' which is a special use (deviated) from the original idiom (marriage).	*The Statesman*, 14 Oct. '99
68.	Buckle under A new phrasal verb that means 'at a state of'. Context: BJP *buckles under* Sena threat.	*The Statesman*, 16 Oct. '99
69.	Marketing Karishma A case of fusion (code mix), 'Karishma' means miracle.	Kanwaldeep Singh *TOI*, 10 Oct. '99

70. Cumeuppance — Editorial, *TOI*, 11 Oct. '99
Context : Laloo's comeuppance.
Here a whole clause is compressed into one term by metanalysis(coming up chance).

71. *age axe* — *The Telegraph,* 17 Nov. '99
Context: "Governor's age axe"
It refers to Governor's sacking of a minister due to under age.
The phrase can be manipulated otherwise also. Example : 'honesty axe', 'tax axe', 'equality axe' and so on.

72. (i) *Super Cyclone*
'Super Cyclone' is a phrase used by weathermen and opposing cricket sides to describe the experience of being battered and blown away by an event. So it serves the purpose of both a word and a structure.

(a) All national, regional English newspapers and journals coined it, especially for the Orissa Cyclone since it is of a greater magnitude. Newspapers like *The Times of India, The Telegraph, The Statesman* between 28-29 Oct.'99, till 23 Nov. '99 and afterwards.

(ii) *Coal Tender*
Short form of 'Coalition Tender', with the coalition rule literally coming to rule. It refers to the one who can keep the engine of state running.

(b) Also *India Today,* 22 Nov. '99 gives a list of new phrases, one of which is this one, says Dilip Bobb. He says these new phrases are to be used now in the next millennium and *The New India Dictionary* contains this phrase.

(iii) *Readership qualities*
It says, the latest qualification to become the Prime Minister of India is to become a good reader (ironically)
Context : the CWC resolution that 'Readers' should be leaders in India, referring to Sonia Gandhi, reading Hindi in Roman script appropriately. It becomes a new idiom that way.

(c) *The Times of India* (20 Nov. '99) also reveals that this term 'Super Cyclone' is coined only after seeing the severity of the storm in Orissa by weather personnel and henceforth the phrase would be used for a cyclone of more than 200 km. wind speed.

(iv) *Walk-in Heads*
The new phrase has replaced the old phrase 'talking heads'

(d) Dilip Bobb, (for i, ii, iii, iv, v, vi, vii) *India Today*, 22 Nov. '99 that gives the list of all these.

which stood for the leaders in TV interviews. There have been so many of them in election time that it is like 'walk-in interviews', 'walk in heads'.
It is a case of substitution.

new phrases used by media at present and hopes they will be used more in times to come.

(v) *Beti Noire*
The thing that the opposition is worried about in Priyanka Gandhi; her 'Beti'.

(vi) *Coup de Grace*
It means the final blow, the death of democracy, used so by all countries except in Pakistan where it means a military take over uniformly acceptable.

(vii) *Skin flick*
The original use was pornographic in nature. Now it is used to describe any Bollywood movie, as now instead of the heroine showing lots of chest, it's now the hero who does that.

73. Shoot out — *The Telegraph,* 19 Nov. '99
The actual, original meaning of the phrasal verb is associated with gun, or a penalty shoot out. The context here uses it in cricket to mean bowling.
Context: Aussies shoot out Pak for 222

74. Pump into — *The Times of India,* 19 Nov. '99
The original use meant 'with great effort', 'to put a lot of money' etc.
Here it is used relating to bullets.

Example:
"The gunmen pumped bullets into Singh's chest".

75. Henna — *The Telegraph,* 20 Nov. '99
(used as a verb).
Context: "You can henna your hair"
whereas *The Oxford Dictionary's* 'Indian Supplement' only speaks about it as a noun.

76. Tailenders
Context: "Opening for the tailenders."

This is a deviated use of the phrase since the dictionary speaks of 'tailend' and only as the last part of something. Here it is referred to persons.

The Telegraph, 19 Nov. '99, and used always for the players of cricket who come to play in the lower order.

77. Cyber Shakha
The Phrase uses a mix up of British English and Indian word (relates to the RSS wing).
Context : "Net savvy RSS gets first cyber-shakha"

The Times of India, 26 Sept. '99

78. Took-taak
This phrase stands for smuggling.
Context : "Life along the Indo-Bangla hinges on *took-taak* deals".

TOI, 28 Sept. '99

79. UN diplomatic Annan
Process of substitution, since both 'United Nations', its Secretary General's 'undiplomatic quality' are associated, expressed through one deviated structure. The graphological deviation in all the similar cases cited can be treated as a syntactic deviation since it also results in a deviant structure of the language.

Editorial, *TOI*, 30 Sept. '99

80. (i) Pujor gaan
(a typical Bengali phrase related to Dussehra).
Context: The lost strain of *Pujor gaan* (code mix).

TOI, 6 Oct. '99

(ii) Pujor Shubhechcha
An advertisement of Thomson TV introduces such structures at the time of Dussehra (so it is time specific).

The Assam Tribune, 5 Oct. '99

81. Kattar Hindus
An Indian phrase to substitute the idea of fundamentalist Hindu. 'Kattar' stands for 'a staunch supporter', 'fanatic'.

Swami S. Aiyar, *TOI*, 10 Oct. '99

82. Who cares about elections? — *TOI,* 30 Oct. '99
I *wanna* party.
(The Americanised structure is used for its popularity in the young and globalised generation.)

83. Benazir insists her wealth is not *ill-gotten* — *TOI,* 12 Oct. '99
[The Americanised structure (past participle) is used].
And IE is a mixture of all languages, that is why it accepts any such usage on the body of newspapers.

84. (i) Bash — (i) *TOI*, 14 Oct. '99
The use of 'bash' is frequent in all newspapers in the positive sense whereas the dictionary meaning is pejorative except in the phrasal verbs.
Bash away
bash with
bash on
The context shows that it is used as a noun and in a positive sense which is a deviation; "Cuttack Cultural bash beginning from October 15."
(ii) bashes — (ii) *The Telegraph,* 10 Oct. '99
(in plural form of the noun, also used in a positive sense).
This is a liberal use of the term.

85. Swearing out
It is certainly influenced by 'swearing in' which gives a new structure. — *TOI,* 14 Oct. '99
Context: Two cartoons displayed.
It writes: Atal Vajpayee (swearing in)
Nawaj Sharif (Swearing out);
(Pakistan P.M. Nawaj Sharif's ouster happens when Vajpayee takes oath of office in India).

86. Cyclone Politics — *TOI*, 21 Nov. '99, p. 8
It has become a 'catch phrase' and used so at the backdrop of the Super Cyclone in Orissa.
It weakens the leg pulling politics of politicians over the issue of the Cyclone.

Context: "Cyclone Politics takes over Orissa". (Title of the news item)

87. Flat out [used as a phrasal verb to mean projected flatness (TV here) of something] Context: 'Flat out gorgeous'. — Advertising of Philips TV, *The Times of India,* 26 Nov. '99

88. Phoney connection It stands for the concept of 'recommendations' in contemporary times through telephone between highly connected people in highly placed establishments. — *The Times of India,* 29 Nov. '99

89. 'In order not to' The new collocational rule of changing the place of the elements of the old structure is seen. Context: "Though Mr. Vajpayee insisted that he deliberately chose to see the affected areas from air in order not to disrupt relief and rehabilitation measures..." — *TOI*, 28 Oct. '99

90. To cap it Context: "Prof. Amartya Sen gets one to cap it all on getting the post of 'Master' of Trinity College". — *Outlook*, 26 Jan. '98

91. Do-gooders Context: "Our do-gooders" The V+N structure is changed into a new noun (N). — Tara Sinha in "The Joy Luck Club" *The Times of India*,. 14 Feb. 2000, p-12

92. Fisc out of water Fisc stands for 'fiscal' and water here refers to the 'crisis'. But it follows the old proverbial pattern — 'Fish out of Water', suggesting 'lonely', 'isolated'. — *The Telegraph,* 18 Feb. 2000

93. Adam — teasing In the model of 'eve-teasing', this new term is deliberately coined by the writer to suit to the modern day trend of girls teasing boys. — Dhara Kothari, *The Sunday Times of India,* 27 Feb. 2000

94. Ulta Pulta — Editorial, *TOI*, 28 Jan. 2002
    A commonly used phrase used for 'confusion' and 'mess up' in Indian culture.
95. aman kee seedee — *The Sunday Times of India*, 27 Jan. 2002
    It stands for 'ladder of peace', like 'ladder of success'.
    This structure is used in a sentence without italicization, giving it a very normal ambience irrespective of its linguistic variation.
    Context: "... will provide New Delhi with a splendid opportunity to construct an aman kee seedee..."
96. EU-Phoric — Editorial, *TOI*, 18 March '99
    Context: 'Not EU-Phoric'
    It is exactly similar to that of item no. 46, 47, 48 in this chapter.
    'EU' serves for both 'European Union' and a part of the word : 'Euphoric' or 'Euphoria'.
97. Am-Bushed Again — Editorial, *TOI*, 1 Feb. 2002
    Refers to America (Am), being ambushed by George W. Bush
98. Kiska band bajega? — *The New Indian Express*, 24 Feb. 2002
    (code switch and proverbial in nature).
99. 'Please to be thoda waiting' — *TOI*, 20 Feb. 2002
    This is a twist in the normal syntactic order.

Summary

Though it is not a radical transformation of English structural patterns that we find in the English dailies in India, a smooth drive towards frequent code mixing, proverbialising, functional English is evident throughout all such newspapers. By professing agreement deviation, liberal use of preposition, phrasal verbs, articles, punctuation and idioms suitable to situation, the writers give a valid specimen of English to be beneficial to students and other language practitioners. In the wake of an interest in Indian roots in historical, cultural, civilisational research, it is worthwhile to note that this linguistic experimentation adds heavily towards a specialised, well researched variety of Indian English in future.

REFERENCE

1. T.C. Baruah, *The English Teacher's Handbook* (New Delhi: Sterling Publishers Pvt. Ltd., 1984).

Chapter - 6

SEMANTIC CHANGE AND NEW MEANINGS IN JOURNALISTIC WRITING

We have already analysed the morpho-syntactic change in the body of newspaper writing. The new entries move in a direction of their own. They form a new chain of meaning. Many new words and structural variation clearly strike a semantic shift.

Focus

We categorise a number of such expressions that flood journalistic writing with the exact contextual meaning they refer to strengthening the communicative, functional nature of English in our society.

Meaning at the Grammatical Level

Broadly the form of language has two categories of meanings to be grammatically appropriate.

(i) The structural meaning which refers to the composite meaning coming out of the whole structure: a sentence, clause, phrase or so.

(ii) The lexical meaning that refers to the individual word meaning.

For example, a sentence can be seen as below:

A	young	man	eloped	with	a	pretty	woman.
det	adj.	N	V	Prep.	det.	adj.	N

It is patterned in a systematic order to communicate a message. It speaks about the grammatical pattern of the sentence only. However, our task here is to see the meaning change at the contextual level and not at the structural level.

Patterns of Meaning at the Contextual Level

By this we mean the socio-cultural and individual perception of the meaning of a structure or of words. Over the ages words have changed their meanings and this is a gradual and growing process. With the stress on the individuality and identity of ethnic, regional cultures, changing economic and political processes the words and structures used in the journalistic register seem to carry confusing and multifarious meanings. The newspaper columnists, editors, writers deliberately use words and structures in such a way that they produce a strange and unique message of their own. Through that they attach their own affiliation to specific culture, society and ways of living in to the language. This can be termed as the 'lexico-social', 'semantico-cultural' pattern of language usage which they strive for. The linguistic structure as well as the social structure contribute to such a change of meaning as each (the British English and the Indian English) functions in a cultural setting different from that of the other.

A large corpus of such Indian English as used in the newspapers would definitely give a feel of the cultural notions here and the special meanings that can be derived from them. This study doesn't merely aim at identifying the exact differences between the British English and Indian English but to point out the deviant use relating to the socio-semantic scale which affirms the view that Indian English as it is used in the body of the newspapers, imposes a burden on British English as a result of which there is a shortening of the distance between the English language (as it was previously thought to be elitist) and its Indian users. We cite an example here:

"Ram before Rambo in millennium English".

'Ram' stands for the representative Indian hero. 'Rambo' stands for the representative British hero. The concept of 'Ram' here points at the whole gamut of Indian words, concepts that have been acceptable to English dictionaries of the language in general. The contextual, social scale on which the meaning operates can be divided broadly into certain categories (*The Telegraph*, 22 Nov. '99).

Conceptual meaning

Contextual level categorises itself into different modes, one of which is the conceptual meaning attached to the words and structures of a speech community. The community of people who speaks the same language is known as a speech community. In this case meanings are arbitrarily attached to the words, events and are so described in dictionaries. They refer to the underlying ideas of the speech community about the words.Then comes the idea of 'grammatical word' (the word divided by spaces), for example, a word like 'make' refers to an arbitrarily chosen meaning, but it constitutes another unit of meaning when it gets combined with other grammatically appropriate units as in 'make out' (to understand). Similar is the case with 'cash' and 'cash in on'. The first one is shared under conceptual meaning whereas the combination is out of its reach.

Cultural meaning

As has already been pointed out, the cultural ethos of a community or a country gets reflected in the language which can be comprehended by that community. The same words may refer to different meanings in different societies. The words 'party', 'dinner', 'meeting' (in western sense — a prior scheduled meeting), 'father', 'mess' have such differences in meaning relating to the respective societies.

Individual meaning

When the individual interacts with himself he has his own identity with words and concepts and he understands them in his own ways. It may not always have parallel response to that of the reader or outsider. Also to the outside world he may respond in his own ways of understanding. A 'cat' may strike a note of compassion; 'pretty', 'fondness' to one whereas it may seem to be 'cunning', 'opportunistic' to someone else. Similarly important institutions and events like marriage, festivals, trends like globalisation, market economy may also be perceived in different perspectives. The newspaper columns come heavily loaded with such individual meaning attached to the words very often. An apt example can be cited: "Duel Personalities" (on Sushma Swaraj and Sonia Gandhi, *India Today*, Sept. '99).

The other varieties

Apart from all these there are varieties, the dialects (the regional variety of a language), the registers (particular use of a language relating to a common profession, institution) which have their special meanings and get reflected in the newspapers and journals.

The Semantic Structure of English

The words having the same semantic component belong to a "Semantic Set". The set has one lexical word which can be used for all other components and their distinctive meanings.

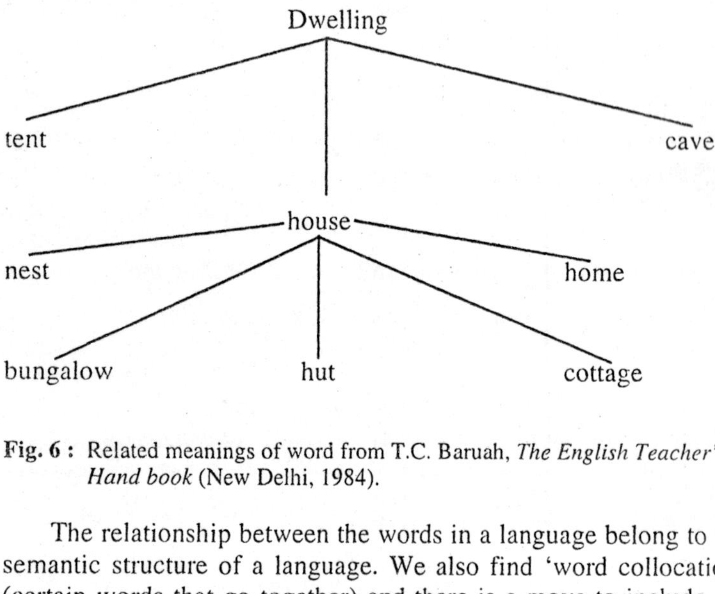

Fig. 6 : Related meanings of word from T.C. Baruah, *The English Teacher's Hand book* (New Delhi, 1984).

The relationship between the words in a language belong to the semantic structure of a language. We also find 'word collocation' (certain words that go together) and there is a move to include the Indian collocations having their special meanings in the newspaper columns.

Some Principles on Semantic Theory

Semantics is taken as a science of symbolism by critics like I.A. Richards and C.K. Ogden[1] in *The Meaning of Meaning*:

"...words may come between us and our objects in countless subtle ways, if we do not realize the nature of their power. In logic... they lead to the creation of bogus entities, the universals, properties and so forth...". It seems the writers do not prescribe the patterns of logic to the patterns of writing English in certain fields like creative work of art, personal discourse. And journalistic discourse is no longer objective, stereotype chronology of events. So such a theory well suits to the requirements of the author for multifarious meanings. Another critic, Wheelwright, suggests a positive term for this multifariousness of meaning to add to the richness of it, *i.e.* plurisignation.[2] In *Philosophy of Rhetoric* (1996)[3], I.A. Richards points out about the new medium of meaning, the new rhetoric:

".. the old Rhetoric treated ambiguity as a fault in language, and hoped to confine or eliminate it; the new Rhetoric sees it as an inevitable consequence of the power of language and as an indispensable means of most of our important utterances". He again adds, "language is a social fact as well as a part of personal experience".[4] Richards is of the view that most of our important discourse is not technically scientific. So it has to be ambiguous. In non-technical discourse words "must shift their meanings". If they did not, "language, losing its subtlety with its suppleness, would lose also its power to serve us."[5]

The Classfocation and Change in Meaning

The change of meaning depends upon manifold factors[6] of which the chief ones are noted below:

Generalisation

This is a frequently seen factor. Usually we generalise about meaning of certain words. For example, 'Journey' and 'Journal' are from the same source 'jour' (from French) which means 'day'. But literally 'journal' means (i) a diary, (ii) a book in which a business firm records its daily transactions whereas 'journey' means a day's ride or walk. Similarly 'companion' (meant a person with whom one shares the bread) and 'comrade' (meant who shares a room with one) have developed the same meaning in modern usage.

Specialisation

To read meant 'to guess a riddle' and to write meant 'to scratch' whereas these meanings acquired new notions gradually. Today by specialisation and restriction of meaning such notions have changed their response. Similar is the case with 'fundamentalism' (a narrower meaning has been attached now a days); that of a 'non-conformist', 'prohibit' etc.

Differentiation, extension

'To give one a ring' (to telephone), 'to drop a line' (a letter), words like 'board', 'book' etc. have the previous qualities like generalisation and specialisation but there is a kind of extension of meaning in them.

Association of ideas

We associate certain ideas to some people like in case of 'a tramp'. Although a tramp moves from place to place, we use it for a person of shabby, careless nature too. It is semi-metaphoric in use.

Affective meaning, colouring

Some words are designed, coloured with an emotional appeal to mean something else. 'Victorian' carries a pejorative meaning. And 'enthusiasm' had a pejorative meaning in 18th century.

Loss of colouring

The opposite has also happened; words like 'politics', 'policy', 'politician' were suggestive of dishonesty to Shakespeare's time and the notion is lost today.

Metaphoric

In every language words are used in figurative, metaphoric ways. This is a field in which writers experiment much evolving new set of metaphors to suit to the occasion. Silly, stupid, dull etc. are used with figurative force from time to time.

Euphemism

Every language has its euphemistic words. Pass away (die), kick the bucket (die) and so on. This is an area in which writers carry on their use of new euphemistic words. For example, in Indian politics 'Saffronite' is a word which defines a person having an alliance with the RSS or VHP and is supposed to be a fanatic.

Reversal of meaning

'To scan' meant reading carefully initially, which today means reading rapidly and a little unenthusiastically.

False euphemism

Some writers use false sense of idealising and creating words instead of the actual word. 'Lavatory' originated as an euphemism which is used as a normal word today. So is the case of 'handkerchief', 'toilct' etc.

Misunderstanding

'Premises' referred to property in legal usage. Now we use it as a house, a building etc. 'Preposterous' means a person intolerably absurd to us today. That was not its actual meaning when it originated. It referred to 'an absurd situation a professional or any person may fall into'. Similarly 'emergency' referred to something that emerged suddenly. The meaning is not so today.

Proper names being used as parts of speech

In course of time the names of persons have acquired a different stature. Example: words like 'guy' (originally Guy Fewkes — a notorious man), 'dunce' (Duns Scotus — the medieval philosopher) etc. The above mentioned categories of meaning have been taken from the analysis of F.T. Wood from which one can easily draw the view that change of meaning is the nature of any language. So many of the words used in journalistic English subscribe to these factors and many are influenced by the local, regional, national factors of a respective country where the English language is used.

"There is a challenge to the standard English", says F.T. Wood[7] as the respective elitist language of a particular social class. The concept of standard English will vary from time to time depending upon the social contexts in which the language is operating.

Conceptual meaning[8]

This has been discussed before too. And it is observed here that for the analysis of any sentence we need to establish a 'phonological', 'syntactic' and 'semantic' representation. Conceptual meaning interprets the meaning of the sentence which is different from all other meanings in the same language and that goes like:

Semantics (C) -----------→ Syntax (B) -------------→ Morphology (A)
[while encoding a message]
Morphological (A)--------------→ Syntactic (B) -------------→ Semantic (C)
[while decoding a message]

It is denotative, logical and cognitive. So conceptual meaning is an essential and enextricable part of the language.

Example: '+ Human, + adult, - male' is the conceptual meaning of a 'Woman'.

Connotative meaning

It is the meaning which exists by reference to something over the conceptual meaning. This meaning is open ended unlike the previous one; a 'woman' may refer to someone who is shy, feminine and so on, depending on the views of the writer and the reader.

Social and affective meaning

It is the recognition of the meaning at the social level and stylistic level of the reader and the writer. It is dialectal, the meaning might speak about the geographical origin of the speaker, the writer reader relation about the 'Status' of the language in use, which may be formal, literary, colloquial etc.The affective meaning speaks the feelings and attitude of the speaker, writer. Affective meaning depends, often associates itself with conceptual, connotative meaning.

Reflected and collocative meaning

Reflected meaning comes out of multiple conceptual meaning, says Leech, where one sense of the word creates our response to another sense. Words like intercourse, ejaculation, erection, cock are taboo words. Since their use often takes the sexual connotation into account collocative meaning is the meaning out of association of the word with its environment.

'Pretty woman' and 'handsome woman' both are suggestive of good-looking women, although taken their collocational property, they suggest different kinds of attractiveness; 'pretty woman' referring to a cute, loving woman whereas 'handsome woman' is suggestive of an assertive, strong willed and smart lady.

Associative meaning

It covers all the meanings discussed before except the 'conceptual meaning' since the later is specific in its representation of the language and the human species. Associative meaning comes out of our experiences which relate us to the meanings we draw. It is more variable and is concerned with the differences rather than the commonness of the analyses or understanding of individuals. It is the meaning established by contrast.

Thematic meaning

It is the meaning that the writer or speaker arranges, organizes through the message. For example between an active and a passive sentence, the stress and focus of the meaning vary. The emphasis changes from one to the other in the process.

Example: "The Professor addressed the conference".
(Here the emphasis is on the 'Professor').
"The conference was addressed by the Professor."
(Here the emphasis is on the 'conference').

The seven types of meaning are categorised in a diagrammatic way here:

1. Conceptual Meaning		Logical, denotative cognitive.
Associative meaning (2-6)	2. Connotative meaning	The idea communicated by virtue of what it refers to.
	3. Social meaning	What is communicated of the social circumstances of the language use.
	4. Affective meaning	What is communicated out of the feelings, attitudes of the writer/speaker.
	5. Reflected meaning	What is communicated through association with sense of the same expression.
	6. Collocative meaning	What is communicated through association with words which tend to occur in the environment of another word.
7. Thematic meaning		What is communicated in terms of order and emphasis of the message (its organisation).

Fig.7 : Seven types of meaning from Geoffrey Leech, *Semantics* (Harmondsworth and Middlesex, 1974).

The semantic knowledge fulfils the social needs through a number of stages.[9] Language functions in certain ways such as:

1. Informational — Passing the information neutrally.
   (Uses the conceptual meaning)
2. Expressive — Communicating the writer's feelings and attitudes.
   (It uses the affective meaning)
3. Directive function —That tries to influence the behaviour or attitude of others. It deals with commands and requests. So like the previous one it also gives less importance to the conceptual meaning and tries to mean more connotatively and affectively.
4. Aesthetic function — Although the language of poetry and other arts involve the expressive function, a separate status is given to it through this function which stresses the communication between the reader and the writer to as many avenues, variations as possible. A heightened sensitivity is at work here.

5. Phatic function — It keeps the communication open, meaning at the lightest and not the heightened level as in the aesthetic function. It fulfils the requirement of keeping the social relations intact.

But a piece of language does not always just express one function but uses a number of them although its orientation may be towards one.

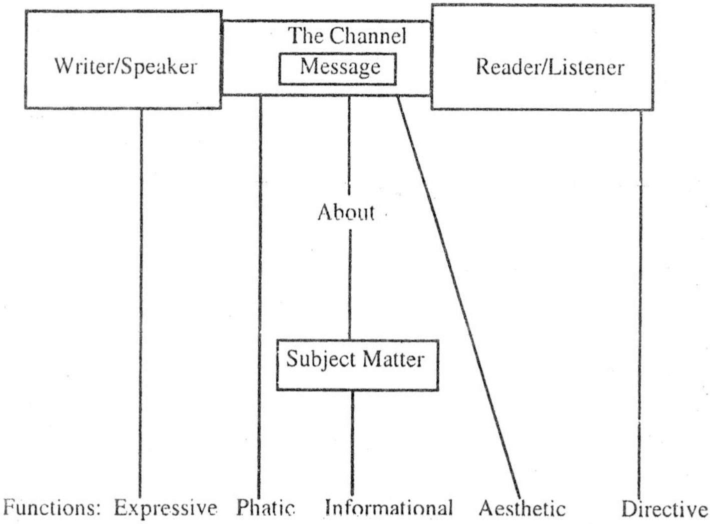

Fig. 8 : Functions of meaning in language from Geoffrey Leech, *Semantics* (Harmondsworth and Middlesex, 1974).

Meaning Content in Journalistic English

The newspaper variety of English constitutes more or less a separate meaning content very often. We can categorise it under the column of 'Associative Meaning'. But our interest is that how far the message succeeds in deciphering the intended meaning which one learns from it to utilize in the fields, day to day use of English. Getting deviated from the prescribed meaning types, they influence the reader in a subjective, tendentious manner to build up a special kind of meaning of words in association. "When I use a word, it means just what I chose it to mean, neither more nor less", says Lewis Carroll (*TOI*, 25 Aug.'99). That justifies the intention of the journalist. We list certain items with the special meaning that the words and structures propagate to the readers in particular and to the English language in India in general below. Depending upon the context, the meanings are categorised.

For example, words and expressions like saffron, butterly, dreamgirl, set water, line the pocket, Kargilonomics, stunner, blocobuster, pawar crisis etc. project new meanings, added meanings, and new usage depending on the occasion and so on. For easy access of the different categories of meaning they are related to, we give a reference of some of those varieties.

Categories	*Serial Nos.*
New euphemism	1, 19, 29 etc.
Proper names	2, 6, 7 etc.
Thematic meaning	4, 6, 8 etc.
Reflective/collocational	5, 13, 15 etc.
Connotative/metaphorical	8, 11, 17 etc.
Affective	10, 37, 54 etc.
Extension	26, 35, 36 etc.
Indian metaphors	27, 29, 38, 44, 85 etc.

It is found that most of these categories come under associative meaning (affective meaning being the major part of it) and extension of meaning. The examples below refer to their thorough analysis.

		Terms and Structures	*Sources*
1.	(i)	Saffron Juggernaut in Orissa	*The Telegraph,* 7 Oct.'99.
	(ii)	Heartland Stalls Saffron March	*The Telegraph,* 7 Oct.'99
	(iii)	Softening the Saffron	*The Telegraph,* 9 Nov.'99.
	(iv)	Blood ties Saffron and Red in death	*The Telegraph,* 9 Nov.'99.
	(v)	Saffron Muslims	*The Telegraph,* 10 Oct.'99.
	(vi)	On the Saffron side of rationality	Editorial, *The Times of India,* 5 Dec.'98.
	(vii)	Wearing Saffron badges	Editorial, *The Hindu,* 4 March 2000.

The term 'Saffron' has got a shift in meaning. Earlier it stood for a colour that is on our national flag that stands for purity and a positive thing. Now the newspapers sound pejorative, specifically pointing towards a political party (BJP and the Shiv Sena, its ally) and its ideology which is communal according to the columnists. So a new euphemism is created.

2. Washing dirty linen in Public
   The Times of India, 6 Aug. '99.
   The structure tells us something of which the conceptual meaning is of no use but the metaphoric, affective meaning. It is about the controversy between two washing machine manufacturers; LG and Samsung. Proper names that refer to important personalities give a scope to the writers to twist them into new meanings.
3. (i) Pawar Play
   Editorial, *TOI*, Aug. '99
   Refers to the power play in the Congress Party and the position of Sharad Pawar, a politician.
   (ii) Pawar Cut
   Editorial, *TOI*, 8 Sept. '99
   (again refers to the politician's position which is at a crisis).
   (iii) "An acute Pawar Crisis ~~would seem to have gripped~~ the Congress in Maharashtra."
   Title of an article in *TOI* 19 Sept. '99
   It also refers to the confusion over the politician Sharad Pawar in the Congress. It refers to the associative (Leech 1974) meaning and then proper name as a part of speech (F.T. Wood 1941) also gives it validity.
4. "Swaraj is our Worth-Right and we can all have it".
   TOI, 15 Aug. '99
   The above proverbial sentences echo the historical speech of Bal Gangadhar Tilak and then talk about Swaraj Paul, NRI and the investment issue in India. This evokes a meaning beyond the grammatical structure. This is a part of the thematic meaning.
5. Swaraj's berthright
   TOI, 25 Aug. '99
   This is another sentence echoing the above where the name refers to Sushma Swaraj, politician and her berth from the Bellary constituency. The word berth is also taken from the train berth which Sushma occupied that was reserved for Smt. Indira Gandhi (1978).

So a composite meaning structure comes out of it.
This is reflected and collocative meaning.

6. Not just a Preity face. — *TOI,* 31 Aug. '99
   The interview with Preity Zinta, film actress titles her name in the place of Pretty. Here the associative meaning is at work. Also proper names as parts of speech (F.T. Wood 1941) come to play here.
7. Will the famished roads Pilot him to Power. — *TOI,* 8 Sept. '99
   (It refers to Rajesh Pilot, another Politician).
   Both his move to power as well as the person concerned are referred in the same sentence resulting in associative meaning as discussed above.
8. Written in Sand — Editorial, *TOI,* 8 Sept. '99
   'Sand' here refers to Rajasthan, the election, voting there. It is a metaphor.
   So this is an Indian affective meaning that the writer resorts to. This is also a new metaphor and connotative in usage.
9. Eyes Wide Shut Won't open in India. — Nikhat Kazmi, *TOI,* 9 Sept. '99
   The writer means something different than what its surface meaning or conceptual meaning suggests. She means the film *Eyes Wide Shut* cannot be released in India due to the Censor Board's objection. At the same time she means something by 'shut eyes' (metaphorically the blindness to progressive attitude) on Indian systems of film censorship. Both affective and metaphoric meaning come to play.
10. ''Setting Water on Fire''. — *TOI,* 13 Sept. '99
    A title that relates with an interview with film maker Deepa Mehta.
    'Setting Water' throws a particular meaning, the expressive one since *Water* is a film that the interviewer means.

But the structure resembles that of a phrasal verb; example: set fire, set in, set out etc. The use is metaphoric and affective.

11. Dream girl floors Amethi Seek Support for Vajpayee. — *TOI*, 26 Sept. '99
    This is the socio-cultural meaning that is fixed in people's mind that the writer makes use of since no one outside can understand who the 'Dream girl' is. Obviously the entertainment world which captures the imagination of our people can make out that it is the film actress Hema Malini. This is connotative and socially established.
12. Duel Personalities — *India Today*, 6 Sept. '99
    It speaks about the political fight between Sonia Gandhi and Sushma Swaraj What it means after analysis (that is the electoral contest against each other) is evident in the use of the word 'duel' itself. This is the meaning in contrast, associative and phatic (keeping communication open, social level intact).

There can be also a meaning like syntactic-contextual meaning which is at work below:

13. UN diplomatic Annan — Editorial, *TOI*, 30 Sept. '99
    By offering a syntactic variety (normally it is connotative in nature), 'Undiplomatic' at one hand and combining UN (United Nations) and its Secretary General Kofi Annan, it establishes the purpose. This also comes under collocational meaning.
14. Home Meet on Winter Offensive — *The Telegraph*, 14 Nov. '99
    The message is not clear on the surface. The writer analyses 'winter offensive' as possibility of attack by Pakistan in the winter season

for which the Home Ministry Officials meet. This is a politically charged meaning which the writer exploits since it is a few months after the Kargil attack. The context specific meaning utilises a metaphor for war in Indian context. Thematic and connotative.

15. Utterly Butterly Delicious — *TOI,* 13 Nov. '99
    This advertisement of Amul Chocolate is a popular one that comes frequently on newspaper columns. Utterly is a pejorative word which is used positively here. The term signifies the affective meaning by the author who uses it in a functional way to create a particular sound effect without the strict adherence to the literal meanings. The use of 'butterly' relates to collocative meaning (words used taking their environment into concern). Also a case of generalisation.
16. Sonia Mercy Plea for Mother Nalini — *The Telegraph,* 19 Nov. '99.
    This is an ambiguity which works as a mode of meaning. We can say this to be a special journalistic ambiguous meaning. The exact message is Sonia Gandhi's plea of mercy for the lady, Nalini who also has a child and was involved in Rajiv Gandhi assassination. By syntactic deviation (dropping the possessive and arranges the words in a way to give forth a theme.
17. Indian cricket star Sourav Ganguly is termed 'Maharaj' in most of the columns which Indians do understand easily. And this has a local flavour

since he is addressed so in his native place, *i.e.* Calcutta.

Examples :

(1) In *The Times of India*, 20. Nov. '99 he is referred so.

(2) Crowd drives Maharaj off the ground. — *TOI*, 18 Nov. '99

(3) Between Tests, Maharaj plans Pujas with family. — *TOI*, 10 Oct. '99

(4) Leading from the front, the Maharaj way. — *TOI*, 18 Feb. 2000

This is a case of local metaphor in offering the special meaning. Also proper names are being exploited for the desired meaning.

18. The Plane Truth — *The Telegraph*, 22 Nov. '99

This is an ironic usage as it means 'the truth about the aeroplane' but writes in the model of 'a plain truth'. This is a case of reflected meaning.

19. Red Bhadralok, Bengal Tigress. — *The Telegraph*, 22 Nov. '99

National, local and localized meanings are evident here since 'Red' stands for the communists. So Red Bhadralok refers to Jyoti Basu, the Chief Minister of West Bengal then and 'Bengal Tigress' refers to the radical and verbose Mamata Banerjee; politician and minister at the same time. A case of connotative and euphemistic meaning.

20. A delicious irony. — *India Today*, 6 Sept. '99

This is affective meaning. The adjective does not fit into an objective analysis but gives a very subjective appeal.

21. Wanted Militants ready to Surrender. — *The Telegraph*, 22 Nov. '99

Opposing to the supposed one, the news says, if the militants surrender arms, they will get certain benefits. The meaning in opposition refers to reflected usage.

22. More Missed Worlds to conquer. — Jug Suraiya, *TOI*, 12. Dec. '99
    By missed worlds the writer means the devastated, poverty stricken, ignored world, states, regions.
    On surface it seems as if he is talking about the Miss World beauty pageants.
    Of course he connects to it ironically. This is rhetorical.
23. Sunrise Session after nuclear darkness. — *The Telegraph*, 24 Nov. '99
    The context is on Jaswant Singh's (politician) visit to Japan (that is the sunrise country) which has suffered the nuclear bombardment.
    This is a kind of meaning by virtue of using subjective metaphors.
    This is meaning by extension.
24. Advani Pulls Kargil gun on Pakistan. — *The Telegraph*, 24. Nov. '99
    It creates again an affective meaning by using the Kargil metaphor from the Kargil war.
25. The bare truth — Editorial, *TOI*, 4 Dec. '99
    It speaks about the truth behind baring (getting naked) of some women in protest.
    The word 'bare' here does not speak about the literal but the contextual meaning related to the message and content.
    This is reflected meaning and a case of false euphemism.
26. Up's Bhul-bhulaiya. — Editorial, *TOI*, 28 Feb. '98.
    A political puzzle encircling a politician or state etc. is termed as 'Bhul-bhulaiya'; a historic monument in Lucknow (Uttar Pradesh capital) that confuses, puzzles people.
    A political crisis is explained that way. It is an extension of meaning.
27. Milking Democracy. — Editorial, *TOI*, 27 Oct. '98
    Here milking refers to politicians befooling people

as seen in Laloo Yadav's rickshaw ride to gain popularity. The meaning is arbitrarily chosen and relates it to the cow. The animal that the leader represents by his caste determines the usage. Both thematic and metaphoric meanings are fused together. This is a case of Indian metaphor (milking).

28. Vegetable Soup. This is an ironical treatment of the terms relating to the price rise of onion, something that is unaffordable. Extension of meaning is seen here.	Editorial, *TOI,* 28 Oct. '98
29. (i) Odour of onion in Delhi's air. A temporarily fixed meaning that speaks of price rise of onion at a point of time.	News item, *TOI,* 28 Oct. '98
(ii) Sinha dishes Indian Onion Soup to UK audience. On the same context of onion price rise, but it also gives a scope of creating, using new metaphors that Yashwant Sinha, Finance Minister uses : 'Big onion' (big threats), 'small onion' (small threats). It also creates new euphemism. That means since the onion factor was a threat to the government then, it was chosen for vested interests too. Other such metaphors are Kargil, Kargilonomics, loading Kargil gun and so on.	L.K. Sharma, *TOI,* 7 Nov. '98
(iii) Ode to the Onion. On the same context of anxiety (as in an ode) on onion price rise. This is a	Tanushree Podder, *TOI,* 6 Nov. '98

part of meaning out of the present issue.

(iv) The Onion factor. — Editorial, *TOI,* 5 Aug. '98

Refers to the contemporary context; that of price rise and politics over it.

By being euphemistic and reflective in nature, the meaning content appears funny but effective as seen in the above examples. It serves the purpose of creating Indianised metaphors.

30. Brawn Tennis. — Editorial, *TOI,* 18 June '99

It replaces 'Lawn Tennis'. The motive behind is well expressed; that is brawn (strength) as an essential element for playing Tennis. It is connotative meaning.

31. Chidambaram adds UF Sauce to Manmohanomics. — *The Economic Times,* 22 July '96

Adding sauce can be guessed to adding favour, adopting and extending the same policy. The meaning is tendentious and not objective in nature. So euphemistic and metaphoric.

32. Flames in the water. — Subhadra Sengupta, *The Telegraph,* 20 Feb. 2000

Refers to the special meaning relating to the present context of the crisis over the film *Water.* It is a connotative meaning.

33. PAN Masala — Editorial, *TOI,* 7 Jan. '98

This is a composite expression that refers to two categories:

(i) Permanent Account Number (PAN), and

(ii) the contextual one; that which goes with 'Masala', referring to a mess of the situation. Metaphoric meaning (Indianised metaphor).

34. CAT out of the Bag. — Editorial, *TOI,* 6 Jan. '98

(i) It also refers to a similar meaning like the earlier one (CAT - 1) referring to Central Administrative

Tribunal and its secretary being out of the post.

(ii) referring to the conceptual meaning that sounds proverbial and rhetorical. Old idiom accommodates the new thematic meaning.

35. (i) Mounting Pressures. — Editorial, *TOI,* 12 Aug. '98

The entire editorial sounds tendentious, more like witty discourse than objective analysis:

"With the build up of steam generated by pressure cooker politics, the BJP led government must convincingly show that it can take the increasing heat in the Kitchen".

It is again a metaphor out of contemporary politics.

(ii) Pressure cooker world. (Means the modern world). — *TOI,* 15 March '99

36. Dr. Gandhi's diagnosis — Ranjit Hoskote, *TOI,* 15 Aug.'98

The title is ambiguous since its conceptual meaning is not that which the writer means, one is kept under anxiety and in actuality he talks about Mahatma Gandhi whom he addresses as a doctor since he gave a real diagnosis for all on spiritual, religious, cultural, social matters that can work like medicine for our individual and social being. This is extensive meaning.

37. "... She would have had to have recourse to *deter gents.* Ms Lewinsky was very accommodating and would never want to deter gents, particularly those helpful to her career." — *TOI,* 23 Aug. '98

The writer also refers to

detergents which could wash the dress of Monica Lewinsky washing the scandal away.
This is an extension of meaning.

38. To Sir, with love and more money. — *TOI,* 23 Aug. '98 (Special report)
The title subscribes to a novel *To Sir with love.* The writer adds 'money' to speak about the teacher's strike for increase in pay. The kind of meaning he wants to convey is ironic and witty. This is again situational and contextual meaning and is affective in nature.

39. The 'One black coffee woman', does she exist ? — *TOI,* 24 Aug. '98
The writer writes about the modern, glamorous, smart woman of the 90s and addresses her as 'black coffee woman'. This is a purely subjective expression, bold and innovative in coinage. He creates a metaphor.

40. UN-fair and dangerous. — Editorial, *TOI,* 26 Aug. '98
As stated in the earlier instance, here is again a load of extra meaning since it writes both about the United Nations and the unfair attitude of the UN Secretary Council (indifference to Sudan's plea). This is an extension of meaning.

41. NAM by-Pamby Reflex. — Editorial, *TOI,* 5 Sept. '98
Just like the above case, here both the idiom 'namby-pamby' and 'Non-Aligned Movement' (NAM) come together in the same structure. Also the use of the phrase 'namby-Pamby' is appropriate to speak about the over reaction of India on UN Secretary General's

use of the 'K' (Kashmir) word. Extension of meaning.	
42. Silence Action Cut. Since the occasion is of an interview with a film maker, such a filmy cliche is chosen for the title. Here it refers to connotative category. It is a meaning that targets the wit of the readers too.	Title of an interview, *TOI*, 5 Sept. '98
43. A Gift Horse in the Mouth. The writer relates it to the context of Clinton-Monica scandal and refers to oral sex by using the horse metaphor for the phallus. This innovative and arbitrary meaning comes under the category of metaphoric meaning, *i.e.* putting extra meaning to existing words.	*TOI*, Special report, 13 Sept. '98
44. India and Pakistan are termed as 'Nuclear Twins' by the media in the wake of their nuclear test. ~~Earlier they were 'midnight twins'~~ for the media. This is an extension of meaning.	The Print media in general.
45. Cesspool of Atal's highways. It is a figurative use that communicates the idea of a levy on diesel. This is Indianised metaphoric meaning.	*The Telegraph*, 21 Nov. '98.
46. Vajpayee stings Congress with emergency blast. This is also metaphoric meaning. The anger of the snake and its threat is highlighted here.	*The Telegraph*, 22 Nov. '98.
47. Insecurity Council. It writes about the UN Security Council's bias for USA. This is meaning in opposition since it challenges the fixed terms. This is a case of false euphemism.	*TOI*, Editorial, 26 Nov. '98.
48. Steal frame. Indian bureaucracy is termed as the 'steel frame' traditionally for its non-transparency and rigidity. The writer makes a slight change to express the rampant corruption in it.	Editorial, *TOI*, 23 Nov. '98

Extension of meaning with metaphoric appeal.

49. Salaam Masala Mira — *TOI*, 24 Nov. '98
This is an interview title. Mira Nair, the film maker is interviewed and *Salaam Bombay* and *Mirch Masala* are two of her films attached to her name forming a strange structure. Proper names give rise to a meaning which is reflective in nature.

50. Madam versus Behan — V. Radhika, *The Week*, 22 Nov. '98
Refers to two important contemporary women political personalities, Sheila Dixit and Sushma Swaraj who were chief contenders for the Delhi Chief Ministerial berth and are addressed so respectively. This is Indian contextual meaning.

51. Some good home cooking. — John Maria, Special review, *TOI*, 13 Dec. '98
The news reveals that 'home cooking' is a music album But to keep guessing the writer does not write it in bold letters or with inverted comma. This is a reversal of meaning too as it does not mean what it says surfacially.

52. A similar case is with — *TOI* 13 Dec. '98
'The goodbye girl's which is also an album of music. An extension of meaning.

53. The biznizz of Dance. — *TOI*, 28 Nov. '99
On looking at the structure it seems as if the writer writes about 'business of dance' with a graphic deviation to attract. But the analysis reveals that it adds another information; that of the surname of a singer. This is a case of proper names being used as a meaning content.

54. Steel of the Iron Man. — Jagmohan, *TOI* 6 Nov. '98
It is easily guessed that of the identity of the Iron man of India;

Sardar Patel. But here 'steel' is used to mean strength which shows poetic usage. This is a part of reflected meaning and also connotative in nature.	
55. Sleep well Mantriji. Here the reader may mean 'sleep' to be laziness, the lethargic Indian politicians and so on. But the writer means 'sexual involvement' of our ministers, politicians in the context of Clinton-Monica scandal and tells that our ministers are more scandalous than Clinton who now raise a cry against him. A heavy load of meaning is put here. This is metaphoric and affective in nature.	Jerry Pinto, Special report in "Sunday Review", *TOI,* 20 Sept. '98
56. Son rise Industry. The idea is taken from 'sunrise' and is used in the context of the dynastic rule; rise of sons and daughters in political circles throughout India (kiths and kins). This is a special metaphor in Indian political context.	Editorial, *The Times of India,* 18 March '99
57. (i) Pak snatch win from Sachin's Jaws.	*The Telegraph,* 1 Feb. '99
(ii) Sachin's ton goes in vain. They all refer to the subjective, expressive meaning that the writer chooses to mean. So a part of the reflected meaning.	*The Times of India,* 1 Feb. '99
58. Progressive Middle Kingdom. It refers to Madhya Pradesh since it is in the middle of the country. It has an affective note.	*TOI,* 1 Feb. '99
59. Singhal-minded agenda. This meaning is associated with a person heading a political, social, cultural organisation.	*The Sunday,* 10 - 16 Jan. '99.

This may not be comprehended by all who do not know what it is to be Singhal minded. It refers to the RSS, Hindutva mission. So it is affective in nature.

60. "Filmfare helped me rise head and shoulder above the rest". — *TOI,* 2 Nov. '97
This is an advertisement that quotes actress Urmila Matondkar.
meanings:
(i) rising head and shoulder — conceptual meaning.
(ii) advertising the shampoo brand : 'Head and shoulder'.
This is extension of meaning, metaphorical in application which means the shampoo 'Head and shoulders' is above the rest of the brands.

61. Colourful facts. — Samita Bhatia, *The Telegraph,* 5 Dec. '98
Facts cannot be colourful. So it is used in an affective sense to mean exaggeration in facts.

62. Talking Turkey. — Editorial, *TOI,* 30 Sept. '99
Assertiveness that is seen in our PM Vajpayee's speech which the writer means in a roundabout manner. Metaphoric, affective in nature.

63. Bad time for a hit wicket. — Vir Sanghvi (Editor of *Hindustan Times*) in The Telegaph, 22 Sept. '99
This is on Bihar's case of President rule which rebounced for the BJP; that is termed to be 'a hit wicket'. Extension of meaning.

64. Satanic years — *The Telegraph,* 27 Sept. '98
(the years Salman Rushdie, novelist spent in exile); this is an intelligent coinage, witty in appeal, connotative in nature. Also the news writes:
(i) now Rushdie to pen Satanic years
(ii) now Salman Rushdie born again midnight's child.
His novels, *Satanic Verses* and *Midnight's children* influence such usage.

65. 'Midnight's End' — *The Telegraph,* 27 Sept. '98
(on lifting of the death sentence on Salman Rushdie, the novelist).

Meanings that are wittily chosen taking the writer's own work into concern. So this is again metaphorical and connotative.

66. Here is a piece of writing that shows a subjective, poetic, allusive model of writing:
"'Picture these scenes: 'An Othello in banian and Pyjamas looking daggers at you from across his balcony; a loony careening down the city streets; a caligula conducting a football match...'
No it is not as kooky or Kafkaesque as that. There are not voices in our heads; some asinine rap is not playing in our brains. But there is no symphony in our spirits either. The sweep of social change has caught our younger minds in its maelstrom. We have, indeed, been living in a pressure cooker for the last decade."
The whole context of modern man's traumatic life is categorically expressed in a broad metaphorical cover, subjective and affective language. The writer discusses the anxiety, stress, schizophrenic attitude of modern desolate man in a poetic discourse.

Jayanth Kodkani, in a special report, *The Sunday Times of India,* 27 Sept. '98

67. A close shave for Shabana.
It is related to the present context of actress Shabana Azmi shaving off her hair for the controversial film *Water.* And here the writer gives the semantic context a load of individual metaphor; 'close shave' referring to close scrutiny of the actress's attitude to art and life.

The Telegraph, 26 Feb. 2000, p.3

68. Once there was a Lion
(Refers to Laloo Yadav, Ex-CM of Bihar). It results in semantic ambiguity.
This is a temporary metaphor coined for an individual.

Outlook, 21 Feb. 2000, p. 78

69. Arty Facts. — *Outlook,* 21 Feb. 2000
Refers to facts that are related to art. There is a semantic shift (arty means artful). Conceptual meaning works here.

70. An 'Unreasonable' Man. — *The Times of India,* (interview with N. Vittal, Chairman, Central Vigilance Committee by M.P.K. Kutty on 1 March 2000, p.10).
It is also a case of semantic deviation because the conceptual meaning is evident that Mr.Vittal is not an unreasonable man (in the context of the news).
But the content shows that in today's world, the unreasonable, individualistic and arbitrary stand taken by such personalities only can restore the good when the so called reasonable lot is driven by stereotype values.
The title definitely plays with false euphemism and teaches the reader the meaning in contrast unlike the strict, objective use of the language. This is a sort of reflected meaning.

71. Educating Zobaida. — An interview title, *The Times of India* (interview with Bhaskar Roy on 7 March 2000, p.14).
The conceptual meaning has nothing to do with the content here since it does not actually mean educating the person concerned; Zobaida Jalal, the Education Minister of Pakistan. So this is connotative in nature.

72. Police to welcome Poila Baisakh in Bangla. — *TOI,* 1 April 2000
Whether it is the Police welcoming the new year day in West Bengal or anything is not quite clear. It actually means West Bengal Police department has planned to begin its official function in the regional language, *i.e.* Bengali. This ambiguity depends upon the associative, context dependent meaning.

73. Seeking a fool proof formula for Kashmir. — Headline, *The Times of India,* 19 June 2000
In the place of 'full proof' the reporter uses the cynical term which serves both the function.

(i) The event,
(ii) The condemnation of the event by media.
The meaning out of the message is that of a cynical condemnation of the government policy and is connotative in nature.

74. India crawl out of Deep hole. — *TOI*, 5 Dec. 2001
It first refers to a plural subject (Indian cricket team); the term 'deep hole' is written in capital to serve the purpose of the word 'deep' and the name 'Deep' (Deep Das Gupta who scored runs to bring India into a strong position). Here surface ambiguity is cleared by context analysis. It comes under associative meaning and proper name is also converted to communicate the message.

75. Bubblegum campuses. — *The Times of India*, 27 May 2001
The word 'bubblegum' has represented the young, often adolescents, their childishness, infatuation. The college campus is the bubblegum campus. It is also true that the teenagers chew bubblegums more than the elderly. New meanings get attached to existing words by this. This is metaphorical in nature and an extension of meaning.

76. Aussie Victory Soured by Bevan Can attack. — *TOI*, 26 June 2001
This structure has been already discussed in Chapter-5. And here we can see the ambiguity that is evident in meaning. Whether 'Bevan attacked some one with the can or was attacked by it is a confusion. So it creates a meaning gap deliberately so that one would get into the details. Associative meaning plays its role here.

77. "Can't wait to be Sun kissed; every shade a woman wants to be." — Advertisement, *Femina*, 1 May 2001

Here we find a figurative use of the word (here 'sun kissed' is pejorative; skin allergy due to sunrays). Poetic use of the language is seen here with a reversal (false euphemism) of meaning. Here 'Sun kissed' is in contrast to the original meaning.

78. It's all kiss-met for Parizaad. *TOI,* 24 Nov. 2001
Actually Parizaad is an actress in a recent movie. The news item means both 'Kismat' (a Hindi word that means fortune) and her kissing scenes in the film. This is a case of metaphoric and affective meaning.

79. The Magical Powers of Mumbai Masala. It is an Indian metaphoric meaning. (Masala referring to something rubbish, gossiping, nonsense, but simultaneously entertaining). *TOI,* 25 Nov. 2001

80. Words like Talibanise, Talibanising are frequently used. Readers as well writers understand what they refer to i.e., 'fundamentalism', 'terrorism', 'Jehad', 'fanaticism' etc. A political regime (Taliban) means all the above notions. *TOI,* 24 Nov. 2001, 25 Nov. 2001 and so on.

81. Diya Diya Burning Bright. *TOI,* 4 Nov. 2001
This catchy, attractive, poetic structure reminds us of Blake's 'Tiger Tiger Burning Bright' (from the poem "The Tiger").
The writer thus uses the associative meaning to mean something speacial.
In this case it refers to an actress, Diya Mirza at the backdrop of 'diya's' (lamps) on the eve of Deewali.

82. A (tom) B (omb) Vajpayee. *TOI,* 9 Aug. '98
The possession of nuclear power by India under the leadership of our P.M. (Vajpayee) is expressed through an associative meaning.

83. Sonne (means zero). *India Today,* 6 Sept. '99
This metaphor is used for the politician Sonia Gandhi who is termed politically to be a Zero.

84. Salmans run amok in M.P. *The Telegraph,* 17 Oct. '98
Salim one up on deer son Salman. Here the word 'deer' replaces 'dear'. It refers to the deer killing controversy. This is an example of connotative meaning.
85. Certain advertisements display a new set of meaning. Job advertisements create a group of lexicon with contrasting, opposite, often ironic levels of meaning as found in the column by Simon Howard in *The Sunday Times* (appeared in the "Ascent", *The Times of India* on 1 Sept. '99):

Ambitious	:	young enough to think it is still possible
Attractive Salary	:	probably not
Bottom line focus	:	nothing else matters
Career-minded	:	crawler
Challenging	:	impossible
Developmental role	:	paying less than we should
Direct and communicative personal style	:	rude
Enthusiastic	:	naive
Exciting opportunity	:	probably not
Experience of implementing cultural change	:	blood on your hands
Friendly environment	:	cramped offices
Hands-on managment style	:	Interfering by another name
Initially on a contract basis	:	This is all a bit of an experiment
Innovative approach	:	the ideas will be yours, the glory ours
Intuitive	:	able to read the boss's mind
Key position	:	you will take all the flak
Liaise at all levels	:	piggy in the middle
Motivational skills	:	enough charm to get people to forget their problems
Opportunity to develop new skills	:	expect to be thrown in at the deep end
Pragmatic	:	unprincipled
Self-motivated	:	you will be on your own
Tact and understanding	:	the politics are a nightmare
Undergoing radical structural change	:	fighting for survival
Unique opportunity has arisen	:	previous incumbent was fired
Work under pressure	:	inadequate resources to achieve the impossible

The above captions are euphemistic in the sense that they hide the opposite and rude message underneath.

86. Vandana Agarwal and Nikhat Kazmi record a number of words from the lingo of the under-13 group as used now-a-days. The boys use such words which can be treated as slang or as the journalists say: 'brawn words'. They originate from wrestling and fighting. But whatever may be the effect, they form a separate communicating mode.The list is given below. They represent a list of Indigenised metaphors.

Source: *The Times of India,* 10 April 2000.

Words		*Meanings they refer to*
Stunner	-	Jam the neck of the opponent in your arm, jump and sit down.
Rock Bottom	-	Throw the opponent on the ring by holding his arms and swinging him around.
Blocobuster	-	Leap on the opponent and get his head between your legs.
Low Blow	-	Leap on the opponent and get his head between your legs.
Pedegree	-	Get his head between your legs, hold up his hands and sit down on the ground.
Choke Slam	-	Hold him by the neck and fling him on the ground.
Tombstone	-	Lift the opponent with his legs and fling him, face downwards.

These words are also discussed in Chapter-4 of this study as a part of the new lexical entries.

The New Approach to Meaning

We can conclude that present day English journalistic content opens a wide scope for the inquiry of meaning. The theoretical frame of semantics no longer fully copes with the requirement of the writer's message. Although it forms the basis of understanding the general meaning content of all such writing, there are certain areas which are noteworthy for the researcher to pay attention to. One can get a variety of meaning outside the strict theoretical boundary of the English language. More than that, the context of India, the local and circumstantial issues more often capture the attention of the writer to utilise those areas. He works as a manipulator in creating new codes out of known words which carry extra weight of meaning. So we find certain words carry a load of meanings which at times go beyond the comprehension of the reader unless he/she goes deep into the matter. We categorize our findings on the nature of semantic change below.

(a) Ambiguity as a method

That is, the writers and editors choose an ambiguous patterning of words, deliberately make the words carry confusing meaning content. This creates a command of the use of language on the part of such writers which may form a model for the curriculum also creating enough space for the young learners of the language to decipher meaning in context.

(b) Semantic liberty

It also makes writing vague in general. The writers of journalistic content enjoy the freedom of writing absurd too. If this liberty is given to the practitioners of the language in other fields it will not pose a big threat to the language. Rather one can be comfortable with it in making the language more intimate to our culture.

(c) Time dependent meaning

A large part of the meaning out of the journalistic writing covers the issues that are time specific. So more or less, one can comprehend the message if one is aware of the contemporary issues. The crisis over the film *Water* becomes a metaphor for so many things as analysed before. Similar is the case with 'Onion' (price rise), 'Monica gate' (sexual scandal) and many more. And although as time advances the issue gets vanished, the wide range of metaphors and new meanings remain alive and can also form the writing corpus for specific usage. No one can challenge their validity. So new meanings can be created out of such contextual issues in any field.

(d) Urbanite, consumeristic

At the advent of a consumeristic culture and more material, global society, the meanings and message also get loaded with such values. The American way of life of urban youths get reflected in the language of the newspapers. So the stylistic content of journalese is more dependent upon the urbanite mind set.

(e) Semantic excessiveness

It covers the writers'/editors' impulsive drive to shape the journalistic register as productive content. Even the words here can have a market value, to weigh and appear saleable, consumerable in the changing economy. Otherwise stress would be shifted from the stereotype literary and linguistic content of English. In order to compete with electronic journalism(e-journalism), words have to mean excessively, creatively and keep changing so that they can be superior to the mechanically defined meanings of their counterparts.This excessiveness creates more avenues, more space for meaning.

(f) Poetic and subjective

Newspapers come overloaded with highly poetic expressions, *i.e.* instead of being objective in approach like the legal and science registers, they show a remarkable orientation towards subjectivity of the writer. Most of the titles also show a rhythmic pattern. Meanings are also more affective than being a carrier of the factual news.This is a possible area of concentration on the part of the learner. A poetic frame accommodates more metaphors that are readymade and suitable to the occasion. The learner can follow a list of such items including the highly patterned use of the advertisement captions for a package in language learning behaviour.

REFERENCES

1. I.A. Richards and C.K. Ogden, *The Meaning of Meaning* (New York: Hercourt, Brace and Company Inc., 1923) 45.
2. Philip Wheelwright, *The Burning Fountain* (Bloomington:1954) 61.
3. I.A. Richards, *Philosophy of Rhetoric* (London: Oxford University Press Inc.) 40.
4. *Ibid.,* 54.
5. *Ibid.,* 73.
6. F.T. Wood, "*Change of Meaning*", *An Outline History of the English Language* (Macmillan India Ltd., 1941) 149-95.
7. Ibid.
8. Geoffrey Leech, *Semantics* (Harmondsworth and Middlesex: Penguin Books Ltd., 1974).
9. *Ibid.*

Chapter - 7

THE LAST WORD

Review

After analysing the new entries with their lexical, structural and semantic implications it is observed that the new words ultimately lead to the required meanings that the editors and writers seek to transfer. Newspapers successfully represent the major source of linguistic change. The idea of language as power is well evident in the body of our English newspapers. So what traditionally was considered vague and ambiguous becomes the real expression of the people. The content of the newspapers provide the actual text of our cultural history. They offer a text which can be practically utilised in the curriculum. So we may not have to borrow the history and culture from outside. Rather than burdening the learner with loads of other cultures and history through the traditional text books, newspapers appear to have become more accessible and comfortable for the learners' interest.

When language achieves the status of a commodity, (as it has been in the era of globalisation), it certainly aspires to be acceptable to all kinds of markets; outside and inside. In the context of the global village, words and the different modes of communication are saleable and exportable. So when such usage gets ample attention (both by the writers/editors of newspapers/journals) influencing the readers, it gets acceptability automatically.

Findings

1. The English print media in India is an effective body of experimentation in Indian English (IE).
2. The newspaper English takes the major role in standardising Indian English in different spheres of society and across the world.

3. Journalists create wide choice for the reader/learner by manipulating numerous processes to create new entries.
4. This ultimately enriches the language which is on a very fast move.
5. The variety of English that has emerged by this process has currency in the rural as well as urban setting.
6. Taken together, the new words, structures with their associated meanings meet the varied requirements of the readers with economy. This is a strong assertion of ethnically rich India.
7. The kind of English thus generated, gives a framework for learning different forms and techniques of literature and language study in general. So the model seems to be fit enough to be utilized by the students across the country for their competence in the respective language and creates room for its entry into the curriculum.

Views from Seminars, Conferences, Books and Articles

We may well judge the validity of our claim of Indian English as a distinct, influential form towards its standardisation, use in curriculum from the strength of views expressed below.

Whitman[1] says about language as "something arising out of the work, needs, ties, joys, affections, tastes of long generations of humanity and having its basis broad and low, close to the ground". And according to Emerson[2], "Language is a city to the building of which every human being brought a stone". A news item in the daily *Telegraph*[3] reads : "Ram before Rambo in Millennium English". It goes on further with reference from the *Encarta World English Dictionary* which has hundreds of Hindi, Tamil, Bengali and words from other Indian languages contained in it. It says since 'Rambo', 'Ramboism' and 'Ramboesque' have been included for 'a person of vigour, anger and revolutionary mindset', 'Ram' is similarly included as the 'ideal man' in the Indian context. It also cites words like achar, korma, samosa, tandoori, masala etc. It says, the *Encarta World English Dictionary* is the "first dictionary to be able to reflect the new world status of English". It contains 3.5 million words of text, 1,00,000 head words, 4,00,000 references and 4,000 illustrations. It also contains the Hindu calendar, list of festivals like Holi, Diwali, Dusshera, Shivaratri and Ganesha Chaturthi. It is also a great achievement that the *Oxford English Dictionary* (1996) has given special space to a number of such entries that are popular in Indian culture. But we cannot always look towards an acknowledgement by any such outside authority for the validity and existence of our use of English. We can do it under our cultural norms. This is a fast growing process in this part of the world. That itself is a guarantee of acceptability in future. In this context a journalist says sarcastically[4]:

> "the dependence on alien bodies of approval, this need to be validated by hoary institutions and foreign sensibilities underscores in real our low self-esteem; our inability to come anywhere near self-validation. A lack of confidence in the quality of our creations. Moral authority as an exclusive foreign held asset." This is the representative voice of our intelligentsia. There is enough encouragement to create, innovate, play with the tricks of language, make it the daily, habitual voice and written medium, and accessible to our teaching curriculum. We here put the view of John Wells, an eminent Professor of English in UK who is a member of Linglex, the board for the study of linguistics and lexicography.

The Professor speaks in an interview[5] with Ratnottama Sengupta, journalist:

> "The use of the word changes from society to society, from generation to generation. Computing has given us terminology like hyperlink, multitasking. Internet has made 'homepage' a familiar word, or e-mail. Media has added words like edutainment, infotainment, infomercial, and docudrama. New concern or the accent on market economy has also given us new words. We are now 'eco-friendly". To quote another writer[6]:
> "English has already been enriched by more than one million words from different languages. It is guessed that after the languages, the possible area to form a sound source for its borrowing is science and technology".We can well realize how the popularization of those new words depends upon the familiarity drive that the newspaper columns materialise. Infotech has been a very popular section in all leading newspapers through which the mass is aware of the new product as well as the newly coined word. The common man uses a variety of Englishes around

him without knowing the intricacy of the language and its grammar. If we take the examples of a train journey, we find the use of words like 'time pass', 'waiting list', 'RAC', 'halt karna', 'A.C. Coach', 'signalling', 'berth', 'reservation' and many more. Similarly in all fields certain words are so common that they are used by everyone concerned to it irrespective of the command of the language, grammar, spelling etc. And the way they are used, significantly tells about the acceptability of the English words used in the Indian way with a mixture of words from indigenous languages. This can never be challenged by any outside authority.

The Welsh linguist David Dalby[7] is quoted in *The Times of India* : "the initiative for the future evolution and planning of the 'new global English language' should properly be with China and India which will harbour more speakers of the language than elsewhere." The editor continues : "We feel 'Global English' needs a brand new transitional image, with its trademark different from the British Union Jack and the American Stars and stripes". Regarding the reader response, Timothy Balding,[8] Director General of World Association of Newspapers (WAN) says in an interview with *The Times of India* (interviewed by Rachna Burman): "the readers want to be not just informed, entertained but also moved by their newspaper". Again he reminds that it has to be easy for people to go out and get it. "Newspaper companies must market themselves like any other brand, market themselves like biscuits if need be".

Two points can be drawn from the above views:

1. The writers/editors have to be tendentious and not just factual; that shows in the process they have to also evolve an idiom, a medium of their own, for the reader, taking the contemporary age into consideration.
2. Marketing newspaper as any other material product. This shows words are saleable and can compete for existence, the point that we have already mentioned.

There has been always a positive response from the English speaking community both inside and outside the country regarding a drive for plain, functional use of English. It is realized from the following views : Saheli Mitra's[9] response from a workshop in this regard:

(i) to make the everyday English language as user friendly as possible.

(ii) John Wild of the PEC (Plain English Campaign) says "English is fast becoming the global language, the language of the market. But, that English will have to be plain and easy for all to understand."

(iii) Ishita Bose, a senior teacher says : "Not only in official forms, plain English should be used in school text books too. After all English should be accessible to all".

(iv) Pulak Lahiri (Prof. of Zoology, Calcutta University) says that "plain English is particularly needed in Science, otherwise it remains beyond the understanding of the common man".

(v) Advertisement consultant Moy Roy says: "Communication with clients is always easier in simple English. And we are today better understood than our grandfathers were." He also remarks : "plain English in our country will work only if it starts from school".

In a symposium held on English studies in India at CIEFL (Central Institute of English and Foreign Languages, Hyderabad) Prof. Sukanta Choudhury of Jadavpur University said that I.E. has slowly gained respectablity and free entry into the curriculum. There is a new status for Indian English and other English literatures from former English colonies. Prof. Meenakshi Mukherjee was of the opinion that the transactional nature of English is of crucial interest.

Hasan Suroor writes : "A fizzy touch to new English" in *The Hindu* (24 July 2000) and says that "the latest edition of the *Oxford Advanced Learners' Dictionary* (OALD, sixth edition, 2000) has canonised almost every word and usage that is spoken in the name of English around the world. We should not connect the issue of language with narrow parochial assertion of one's tongue. English and not Hindi—has been the *de facto* national language of communication in India. It is the only available language of communication between people from the North and the South and Eastern States. It is no longer a language of the Raj and we have developed an English with our regional flavours. Increasing instances of inter-regional marriages make English—at least the naturally Indianised version of it—the only practical "mother-tongue" ("English Vazhga", *TOI*, 28 April 2000). Bryan Appleyard is of the opinion that e-English would change the nature of English language. He says the instant addition, new alternations will break the solidity, immobile status of *Oxford English Dictionary* by making it alive, reacting to the vernacular instantly. The website offers the possibility of a dictionary as dynamic as the language itself. He remarks:

> "It throws out of the window any idea of standard English. Neither the English nor anybody else owns the language. Purists writing to newspapers to complain about split infinitives have been swept aside by the sheer success of an English that belongs to all users and they can, it seems, do what they like with it" ("e-English rules the waves", *The Times of India*, 30 March 2000). Even about SMS (Short-text Message Service) Vinay Kamat (*The Times of India*, 2 Sept. 2001) says that it modernises, popularises, enriches and globalises English. "It is younglish (young English), it is art, it is fusion and it is brewitty (bravity)"; opines the writer. Jug Suraiya (journalist) in "Televised Terror" (*The Times of India*, 15 Sept. 2001) remarks : "words, the particulate matter of language, seem to lose their gravity and float away from the things we try to fix them to". He is of the view that media images shape our ethics and our actions.

To quote Sally Wehmeier, editor of *Oxford Advanced Learner's Dictionary* (sixth edition):"Every dictionary has to reflect the language that is currently being used. That's why the 'standard English' we are presenting to foreign learners now includes a wider range of influences and uses." She says that people reading specific journals, magazines or periodicals mark new words and then send them to the OAD for assessment and is of the opinion that "inclusion of foreign words is not a threat to the purity of the language. English has always incorporated words from other languages. Like clothes, even language has a fashion." (In an interview with Suchitra Behal, *The Hindu*, 20 Aug. 2000). In another interview we find the Chief Editor of *The Oxford English Dictionary*; John Simpson spoke to Anita Joshua (*The Hindu*, 18 Feb. 2001) about the decline of the dominance of British English and an equal rating of British English with other varieties as used in different countries including Indian English. Finally, he is of the view:

> "I think I'm much more aware that we need to keep a close look out at idiomatic developments in Indian English—not just the

loan words from Indian languages." Rajeswari Sunder Rajan, Reader in English, Wolfson College and Fellow, Oxford University writes in *The Hindu* (18 Feb. 2001) about the colonial status of the English language during British rule here and contrasts it with the decolonised, antielitist status it has today. We can see certain representative British writers using Indian words thereby legitimising their entry here:

1. Harold A. Gould, visiting Professor, South Asian Studies at University of Virginia writes:

   "Doer Clinton rescues Sinner Clinton. The principal basis for Clinton's resilience reflects neither his *karma* nor his *tabiyat* but the brilliance of his socio-political vision" (*The Times of India*, 5 Dec. '98).

2. *The Times*, London writes:

   " ...Parents are better equipped than *nannies* to raise children, especially when the *nanny* is either the government or the Court" (*The Times of India*, 8 Oct. '98).

3. Michael McGhee uses the terms 'Dukkha', 'Klesha', 'Shraddha' in his article (*The Times of India*, 5 Dec. '98). What could be more exhilarating than the projection of our words and cultural ethos by foreign writers ?

The Curriculum

It is found that this variety of English produces an alternative text. Language learning can go along with learning certain relevant functions of literary forms; that of the alliteration, poetic expression, the conative, expressive, referential functions of language. It acts as a great motivator being eco-friendly and easy, down to earth in nature. We cite certain statements in the form of news which acquaint the students with the great literature of the world and language learning simultaneously.

1. "Prometheus Unbound" — Narayani Ganesh, *TOI*, 30 Jan. 2002
   The news item is about something else but echoes the great Greek

myth, drama and P.B. Shelley's famous poem.

2. Sen and Sensibility (echoes *Sense and Sensibility* by Jane Austen).
   Talks about Amartya Sen, the economist.
3. Lab's Labour Lost (Shakespeare wrote *Love's Labour Lost*).
4. Much Adoor About Something *TOI*, 13 Jan. 2002
   (Shakespeare wrote *Much Ado About Nothing*)
   Great proverbs are also learnt in similar fashion.
   A student understands the meaning of 'ode'(being inquisitive) from :
5. Ode to the Onion *TOI*, 6 Nov. '98

Language learning becomes a process mostly facilitated by one important variety of register; the newspapers and journals. The earlier textbook approach of teaching language can find an abler alternative by introducing this variety into the class room. It can make learning more interesting like a game, with greater involvement, appear more relevant to the world and our immediate environment.

Prospects

The above observations confirm the fact that we need a plain, functional English. And we draw the conclusion that in order to make English plain, we have to associate it with the local, regional, national ethos and tongue, our language, our culture. The English newspapers which project such a stand, wherever do they practise it; either in the editorial or in their different sections, do a brilliant task in this regard. The content of the newspaper can be an alternative text for the language learner. In other words, the text can be built taking the words, structures that appear in the newspapers as we have seen in our examples. The students can easily take up the nuances governing the new entries and their associated meaning.

In the process, the cultural burden that we often bear in the form of textbooks, history of another country can be lessened. The disadvantage of making a student alien from his background can be compensated by it. Language practice according to convenience can be our real motto rather than language as a load. Day to day events can be taken up and the kind of words, structures used there in may be taught. The Indian imagery, syntactic deviation can be easily put into use. Since the writers have been bold enough[10] to borrow words from Sanskrit, Hindi and other regional languages by way of translation and transliteration, the learners can smoothly pick up those words for their benefit in the form of a comfortable learning material and for the purpose of functional, communicative English.

In the context of inter-disciplinary approach in every field, Indian English as appears in the newspapers and journals give the most composite stuff of Indianness. It is time this kind of English became more official and a standard one making it accessible to the formal, curricular fields.Our print media offers the finest area of experimentation and assertion of Indian English.We need to look at them as one of the primary, suitable mediums of language development.

REFERENCES

1. Walt Whitman, *The Story of English*, ed., Robert McCrum, William Cran, and Robert MacNeil (London: Faber and Faber Ltd., 1986).
2. R.W. Emerson, *The Story of English*, ed., Robert McCrum, William Cran, and Robert MacNeil (London: Faber and Faber Ltd., 1986).
3. *The Telegraph,* 22 November '99.
4. C.P. Surendran, "Currying favour with the Brits", *The Times of India,* 11 Feb. '98.
5. John Wells, "Downsizing Queen's English", *The Times of India.*
6. Mukul Sharma, "August English", *The Times of India,* 5 Dec. '98.
7. Editorial, *The Times of India.*
8. Timothy Balding in an Interview with, *The Times of India,* 12 April '99.
9. Saheli Mitra, *The Telegrah*, 16 November '98.
10. Sheo Bhushan Shukla, "Indianness of Indian Fiction in English", *Studies in Contemporary Indian Fiction in English*, ed., A.N. Dwivedi; (Allahabad: Kitab Mahal, 1987).

BIBLIOGRAPHY

Allen, W.S. *Living English Structures*. London: Longmans, Green & Co., 1959.

Anand, Mulk Raj. *Coolie*. London: Lawrence and Wishart, 1936.

—. "Pigeon Indian: Some Notes on 'Indian English' writing". International Seminar on Australian and Indian Literature. New Delhi, 12—16 January 1970.

—. Speech. *Soviet Revie* . 26 March 1968. 92.

—. *T o Leaves and a Bud*. London: Lawrence and Wishart, 1937.

—. *Untouchable*. London: Wishart Books Ltd., 1935.

Balding, Timothy. Interview. *The Times of India,* 12 April 1999.

Bansal, R.K. "The Intelligibility of Indian English". Diss. University of London, 1966.

Barooa,.G.S. *A Comprehensive Manual of Current English*. New Delhi: Cosmo Publication Pvt. Ltd., 1989.

Baruah, T.C. *The English Teacher's Handbook*. New Delhi: Sterling Publishers Pvt. Ltd., 1984.

Basu, Sudipta. "Mind Your Language". *The Telegraph,* 5 Dec. 1998.

Baugh, Albert C. *A History of the English Language*. 1968. New Delhi: Allied Publishers Pvt. Ltd., 1988.

Bloom, J.P., and J. Gumperz. "Social meaning in Linguistic Structure: Code Switching in Norway". *Directions in Sociolinguistics*. Ed. J.J. Gumperz and D. Hymes. New York: Hold, Rinehart and Winston Inc., 1972. 407-34.

Bolton, W.F., and David Crystal, eds. *The English Language: The Penguin History of Literature*. 1975. London: Penguin Books Ltd., '93.

Bright, W. "The Dimensions of Sociolinguistics". *Sociolinguistics*. Ed. W. Bright. Mouton: The Hague, 1966.

Burgess, Anthony. Introduction. *All about H. Hatterr*. By G. V. Desani. London: Penguin Books Ltd., 1972.

Chand, J.K. "Making Rag Pickers of Decent Learners". National Seminar on Curriculum Renewal. ELTI. Bhubaneswar, 21 Jan. 1999.

Chomsky, N. *Aspects of the Theory of Syntax*. London: Mass, MIT Press, 1965.

Corder, S. Pit. *Introducing Applied Linguistics*. Middlesex: Penguin Books Ltd., 1973.

Das, Kamala. "An Introduction". *Summer in Calcutta*. New Delhi: Everest Press, 1965.

Dasgupta, Sanjukta. "Politics of language and Post Independence Indian English Poetry". *Indian Literature*. 52 ('98) : 207-17.

Desani, G.V. *All About H. Hatterr*. 1948. London : Penguin Books Ltd., 1972.

Dubey, Vinod S. *Ne spaper English In India*. New Delhi: Bahri Publications, 1989.

—. "The Republic of Orissa : Annals from the pages of the Twentieth Century". *Saturday Evening Harkaru*, 25 May 1845.

Dustoor, P.E. *The World of Words*. Bombay : Asia Publishing House, 1968.

Dutt, Michael Madhusudan. *The Captive Ladie*. Madras : n.p., 1849.

Dutt, Sochee Chunder. *The Young Zemindar*. London : Remington, 1885.

Firth, J.R. *Papers In Linguistics*. London : OUP, 1964.

Fishman, J.A. "The Sociology of Language : An Interdisciplinary Social Science Approach to Language in Society". *Advances in the Sociology of Language*. Mouton : The Hague, n.d. 204-17.

Friedlander, E.J., and J. Lee, *Feature Writing for Ne sp apers and Magazines*. New York : Harper and Row, 1988.

Goetz, Philip W., ed. *The Ne Encyclopaedia Britannica*. 6 vols. Chicago and London : Encyclopaedia Britannica Incorporated, 1768.

Goffin, R.C. "Some Notes on Indian English". *S.P.E. Tract*. 51 (1934) : 21

Gokak, V.K. *English in India, Its Present and Future*. Bombay : OUP, 1964.

—. *In Life's Temple*. N.P.: n.p., 1965.

Grey, Elizabeth. *The Story of Journalism*. London : Longmans Young Books, 1968.

Halliday, M.A.K., A. McIntosh, and P. Strevens. *The Linguistic Sciences and Language Teaching*. London : Longmans, Green and Co. Ltd., 1964.

Harris, J.W. "Diphthongization, Monophthongization and Metaphony revisited". *Diachronic Studies in Romance Linguistics*. Ed. M. Saltarelli and D. Wanner. Mouton : The Hague, 1957. 537.

Haugen, E. "Linguistics and Language Planning". *Sociolinguistics.* Ed. W. Bright. Mouton : The Hague, 1966.

Holloway, J. "I will Tell You One thing, a letter from India". *Hudson Revie* . (1959).

Hornby, A.S., ed. *Oxford Advanced Learner's Dictionary.* London : OUP, 1996.

Hymes, D. "On Communicative Competence". *Sociolinguistics.* Ed. J. Pride and J. Holmes. London : Penguin Publications Pvt. Ltd., 1972. 269-93.

Iyengar, K.R. Srinivasa. *Indian Writing in English.* 1962. New Delhi: Sterling Publishers Pvt. Ltd., 1990.

Jespersen, Otto. *Gro t h and Structure of the English Language.* 1938. London : Basil Blackwell, OUP, 2000.

Kachru, Braj B. "Analysis of Some Features of Indian English : A Study in Linguistic method". Diss. University of Edinburgh, 1962.

—. "Indian English : A Study in Contextualization". *In Memory of J. R. Firth.* Eds. Bazelletal. London : Longmans, 1966. 256-87.

—. "Some style features of South Asian English". *National Identity.* Ed. K.L. Godwin. London : Heinemann Educational Books Ltd., 1970. 130.

—. *The Indianization of English : The English Language.* New Delhi : OUP, 1983.

—. "The Indianness in Indian English". *WORD.* 21 (1965) : 408-09.

Kemenade, Ans Van, and Vincent Nigel, ed. *Parameters of Morphosyntactic Change.* London : Cambridge University Press, 1997.

King, Bruce, ed. *Literature of the World in English.* London: n.p., 1974.

Labru, G.L. *Indian Ne sp aper English.* New Delhi: B.R. Publishing Corporation, 1986.

Lal, P., ed. *Miscellany of Creative Writing.* Calcutta: Writers Workshop, 1960.

Land, G. *What is in the Ne s?* London: Long man Group, 1986.

Leech, Geoffrey. *Semantics.* Harmondsworth and Middlesex : Penguin Books Ltd., 1974.

Maison, Margaret M. *Examine Your English.* Calcutta: Orient Longman Ltd., 1964.

Matthew, Mammen, ed. *Manorama Year Book.* Kottayam: Malayala Manorama Co. Ltd., 1997.

Matthews, H. *Morphology*. London: Cambridge University Press, 1974.

McCarthy, Michael. *Discourse Analysis for Language Teachers*. London: University of Cambridge Press Syndicate, 1991.

McCrum, Robert, William Cran, and Robert MacNeil, ed. *The Story of English*. London: Faber and Faber Ltd., 1986.

Mencher, M. *Basic News Writing*. New Delhi : Universal Book Stall, 1990.

Mitra, Saheli. *The Telegraph,* 16 November 1998.

Mukherjee, Meenakshi. "Style in Indo-Anglian Fiction". *Indian Writing in English*. 4 (1970) : 6-13.

—. *The Twice Born Fiction : Themes and Techniques of the Indian Novel in English*. New Delhi : Heinemann Educational Books Ltd., 1971.

Nehru, Jawaharlal. *Glimpses of World History*. 1934. New Delhi: OUP, 1982.

Palmer, F.R. *Semantics: A New Outline*. London: Cambridge University Press, 1976.

Parasher, S.V. "Certain Aspects of the Functions of Indian English: A Sociolinguistic Study". Diss. CIEFL of Hyderabad, 1979.

—."Communication Styles in Indian English". *Language Matters*. Ed. K.V. Tirumalesh. New Delhi: Allied Publishers Ltd., 1999.

—. *Indian English: Functions and Form*. New Delhi: Bahri Publications, 1991.

Parthasarathy, Rangaswamy. *Journalism in India : From the Earliest Times to the Present day*. New Delhi : Sterling Publishers Pvt. Ltd., 1989.

Pountain, Christopher J. "Structures and Transformations". *The Romance Verb*. New York: Barnes and Noble Books, 1983.

Quirk, Randolph. *The Use of English*. 1962. London: Longmans, 1967.

—. and Sidney Greenbaum. *A University Grammar of English*. London: Longman Group Ltd., 1973.

Rao, Raja. *Kanthapura*. 1938. New Delhi: OUP India, 1989.

Richards, I.A. *Philosophy of Rhetoric*. London: OUP Inc., n.d., 40.

—. and C.K. Ogden. *The Meaning of Meaning*. New York: Hercourt, Brace and Company Inc., 1923. 45.

Robins, R.H. *General Linguistics. An Introductory Survey*. London: Longman Group Ltd., 1964.

Rubdy, Rani. "A study of some written varieties of Indian English". Diss. CIEFL of Hyderabad, 1981.

Rushdie, Salman. *The Moor's Last Sing*. London: Jonathan Cape Ltd., 1995. 135.

Sarma, G.P. *Nationalism In Indo Anglian Fiction*. New Delhi: Sterling Publishers Pvt. Ltd., 1978.

Sefali, Sasmita. "Typical Features of Newspaper Headings." PGDTE Project. ELTI of Bhubaneswar, 2000.

Seth, Vikram. *A Suitable Boy*. Penguin Books India Ltd., 1993.

Sharma, Mukul. "August English". *The Times of India,* 5 December 1998.

Shipley, Joseph Twadell. *In Praise of English*. New York: Times Book Co. Inc., 1893.

Shukla, Sheo Bhushan. "From Indianness of Indian Fiction in English". *Studies in Contemporary Indian Fiction in English*. Ed. A.N. Dwivedi. Allahabad: Kitab Mahal, 1987.

Simeon, Potter. *Our Language*. 1950. London: Penguin Books Ltd., 1990.

Smith, L., ed. *English for Cross-Cultural Communication*. Hongkong: Macmillan, 1981.

Spencer, J.W. "A Multilingual Commonwealth". *Books*. n.p., 1965.

—. "Language and Independence". *Language in Africa*. Ed. J.W. Spencer. London: Cambridge University Press, 1963.

Steffenson, Margaret S., and Chitra Joag Dev. "Cultural Knowledge and Reading". *Reading In Foreign Language*. Ed. J. Charles Alderson and A.H. Urquhart. Essex: Longman Group Ltd., 1984.

Surendran, C.P. "Currying Favour with the Brits." *The Times of India,* 11 Feb. 1998.

"The Anglo-Indian Tongue". *Black o od's Edinburgh Magazine*. 121 (1877).

Umamaheswari, S. " The Role of Newspapers in the present society." *The Competition Success Revie* (1994) : 13-14.

Weinreich, U. *Language in Contact*. Mouton: The Hague, 1968.

Wells, John. "Downsizing Queen's English". *The Times of India*.

Wheelwright, Philip. *The Burning Fountain*. Bloomington : n.p., 1954. 61.

Widdowson, H. *Teaching Languages as Communication*. London: OUP, 1978.

Wilkins, D.A. "The Social Function of Language". *Linguistics in Language Teaching*. Ed. D.A. Wilkins. London: Edward Arnold Publishers Ltd., n.d.

Wimsatt, William K. Jr., and Cleanth Brooks. *Literary Criticism, A Short Reading*. London: OUP, 1957.

Wood, F.T. *An Outline History of the English Language*. 1941. Madras : Macmillan India Ltd., 1969.
Wren, C.L. *The English Language*. London: Methuen, 1977.

Newspapers and Journals

The Times of India, New Delhi.
The Hindustan Times, New Delhi.
The Hindu, New Delhi.
The Telegraph, Calcutta and Guwahati.
The Statesman, Calcutta.
The Economic Times, New Delhi.
The Ne Indian Express, Bhubaneswar.
The Sun Times, Bhubaneswar.
The Asian Age, Bhubaneswar. *The Samaj* (Oriya daily), Cuttack.
The Assam Tribune, Guwahati.
Frontline.
India Today.
Outlook.
Sunday.
The Ne Woman.
Cricket Talk.
Politics India.
Femina.
The Week.
The Competition Success Revie
Sportstar.
Filmfare.

Index